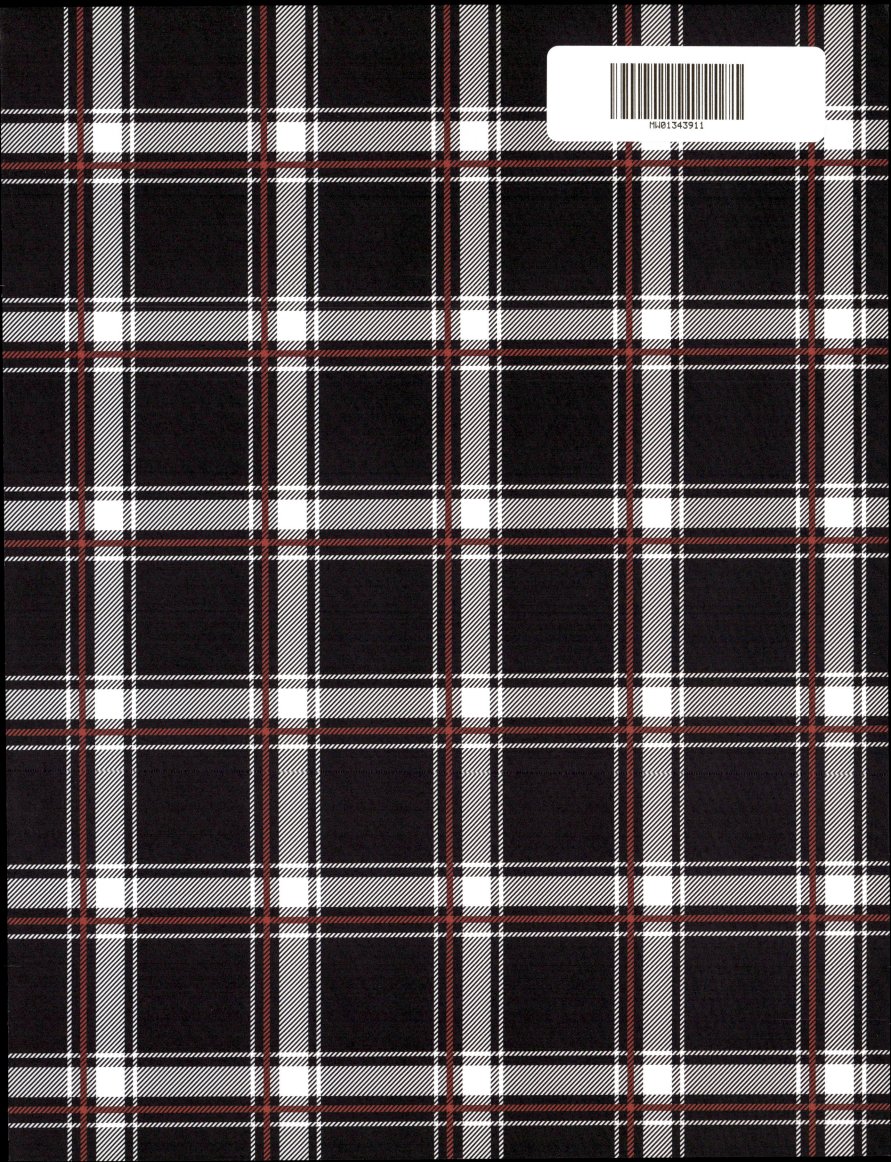

THE COMPLETE BOOK OF VOLKSWAGEN GTI

EVERY MODEL SINCE 1976

RUSSELL HAYES

CONTENTS

Introduction 5

Chapter	1	2	3	4
Model	Golf GTI Mk1	Golf GTI Mk2	Golf GTI Mk3	Golf GTI Mk4
Model Year	*1976–1983*	*1984–1992*	*1991–1997*	*1997–2003*
Page	6	34	68	90

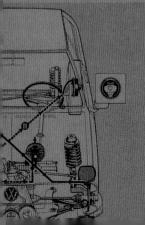 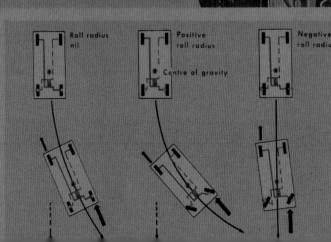 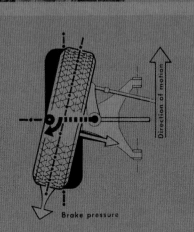 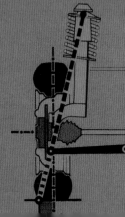

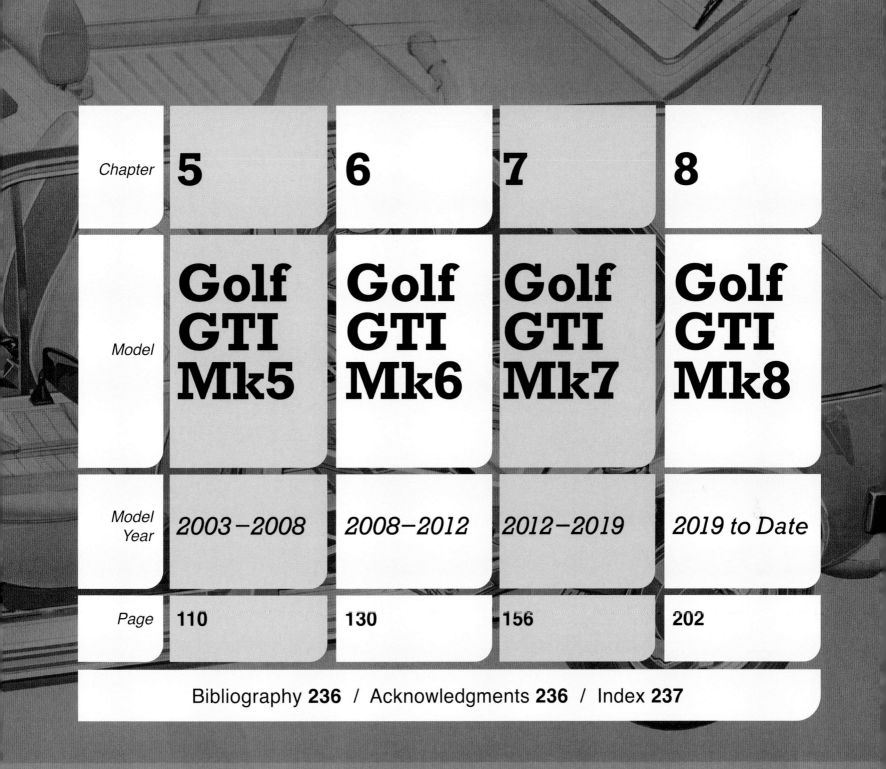

Chapter	5	6	7	8
Model	**Golf GTI Mk5**	**Golf GTI Mk6**	**Golf GTI Mk7**	**Golf GTI Mk8**
Model Year	*2003–2008*	*2008–2012*	*2012–2019*	*2019 to Date*
Page	110	130	156	202

Bibliography **236** / Acknowledgments **236** / Index **237**

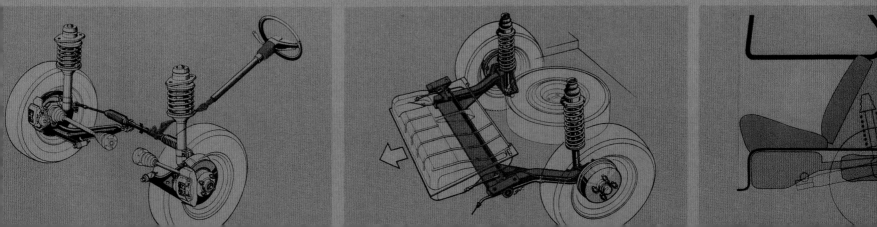

A NOTE ABOUT ENGINE POWER IN THIS BOOK

It's complicated. The popular ways to express a car's power output have changed in the lifetime of the GTI and still differ depending on what country you're in. For the 1970s and 1980s I've followed British car magazines and brochures that used brake horsepower (bhp) to the German DIN standard (*Deutsche Industrie Normen*) reflected net horsepower. Net horsepower is the power output measured on a test bed with the engine still fitted with ancillaries such as the gearbox, pumps, and exhaust systems. North America also used bhp for its Volkswagens, although the figure was usually lower than Europe due to emission control apparatus. This was the American Society of Automotive Engineers (SAE) net figure, and from the 1990s became referred to as just hp. In 2005, the SAE issued a new power and torque rating standard, J2349, which made some cars appear to lose power because the power steering pump was added.

For Euro-GTIs from the late 1990s (GTI Mk4) I'm using the German metric measure for brake horsepower PS, for *Pferdestärke*, or horse-strength, as from that point it has been used by the Volkswagen Group to describe the outputs of its cars—the PS number is still sometimes in the model name (TDI 110, etc.). One PS is equivalent to 0.9864 bhp, and the British motoring press still largely converts the PS figure back to bhp (for example, 265 PS becomes 261 bhp).

INTRODUCTION

GTI: three magic letters. Few things have lasted like the Volkswagen GTI. It was a backroom project that turned the talented Volkswagen Golf into a sports car for all—affordable, practical, and, above all, fun. Debuting in 1975 as a 1976 model, Volkswagen's GTI joined the Scirocco as one of the company's first performance cars, blasting away its staid image and making the words "hot hatchback" part of the dictionary.

With the years, the GTI gave us more and more models: the Corrado, the Jetta GLI, and those four-wheel-drive pocket supercars, the Golf Rs. Other hot hatches came and went over the decades with new names, new tricks but never really beating the evergreen GTI.

Just why is it so beloved? Perhaps it's that unique blend of discretion, crushingly capable on-road manners, and the perfect blend of comfort and sportiness. Of course, like any long-running rock band, there have been albums that don't quite hit the mark, but the GTI magic usually returns with the next generation.

A new GTI is like meeting up with an old friend and starting where you left off years ago. It has its own folklore of seat patterns, wheels, body shapes, and golf ball gear shifts. Few designs of car on sale today have visual references dating back to a series that started over half a century ago. And if you want more individuality, the GTI has always been a blank canvas for tuners and customizers the world over.

Eight generations of GTI have tracked the evolution of the car. The journey from Mk1 to Mk8 has seen it double in weight, almost triple in power, go from an optional radio to a digital cockpit powered by AI, go from fuel injection to minutely managed turbochargers and from a four-speed gearbox to a seven-speed automatic that can change faster than a racing driver. Now as the electric age beckons, the badge is ready for the future.

Russell Hayes
London, 2025

1.
SOMETHING SPECIAL: THE MK1 VOLKSWAGEN GOLF GTI 1976–1983

On March 29, 1974, the first-ever Volkswagen Golf came off the Wolfsburg production line. It had to do nothing less than save the company from massive debt (the US market had collapsed) and pull it out of the Beetle era. After years of wrong turns, Volkswagen had arrived at the perfectly proportioned hatchback styled by Italy's Giugiaro with a new transverse-mounted water-cooled engine and front-wheel-drive.

Through the 1960s, dozens of prototype Beetle successors were built and abandoned. The nearest one to get to production was developed from scratch by Porsche's engineering department with little help from Wolfsburg. The EA266 three-door hatchback had a water-cooled four-cylinder engine laid flat under the rear seat and drove the rear wheels—yes indeed, a mid-engined family car. However, there were problems with cabin smells and service access. Although cleared for production in 1972, EA266 was canned by new Volkswagen boss Rudolf Leiding in 1971, having seen the Golf. According to Germany's *Der Spiegel* 50 cars had been completed (most were then crushed) and it was said that the decision cost the company £21 million in written off research and development.

RIGHT: Volkswagen's past and future in 1974. The new Golf middle second row; the Passat, Scirocco, and K70 third row, left to right. Back row left, the Type 181—or "The Thing" to American buyers. *(Volkswagen UK)*

CHAPTER 1. SOMETHING SPECIAL: THE MK1

However, Volkswagen's own EA276 from 1969 was closer to the future Golf with a front engine, hatchback with large trunk lid, and torsion beam rear axle. But under the hood lurked a Beetle engine. But it didn't look very inspiring, hence the call to Italy for help. Giugiaro landed the contract to provide the style for a whole family of new Volkswagen cars: the mid-size Passat, the Scirocco coupé (see page 12), and the Golf. All were named after winds; Golf was to have been Gulf (*Golfstrom*) but morphed into Golf, internally called project EA337.

The Golf's Magic Ingredients

Having only been able to bring out bigger and more expensive versions of the Beetle—the Type 2 and the 411—Volkswagen finally conceded that front-wheel-drive was the way of the future for European cars and bought its way into a new engineering philosophy.

In 1965 Volkswagen had bought half of Auto Union GmbH in Ingolstadt—now better known as Audi—from Daimler Benz, initially only as a potential extra factory space to build Beetles. But Audi made front-wheel-drive cars, with water-cooled engines from the 1965 Audi onward. When VW fully bought Audi in 1968, it gained the initial studies for the Audi 50, a neat three-door car that embodied the essence of the forthcoming "supermini" class of the 1970s, and the finished Audi 100 executive sedan, launched in 1969 and a hit from the outset.

Also in 1969, Volkswagen absorbed the innovative but cash-strapped NSU into Audi to get access to the NSU K70 (K for *Kolbenmotor*—piston engine), taking the structure of the rotary-engined Ro80 and adding a conventional water-cooled engine. Volkswagen quickly spruced it up and launched it in 1970 as the Volkswagen K70, its first front-drive water-cooled car, an essential testbed.

Volkswagen Safety Construction - in all Models

All our cars have advanced passive safety features, such as rigid steel cell passenger compartments and safety conscious interior planning. However, active safety elements also play a vital role in the new generation cars.

You will find that every one feels good to drive which is as it should be, because they all have the latest in automobile engineering techniques behind them. You'll find individual wheel suspension, torsion beam centre-coupled, self-stabilising, or torsion beam rear axles, make sure of accurate wheel location. All-important when bad road conditions have an uneven effect on front wheels.

The roadholding and complete lateral stability, even in strong crosswinds, are remarkable. This is because the engine, gearbox and differential are combined in a single unit, giving a low centre of gravity. Body roll is therefore restricted, and directional stability is maintained by the improved suspension system. Should a tyre burst or skid at speed, the stabilised steering/braking system will help the car pull up in a straight line.

The new VWs have excellent acceleration, and to match it, excellent braking power. Front disc brakes are standard on all models, and the diagonally linked dual circuit brakes ensure that braking power is effectively distributed should one circuit fail.

No expense has been spared by Volkswagen to provide the ultimate in safety. It's a sound investment, as we want the VW driver to be a confident driver.

Not a big seller, the K70 was a placeholder until the Italian-styled family arrived. In May 1973 Volkswagen's first Passat marked the true start of the new generation (Dasher in the US), rendering the K70 redundant and laying the ground for the Golf.

Volkswagen naturally turned to Audi to power its new water-cooled generation. Audi already had a group of ready-made engines, the EA827 series first seen in the 1972 Audi 80. The 80-based 1973 Passat offered a 55 bhp 1.3 EA827 plus a 75 and 85 bhp 1.5-liter version. For the top-of-the-range Golf, Volkswagen chose the latter 1.5-liter four-cylinder in 70 bhp tune. It had a cast-iron cylinder block and aluminum head with overhead valves actuated by a belt-driven single overhead camshaft and bucket tappets, and was introduced in 1.3-liter and 1.5-liter versions.

In the Audi and the Passat, it was mounted longitudinally ahead of the gearbox and drive shafts and inclined by 40 degrees to fit under the hood line. In the Golf it was turned through 90 degrees transversely and inclined backwards by 20 degrees for balance. The clutch and gearbox were on the left, with the final drive unit at the back of the gearbox, and drive to the front wheels was by drive shafts with constant velocity joints at each end.

For the basic—and big-selling—Golfs, the 1.1-liter EA111 began its development at Audi under Franz Hauk for the Audi 50 (which soon became the VW Polo) but was then taken over by Volkswagen. The 1.1-liter unit differed from the Audi 80/Passat EA827 by having its valves operated by short rockers instead of bucket tappets, and the drive to the oil pump and distributor came direct from the left side of the overhead camshaft. Unlike the EA827 it was specifically designed to be short enough for transverse installation, and the four-speed gearbox was end-on. The 1.1-liter engine/gearbox assembly was inclined forward by 15 degrees, again, for balance.

Factory performance figures claimed a 0 to 100 kph (62 mph) of 16.5 seconds and a top speed of 140 kph (87 mph) for the 1.1-liter and 15.5 seconds/160 kph (99 mph) for the 1.5 manual, with a shorter set of gear ratios on the 1.1. Official fuel consumption figures for the Golf 1.1 ranged from 35.2 to 51.3 mpg and the 1.5 manual from 33.2 to 47.8 mpg.

The Golf's MacPherson strut and lower wishbone front suspension followed Audi, but its rear suspension was a clever and cost-effective design. Already seen on the Scirocco (see page 12), each rear wheel was independently sprung on a trailing arm and coil spring with the trailing arms pivoting on a beam linking them across the car. Seen in profile this beam was a simple T section that fit neatly beneath the fuel tank. It was also very cheap to manufacture.

The design avoided the problem of other dead axles that would transmit abrupt wheel movements from one side or the other, known as "axle tramping" because it was located by rubber bushes and acted as an anti-roll bar to twist in corners, exerting powerful wheel control.

Steering was by sharp rack-and-pinion and, like all the latest VW-Audis, had a negative steering roll radius, so that any resistance on a front wheel due to braking or burst tire turned the wheel inward rather than outward. Braking was by drums all around on the Golf 1100, front discs/rear drums on the 1500, servo assisted.

A Sports Golf?

The Golf's international press presentation was held in Munich in May 1974. Launched into the fuel crisis, it was the right car at the right time. Production numbers had to be increased after three months to meet demand, and it became the best-selling car in West Germany—albeit with some teething troubles. Beetle production was moved to Emden.

A sports version of the Golf was not in the plan, but the essential ingredients were there—well-behaved suspension, sharp steering, and great brakes. The motoring press had noticed that the 70 bhp 1.5-liter Golfs were rather a hoot to wind up and drive fast, and felt quite sporty, especially on the optional alloy wheels with 175/70SR13 radials instead of the 155 section radials normally fitted. Chris Goffey of Britain's *Autocar* (September 6, 1975) wondered why Volkswagen had chosen to downplay the 1500 LS's sportiness. "Certainly, it is one of the most sporting sedans to have ever emerged from Wolfsburg. One can imagine many other manufacturers with such a model on their range labeling it 'GT.'"

But having trouble keeping up demand with the regular models, there was then no need for an overtly sporty Golf to liven up sales, and the groundbreaking diesel was in preparation. Nor was the Scirocco being touted as a sports car.

However, there was some precedent for a sports Volkswagen courtesy of the 1969 Volkswagen-Porsche 914 (although more Porsche than VW), but there was certainly a public appetite for a sporty Beetle. The 1972 1303S *Gelb-Schwarzer Renner* (GSR), or yellow-black racer, had all the latest sporty clothes—finished in yellow with black engine cover and hood, sports seat, and wide wheels—but no more power than the regular 50 bhp. Craftily, German owners were supplied with a list of tuning firms, and 3,500 GSRs were built between December 1972 and February 1973 and taken off to be powered-up if their owners wished.

The path to the first Golf GTI started strictly "off the books." And the two now-famous names associated with it are the development engineer also responsible for the press fleet Alfons Löwenberg and PR director Anton Konrad, both of whom had strong motorsport backgrounds. From 1972, both had agreed that it would be better to support private passenger car racing than continue to fund Formula VEE (Beetle-based engine racing).

While Ford and Opel increased their competition efforts, Volkswagen was not in the mood. Especially so following the oil crisis in 1974, as Konrad told the author in 2013. "When we launched the Scirocco the motorways were closed on Sundays, so the situation was against cars and traffic," Konrad said. "The engineers had to talk about fuel consumption reduction and other things, not making sport cars. The official order was that nobody should have anything to do with creating sports cars."

Löwenberg could already see that the Golf had all the right ingredients and that keen driver favorites like the NSU Prinz, BMW 2000, and Opel Kadett had a similar power to weight ratio to a Golf 1.5. On March 18, 1973, he wrote a memo to six senior managers in the research and development department suggesting that a souped-up Golf could be used to encourage private motorsport entrants. He named his ideal car the Sport Golf. Matching to FIA-Group 1 regulations, these cars would have a 1.6-liter 100 bhp engine, five-speed-transmission, 6 x 15-inch wheels (over 13-inch for the Golf LS), ventilated disc brakes, an oil cooler, and sports seats.

Only chassis specialist Herbert Horntrich and development chief Hermann Hablitzel were receptive to Löwenberg's idea. And so discreetly, the GTI began, according to Volkswagen lore, over beer and

OPPOSITE: The Golf's mechanical layout came from an excellent new parts box. The simple but effective rear axle gave independent suspension. The fuel tank is safely below it and the rear seat. *(Author)*

sandwiches at Konrad's home. With no official backing, Hablitzel set up an unofficial working group led by Löwenberg that included specialists who dealt in wheels, tires, suspension, and bodywork.

Anton Konrad established a link between Horst-Dieter Schwittlinsky (marketing) and research and development. The pair kept their board members onside and were supported by the enthusiasm of the PR managers of the importers, especially Sweden, France, and Italy. Konrad also started to arrange press events at its Ehra-Lessien test track with a "sports" theme, bringing along modified race or rally cars. In 1974 VW Motorsport at Hannover created a 1.5-liter Group 1 Golf for Freddy Kottulinsky, the up-and-coming Austrian racing driver, who campaigned it through 1975.

As Konrad recalled, the basis of the first Sport Golf came from a pre-production Golf (although Volkswagen's account has it as a Scirocco), a number of which were released for experimental engineering. The first prototype had 6 x 13-inch wheels, lower springs, different shock absorbers, and several parts via contacts at tuner Kamei and suspension specialist Bilstein. Special parts were made in the test trials area. In Volkswagen's account, the Scirocco-based chassis prototype had its basic 85 bhp 1.5-liter four-cylinder tuned to about 100 bhp with a two-stage carburetor and a rudimentary exhaust system.

Whether Golf or Scirocco-bodied, the first prototype was simply too raucous to contemplate for production—far more rally than road car, with hard suspension, a sports exhaust, and very wide wheels and tires (205/60 HR 13s when a Porsche 911 ran on 185/70 tires).

ABOVE: The racy looking 1972 Beetle GSR 1303S was frowned upon by German politicians but sold well. Perhaps the start of the GTI idea? *(Volkswagen AG)*

OPPOSITE: The engine bay of a time warp 1979 UK-market GTI. The canted-back engine helped spark plug access, but a 1970s mechanic might have been daunted by the pipework for the Bosch fuel injection system (right, above the gearbox). *(Allen Kenny - Iconic Auctioneers)*

Löwenberg and Horntrich decided to build a calmer version. Löwenberg is said to have showed it to head of research and development Professor Ernst Fiala at the Ehra-Lessien test track in spring 1975, and he was sufficiently convinced to allow the project to continue. At the same time, the sales department now sensed the good market opportunities for a sporty Golf, and Volkswagen still needed a novelty for the 1975 International Motor Show in Frankfurt. The Sport Golf project received official backing in May 1975, its code name EA195.

The project suddenly acquired momentum from all quarters. Six prototypes with different configurations were created, ranging from a car trimmed for maximum sports car performance to a modestly understated version. The initial engine was the 11.6-liter EA827 from the 1973 Audi 80 GT, which produced 100 bhp with a twin-choke Solex carburetor.

Herbert Schuster, the new test manager, had arrived from Audi and would later be dubbed "father of the GTI." To cut costs, he reduced the width of the wheels from 6.0 to 5.5 inches and shrunk the tire size to 175/70 HR 13. He also added front and rear anti-roll bars and honed the winning combination of wheels/tires and suspension settings to give the best combination of sporting handling and comfort.

The evolution of the Audi range brought with it the magic ingredient for the Sport Golf to become the GTI. The Audi 80 GT and Passat were about to adopt Bosch fuel injection as a way of meeting US emission regulations, and the GT's power increased a useful 10 additional horsepower to 110. The additional benefit of electronic fuel injection was that it was maintenance-free and docile in slow traffic, unlike sporting carburetors. Only found in prestige cars at the time, it would bring additional cachet to the new Golf. The system's name, Bosch K-Jetronic, was wonderfully exotic to enthusiasts' ears.

As an aside, the Golf 1500 became a 1600 in 1975 with a carburetor version of the 1.6-liter engine for taxation reasons and to allow the use of low-lead fuel, but the GT engine had bigger inlet valves, Heron-type pistons with dished crowns, plus an oil cooler.

Anton Konrad had discussed the Sport Golf project with Ferdinand Piëch, of the Porsche dynasty, who was then heading Audi technical development. Konrad secured an agreement for Audi to provide 5,000 injected engines before the Audi 80 injected version became public.

Production was cautiously sanctioned on the basis of a minimum of 5,000 sales—enough to spread around the dealer network and also to homologate the car for Group 1 Production Touring Car motor sports. It was not even two days' overall production of standard Golfs. Plus, there was no direct competitor for this extremely fast hatchback with room enough to haul a fridge.

The GTI Name

The initials that came to mean so much were simply the easiest choice for Volkswagen. Herbert Schuster said the Volkswagen was labeled GTI merely to distinguish it from the Audi (the "E" stood for *einspritzung*, German for injection). The Golf's "I" would be copied the world over.

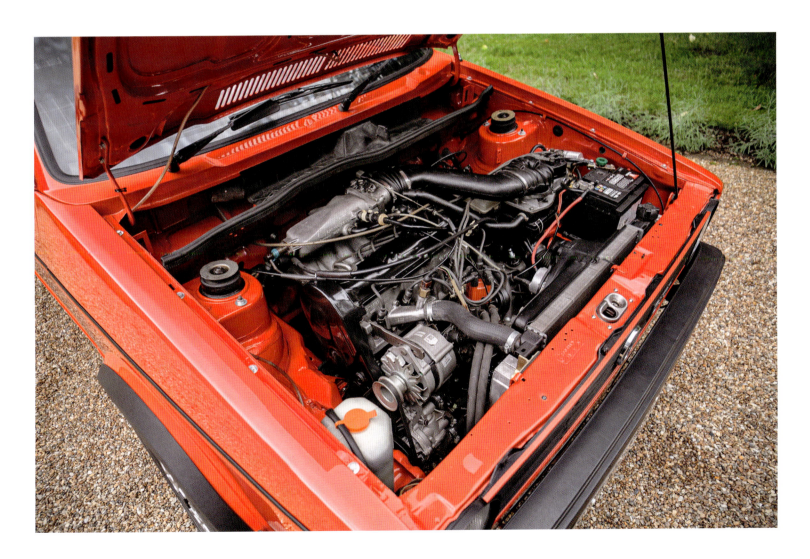

THE VOLKSWAGEN SCIROCCO MK1 1974–1981

Built since the 1950s by Karmann in Osnabrück, the well-loved Volkswagen Karmann-Ghia coupé and convertible were nearing the end of their time at the start of the 1970s.

As author Joachim Kuch recounted in *Golf Story* (Motorbuch, 2015), a successor to the Type 14 Volkswagen Karmann-Ghia had been in discussion since 1969. Every European manufacturer and a growing number of Japanese imports had several sizes of coupé in their ranges, often no more than a fastback roof grafted onto a sedan, two doors less, often no faster, but with a little more style.

In August 1971 Volkswagen decided to base the new coupé on the EA337—the future Golf—and Giugiaro was given the commission to style EA398 as well as the Golf and Passat. It would be the third new Volkswagen named after a wind, the hot Mediterranean one that whisks up from the Sahara. Company records show that when market tested in 1973, the name "Scirokko" brought up "exotic" associations, perhaps a car made by Alfa Romeo. Plans to call it the Blizzard in the US were not pursued. Scirocco it was.

The new model was aimed to launch at the start of February 1974, deliberately about six months before Golfs would be on the roads in the hands of their first owners. The lower-volume three-door coupé had to incorporate as many Golf components as possible to reveal any early problems ahead of time. Dealers would also get used to servicing the new drivetrains on a low-volume model, and it enabled engine production to be brought on stream for the later and much higher Golf volumes.

The German market would be first for the Scirocco, quickly followed by the US, which had been the key market for the Karmann Ghia, and still was for the Beetle convertible, also built by Karmann.

Karmann largely financed the development of the car it was eventually to build, from May 1972 developing the entire body-in-white (the bare shell), while Volkswagen in Wolfsburg supplied parts such as the engine and transmission, suspension, electrics, and fuel tank. Its 847 kg curb weight would be close to the future Golf's.

At 3.87 meters long, the Scirocco was slightly longer than the Golf (3.72 m) and shared its 2.4 m wheelbase. The extended hood and short fastback with an integrated tail spoiler created—together with a 14 mm larger wheel track—the correct sports car proportions.

The rear seats were only suitable for children—part of the coupé deal—but front headroom wasn't as generous as it might have been, leading to an early redesign of the front seats for some extra centimeters. But it was an airy cabin to be in, with large side windows and good trunk space further increased by a folding rear seat.

The Scirocco was the first of the new generation of cars that Volkswagen had genuinely developed itself without borrowing from Audi (the Passat used a lot of the Audi 80's structure). Its handling was honed at the company's magnificent Ehra-Lessien test track, which had opened in 1968.

As required, underneath the Italian lines mostly was the future Golf—front-wheel-drive transverse engines, MacPherson strut front suspension, and simple trailing arm and coil spring rear suspension with the ingenious new rear beam axle that gave semi-independent rear suspension at very low cost. Like all new Volkswagens it had a negative steering roll radius.

The Volkswagen Scirocco was launched at the Geneva Motor Show on March 8, 1974, the press having had the chance to sample it beforehand at Ehra-Lessien. Public road drives would have been a problem, as 1974, the year of the first oil crisis, brought a ban on driving on Sundays in the early part of the year and rigid speed limits to save fuel: 100 kph (62 mph) on motorways, 80 kph (50 mph) on country roads.

Production began in April 1974. These first Sciroccos were a foretaste of the engine choices for the first Golfs. The range started with its 1.0-liter engine developing 50 bhp then the 1.5-liter Passat/Audi 80 unit developing 70 or 85 bhp. Gears were the same four-speed manual or three-speed auto. The 1.1 was imported into the UK only as the 85 bhp 1500 TS, in right-hand drive from autumn 1974.

Depending on the version (base, L, or TS), a first-generation Scirocco had either a single rectangular or dual round headlamps at each corner. The TS had all the sporty must-haves of the 1970s—corduroy trim and a steering wheel whose three spokes had stamped-out holes.

The most powerful variant, the 85 bhp Scirocco TS, reached 175 km/h, impressive for those times, and it handled the classic sprint from 0 to 100 km/h in 11 seconds. In the more sporty versions, the center console housed a clock and a voltmeter. As one might imagine, the 1.1-liter 50 bhp engine was not a match for the sporty looks. In the first few years, around 77 percent of Scirocco buyers opted for the 85 bhp engine.

By June 1974 the Scirocco was building up to its target of 300 a day and after the summer break, Wolfsburg would be building 3,000 Golfs a day. According to the *Auto Zeitung* newspaper (Joachim Kuch wrote), more than half of the Sciroccos built every working day were being exported.

Over the remainder of 1974 the company sold 24,555 Sciroccos, and in its

OPPOSITE: Flat, square single headlamps denoted a base European Scirocco L of 1974 vintage. With the 1.1-liter Golf engine, it was a case of style over speed. A small front spoiler was designed in. *(Volkswagen AG)*
TOP: The Scirocco dashboard followed the Golf's layout. The sports steering wheel plus center console with an oil temperature gauge and clock came with a Scirocco GTI or TS. *(Volkswagen AG)*
LEFT: The small in-built rear spoiler and cut-off tail were the result of Volkswagen's new wind tunnel. This Scirocco TS has the same alloy wheels later offered on the first Golf GTIs. *(Volkswagen AG)*

first full year of production (1975) 58,942 units were sold. Volkswagen quotes a contemporary survey in which 42 percent of respondents purchased the Volkswagen based on its design, 25 percent due to its sportiness, and a modest 11 percent cited "economy" as the main criterion for their decision to buy.

In 1975 the Scirocco was welcomed into the US market with great enthusiasm. Even though the power of the 1.5-liter motor was limited to 70 bhp by the single Zenith carburetor, air pump, and catalytic converter it was slick to drive and to look at.

Initial sales were strong but drooped after teething troubles emerged. Premature rust was a problem shared with the first Golfs due to poor-quality steel and preparation. In addition to dropping the seat height, the gear change quality received early attention.

SCIROCCO GTI

Upgrades to the Mk1 Scirocco tended to follow the rhythm of Golf or Passat engine production. So, in June 1976 the Golf GTI and Scirocco GTI were launched as a pair, both with the same 110 bhp injected engine. Once again, Volkswagen was spreading its bets with two GTIs—because as mentioned in the main text, there was no obvious mass market for the Golf GTI.

The 1976 Scirocco GTI replaced the TS model in Germany and had a lot of the kit of its smaller sibling: halogen headlights, a twin horn, rev counter, tartan Recaro seats, sports steering wheel, and a center console. It had the wider wheels and tires, the anti-roll bars, heavy-duty dampers, and stiffened springs of the Golf GTI plus the ventilated front disc brakes and the bigger brake servo, but the suspension was not lowered, the standard Scirocco still lower than a Golf. The same 110 bhp injected engine was served up in the GLI version with bronze tinted windows, high-end fabrics, and metallic paint.

The US market missed out on the Scirocco GTI, but from October 1976 it was available to order in left-hand drive to British buyers, in red, blue metallic, black metallic, or silver metallic. Along with the Golf GTI, deliveries arrived in 1977. At £4,638 to the Golf's £3,372, the price premium and left-hand drive steered buyers toward the Golf.

In 1977 the Scirocco received a facelift for the 1978 model year. The front indicators and the bumpers were covered with dark PVC impact protection wrapped around the front wings, and the B-pillars were tinted black. At the same time the radiator grille got a decorative frame. The European engine lineup was now 50, 70, and 110 bhp.

American Sciroccos had a revolving door of engines to keep up with regular Golfs. First to 1.6-liter for '77 with fuel injection and 76 bhp, then with the facelift 1.6-liter and 71 bhp in 1978 for better emissions and economy. It was back to 1.6-liter and 76 bhp for 1979. The luxury Scirocco Storm, with leather seats, was sold in the UK from 1979 to 1981.

When the Scirocco GTI came to the UK in right-hand drive form in 1979 it had become a GLI. It had the same 110 bhp and same suspension set-up but luxury and no stripes. In 1980, the Scirocco was also produced with a 1.8-liter diesel engine just for the US; in 1981, a 1.7-liter was used with a five-speed gearbox.

There were extra-hot Sciroccos from early on. Veteran Volkswagen tuner Gerhard Oettinger coaxed 100 bhp out of the 75 bhp-engined TS in 1975, and in 1976 he presented his version of the Scirocco GTI, extended to 1.8 liters and with many detail engine changes good for 125 bhp.

Joachim Kuch wrote that in 1979 Volkswagen engineered a turbocharged Scirocco, of which 2,000 units were to be built for export in the spring of 1979, but it never went into series production because several pre-series cars caught fire.

Elsewhere, several companies would offer you a turbo conversion (Janspeed was popular in the UK) and stripes and spoilers to match, usually applied to a standard carburetor Scirocco. Germany's Rinspeed offered turbo conversions for the Golf and Scirocco with additional bodykit.

By the end of production in February 1981, 504,153 first-generation Sciroccos had left the assembly line at Osnabrück.

THE MK1 SCIROCCO IN MOTORSPORT

The first Scirocco, like the Golf, would spark a revival in German grass roots racing of largely stock cars by keen amateurs, as Volkswagen reinvented itself as a sporting brand.

In 1976 Volkswagen Motorsport in Hannover created a special series of 50 identical 110 bhp Sciroccos for the newly established Volkswagen Junior Cup, all of them painted black. Drivers included the likes of Manfred Winkelhock, who won the first sea-

LEFT: Launched in 1975, the North American Scirocco retained the European bumpers, but they were mounted on hydraulic impact cylinders. Neatly done, this lengthened the car by only 3.5 inches. *(Revs Institute)*
OPPOSITE TOP: In Germany the Volkswagen Junior Cup started with packed grids of identical production spec Sciroccos. Here at Hockenheim, close racing guaranteed scrapes. *(Volkswagen AG)*
OPPOSITE BOTTOM: With 170 hp and able to hit 150 mph, the Trans-Am Sciroccos were a major image booster for Volkswagen in America, yet were the idea of one dealer. *(Motorbooks)*

son and would go on to become a Formula 1 driver. The Junior Cup then switched from the Scirocco to the Golf GTI, which was built from 1978 onward to Group 1 regulations (which also allowed it to be used in rallies), very close to production Golfs.

In the United States, Bill Scott, a VW dealer from Chicago, had two Sciroccos built for the Trans-Am series with the support of the American VW importer in 1975. It was successful in the VW/SCCA-created Scirocco/Bilstein Cup series and then one of the cars won Category 1 of the 1976 Trans-Am championship for touring cars under 2.0-liters and further rounds of the championship the following year.

In Europe, racing Sciroccos were praised for enlivening Group 2 of the European Touring Car Championship, which the likes of Ford and BMW had abandoned to compete larger-engined cars. There were several private teams with cars developing up to 184 bhp with Kugelfischer fuel injection, and in 1978 Volkswagen Motorsport supported Germany's Willi Bergmeister with Swiss driver Jörg Siegrist, another for Anton Stocker/Hans Nowak.

GTI Style

For a sports model in the 1970s, black details spelled speedy, and the new fast Golf followed the fashion in a tasteful way. Volkswagen chief designer Herbert Schäfer was responsible for what would become the exterior signatures for generations of Golf GTIs: the red stripe on the radiator grille, the larger front spoiler (to counteract nose lifting), modest plastic wheel well extensions, and a matte black frame on the rear window. A black stripe on the lower half of the door joined the wheel arches. At launch the only exterior colors were red or silver.

As a model created on a limited budget, much of the interior was lifted from regular Golfs. The steering wheel was borrowed from the Scirocco TS. All was black inside: headlining, carpets, dashboard, door panels, and even sun visors. However, perhaps the stroke of genius was seats with the now famous tartan pattern chosen by Gunhild Liljequist, a Volkswagen trim and color designer from 1965 to 1992, who often visited Great Britain and admired the quality of the fabrics available. She also had the idea of the now famous golf ball gear knob, playing on the sport (although the golf ball had appeared in Giugiaro's early sketches). An oil-pressure gauge, rev counter, quartz headlamps, and a heated rear window with a rear wash wipe completed the equipment.

Mk1 GTI Technical Spec

The power-to-weight ratio of the Golf GTI was sensational. With a 9.5:1 compression ratio (a standard Golf 1600 was 8.2:1) the 1.6-liter injected four-cylinder produced 110 bhp at 6,100 rpm—57 percent more power than a 1975 Golf 1100 L, and the GTI's curb weight

OPPOSITE TOP: Tartan seats soon spelled sporty in the mid-1970s. This is a 1979 British GTI, the first year of right-hand drive. Silver panel on door is a period electric window kit. *(Allen Kenny - Iconic Auctioneers)*

OPPOSITE BOTTOM: A large rev counter (left) came from the twin dials of the Golf L/LS, plus the dashboard of the base Golf that lacked a glove box lid. Extra instruments in a center console and the steering wheel were shared with the Scirocco. *(Volkswagen AG)*

ABOVE: Marketing pitched the GTI as a practical sporty car in the spirit of small BMWs, smart enough for weekdays but ready for play on the weekend. *(Volkswagen UK)*

of 810 kg was less than the 1100 L three-door's 820 kg curb weight (with half a tank of fuel).

With a four-speed gearbox the claimed acceleration times were 0 to 100 kph (62.5 mph) in nine seconds, a top speed of 182 kph (113 mph), and fuel consumption of 36 mpg. It could take on larger cars with larger engines, such as the newly introduced 2.0-liter Ford Escort RS2000 with 110 bhp but almost 200 kg more weight—tested top speed 112 mph.

The suspension was lowered by 20 mm over a standard Golf with shorter springs and stiffer damper settings, plus twin anti-roll bars as originally conceived. The track was widened by 14 mm to fit 175/70 HR13 radial tires on simple 5½ J 13-inch steel rims. The alloy wheels offered on lesser Golfs were an option. The front disc brakes were ventilated, matched to a larger servo and a rear wheel pressure regulator valve.

Frankfurt 1975 GTI Reveal

On September 11, 1975, the Audi 80 GTE and Golf GTI both appeared at the Frankfurt Motor Show. The Golf was a complete surprise. Nobody had been expecting this sudden move from the manufacturer of hitherto sensible family cars, and some thought it was reckless. "The press was very negative," Fiala told the author in 2013. "They said it's very aggressive, such a light car; 800 kilos with 110 bhp you will have millions of injuries and people killed, but after the press really drove the car they corrected their understanding. This was only for a few weeks and then the discussion was over."

The Audi GTE was for immediate sale, but the Wolfsburg lines were dealing with insatiable demand for regular Golfs, so the Golf GTI went away for durability testing and was not offered for sale until June 1976, alongside the similarly engined Scirocco (see page 12). Volkswagen had benefited from experience with the Audi GTE to tune the 1.6 for smoothness and flexibility.

Meanwhile, American buyers were getting their first taste of the Golf. In its American safety and emissions-compliant form it was renamed the Rabbit in North America (a small, cute, and nimble animal). The Rabbit had square sealed-beam headlamps, impact absorbing bumpers, passive seatbelts, dashboard padding, and crash reinforcement, adding 70 extra kilos. Like the Scirocco, the first Rabbits were fitted with the 1.5-liter engine coupled to a catalytic converter that kept power down to 70 bhp.

On sale in the US at the start of 1975, the Rabbit hit a keen but passing appetite for fuel-efficient cars (the 1976 diesel was the real star). "Best car in the world for under $3,500," said *Road & Track*, magazine, but the currency exchange rate was not in its favor. The same money would buy you an American six-cylinder.

OPPOSITE: Usually an optional extra, a rear wash-wipe was standard on every GTI and much appreciated during a fast drive down muddy roads. This 1979 UK car had only 53,540 miles showing when auctioned in 2024. *(Allen Kenny – Iconic Auctioneers)*

RIGHT: Like any Golf, there was room for two adults in the rear. The backrest folded onto the base, which then pivoted forward to give a completely flat load bay. *(Allen Kenny - Iconic Auctioneers)*

1976—GTI On Sale

The Golf GTI went on sale in mainland Europe in June 1976, accompanied by the new Scirocco GTI with the same engine but not the same suspension setup. At the European press launch at the Hockenheim circuit the company playfully issued each journalist a red silk scarf and black leather driving gloves (this was the 1970s after all).

Anticipating a small production run to a limited market, it carried a large price for a small car at DM 13,850 compared with DM 10,790 for the five-door Golf LS. The idea of right-hand drive versions of either car for the UK was ruled out because the brake servo was said to get in the way, let alone re-engineering the GTI for America. The UK press release was quite plain: special-order left-hand drive Golf and Scirocco GTIs could be had from September, but "For technical reasons it will not be possible to produce right-hand drive versions. Volkswagen (GB), who are investigating the motor sport potential for both cars, are importing them mainly for competition drivers."

The critics loved it from the outset. In its July 1976 edition, *Auto Motor und Sport* was completely won over by the "conspicuously inconspicuous" GTI. The magazine's test figures were 0–100 km/h (62 mph) in 9.4 seconds and a top speed of 185 km/h (115 mph)—better than the official claims.

There was praise for the calm way in which the car handled its power from the flexibility of the engine, the improved fuel consumption from the fuel injection, and only a slight loss in overall comfort from the standard car. "One of the most delightful tasks a driver can have is to climb an Alpine pass in a GTI," said the magazine.

Motorway comfort and stability were equally praiseworthy up until about 170 km/h (105 mph), when the front end of the GTI started to become light, despite the presence of the spoiler. This was a minor point in a test that concluded that the new Golf was the true successor to the small BMW sports sedans.

Homologation was expected to be reached by October 1976, when 5,000 examples would have been assembled. But the high price was no deterrent; production was soon 5,000 cars a month, and Volkswagen was able to maintain the premium price at the increased build rate. According to the 1984 British book *Volkswagen Golf, the Enthusiast's Companion* 10,366 Golf GTIs were produced in 1976 (even though this was only half a year on sale).

TUNING THE FIRST GTIs

As soon as the Golf came out, a whole industry popped up aiming to make it faster or look faster. Kamei soon established itself as the top purveyor of grilles with extra lights, spoilers, and stripes, as did Zender. It was a bolt-on bonanza. ATS and BBS supplied alloy wheels.

For increased engine power there were many German Volkswagen tuners but Oettinger was the biggest name. Since 1951 Gerhard Oettinger's Okrasa carburetor kits (the initials of Oettinger Kraftfahrtechnische Spezial Anstalt) had pepped-up generations of air-cooled Volkswagens across the world.

In the gap between the 1975 announcement of the Golf GTI and the summer 1976 on-sale date, Oettinger jumped in with a conversion of the Golf LS that involved transplanting the 100 bhp 1.6-liter carburetor engine from the Audi 80 GT plus extra sports equipment for almost DM 6,000 more than a GTI at DM 16,258. In 1977 Oettinger presented a 16-valve cylinder head.

While American enthusiasts pined for a real GTI, Rabbit (and Scirocco) buyers could look to tuners such as Power Haus Products of California, which had been importing Okrasa kits since the Beetle era. Kits extended the 1.5-liter Rabbit engine to 1.6 or even 1.8 liters. In 1980 a $2,500 Okrasa 1800 Rabbit conversion was claimed to cover 0–60 mph in 10.6 seconds—as fast as a Porsche 924 and two seconds faster than stock.

Also from California, Porsche-like performance was claimed for the Automotive Performance Systems (APS) Rabbit, which, in 1982, along with upgraded suspension, wheels, and Kamei front spoiler added an Oettinger 16-valve cylinder head and an Okrasa cylinder enlargement kit to 2.0 liters for 112 bhp. The price tag was a hefty $12,000.

GTI-PLUS

In Europe, with the advent of the real GTI, there were some buyers for whom 110 bhp was simply not enough. Nothelle and Oettinger bored-out the engine to 1.9 and 2.0 liters and up to 136 bhp.

In Britain, the pioneer of tuned Golf GTIs and GTI racing (see page 26) was GTi (small "i") Engineering. It was founded in 1978 by racing driver Richard Lloyd and Brian Ricketts, formerly of Broadspeed, initially to convert left-hand drive first GTIs to right-hand drive.

The company imported APS alloy wheels, Bilstein spring and damper kits, Zender spoilers, and a "four door" GTI conversion (denied to the English market). From 1979 it offered a 1.8-liter conversion of the 1.6-liter GTI. The 1.8-liter conversion bored out the standard block to 81 mm

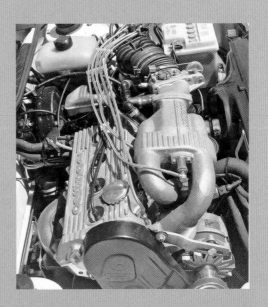

(an increase of 1.5 mm) and increased the stroke using the crankshaft of the US specification 1.7-liter.

The £1,437 conversion then added Cosworth-forged pistons, raising the compression ratio from 9.5:1 to 10.0:1, plus a gas-flowed cylinder head with slightly larger inlet and exhaust valves, special valve springs, and a mildly greater overlap Schrick camshaft. It produced around 135 bhp. A more expensive conversion added a hotter camshaft, more cylinder head mods including bigger valves, and a modified throttle body for 140 bhp.

Also in the UK, the 1982 Toleman GTIs offered 1.8- or 2.0-liter extensions with either an eight-valve or the 16-valve Oettinger head, the latter giving 155 bhp. The 16-valve engine alone was £2,900.

TURBO TROUBLE

As an alternative to enlarging the engine, by the late 1970s adding a turbocharger was a quick slug of power for any car. In Germany in 1980, the Sorgler GTI, with a KKK turbo, became the first Golf GTI to offer 200 kph (124 mph). Janspeed was a popular turbo kit in the UK, while Turbo Technics of Northampton developed a conversion based on a Garrett AiResearch T3 turbo fitted with an intercooler behind the grille.

These early conversions quickly became a handful to drive as these turbos suffered huge "lag" before they cut in. If the car hadn't had a suspension or brake upgrade the sudden boost could shoot it right off the road. On regular Golf GTIs, upgraded brakes were a better use of money than more power.

At the 1979 Geneva Motor Show, Swiss tuner Rinspeed presented its Golf GTI Turbo equipped with a Rotomaster turbocharger, modified pistons for the lower compression ratio needed, and an exhaust system bypass valve to give the 1.6-liter 135 bhp. It was docile to drive at low speeds, but, in common with other early turbos, it suffered dreadful fuel consumption.

THE FIRST OFFICIAL GTI 16-VALVE

In 1981, as the "hot hatchback" race intensified, Volkswagen France looked to keep its GTI at the top of buyers' lists by offering a 136 bhp version, named 16S (for 16 *soupapes*, French for valves) with the Oettinger 16-valve cylinder head.

The conversion entailed special pistons for the higher compression ratio (10.5:1 as opposed to 9.5), a balanced crankshaft and connecting rods, and modified oil sump and pump. The 16S took GTI power from 110 to 136 bhp and a claimed maximum of 121 mph. A BBS bodykit matching the color of the car plus four headlamps and unique badging marked out the French super-GTI.

For the 16S to be sold with a full factory warranty through French Volkswagen dealers, Volkswagen Germany demanded extensive tests. It was also homologated for Group 4 racing (400 examples needing to be produced), whereby Oettinger was sent standard GTIs from Wolfsburg to be fitted with the modified engines.

Produced between August 1981 and July 1983, at FRF 75,000, France's Golf GTI 16S was 50 percent more than the standard car and equal to the price of a BMW 323i. Only around 1,250 were produced.

MORE RABBIT GTI

As the US-only Rabbit GTI was only built between 1983 and 1984, there was little time to demand hotter versions, and the Mk2 Golf GTI had already launched in Europe. However, GMP Inc. of Charlotte, North Carolina, offered a buffet of add-ons, including an upgraded Kenwood sound system, Sachs suspension kit, and European Recaro seats. Its engine alterations included a hotter camshaft, a modified throttle body, and stainless-steel exhaust that nudged power up from 90 to 100 bhp.

OPPOSITE TOP: Typical of the many uprated Mk1 GTIs, a German Zender body-kit and ATS wheels, two-tone paint, and quad lamps marked out the 1982 British Toleman GTI. *(Magiccarpix)*
OPPOSITE BOTTOM: The extra power of the 16S conversion needed a stronger clutch and also had closer ratio gears. It was the fastest "production" Mk1 GTI. *(Volkswagen UK)*
TOP LEFT: The most spectacular Rinspeed Golf GTI Turbo was the 1981 gull winged Aliporta, fitted with a TV and a cocktail cabinet. *(Motorsport Images)*
TOP RIGHT: The 1981 French Golf GTI 16S conversion was sanctioned by Volkswagen in Wolfsburg but ruled out as too fragile for wider production. *(Volkswagen UK)*

BELOW: All-White Golf Cabriolet specials were high fashion in the 1980s. As it had a GTI engine Volkswagen UK's 1984 version added the red grille stripes and extra driving lights. *(Volkswagen UK)*

The 1977 Golf GTI

The British press first got the chance to fully road test a Golf GTI when the special-order left-hand drive cars began filtering through in spring 1977. An opening steel sunroof became an option on all Golfs in 1977.

MKT 512R, finished in Mars Red, was the demonstrator for Volkswagen UK, and *Autocar* gave it the full road test treatment in March, even if some readers might have found the steering wheel on the "wrong" side of the car a bit off-putting. At £3,372 it was expensive for a compact 1.6-liter car, especially only in left-hand drive but compared well against the similarly fast £3,729 Ford Escort RS2000 and the £3,833 16 valve Triumph Dolomite Sprint. Specialists such as GTi Engineering (see page 20) offered conversions to right-hand drive.

At first the suspension seemed stiff, the road testers found. "However, when the GTI is extended, one immediately begins to appreciate all the attention that has been given to the suspension. . . . With so much power, the GTI tends to approach corners at a very high speed and it makes much greater demands on its driver than does the standard car."

As with all front-drivers, the default characteristic was understeer. So, the nose ran wide at very high speeds but when the testers suddenly lifted off the throttle in a corner, they found that "the car suddenly converts to oversteer, which, if allowed to get out of hand, can result in the tail swinging a long way out of line . . . as one becomes more familiar with the GTI, one learns to exploit this trait to great advantage."

At the test track the best maximum speed was 108 mph and 0–60 mph came up in 9.8 seconds, which it judged "a most respectable rate for a 1.6-liter sedan car" at an average of 29 mpg. Practicality was an added bonus: "Even would-be Roger Clarks [the famous British rally driver] have to carry dogs, children, and the odd washing machine around sometime."

1978—The Rabbit Arrives

With much fanfare, the first American-made Golf rolled off the line on Monday, April 10, 1978. To overcome volatile exchange rates, Volkswagen had taken the bold step to assemble the Rabbit in America at an ex-Chrysler plant in Westmoreland, Pennsylvania, the first-ever US factory for a mass-produced non-American automobile.

At full production, 5,000 employees assembled the new Rabbits from parts delivered from Europe as a Completely Knocked Down (CKD) kit. Engines and transmissions were shipped from Germany, and Volkswagen of America (VWoA) sourced most other materials from US and Canadian suppliers (Canada imported German Golfs until 1981).

This was a very US-flavored Golf with its own interior trim and colors—from 1981 the color of the interior matched the exterior paintwork. In 1980 a pick-up version was created for the US and was later made in Europe as the Caddy.

From 1978 Volkswagen of Mexico made its own version of the Golf, called the Caribe, at its Puebla factory. The new name ensured it was not confused with the Golf, which it also made but was a unique model that looked a little like a Golf but had started life with a Beetle engine in the front. It most closely resembled the Rabbit with rectangular headlamps and stayed in production until 1987. The 1984 Caribe GT was almost like a GTI with a red strip around the grille and black rear spoiler, and it had a twin-carburetor 1.8-liter 85 bhp engine.

In Europe, a mild facelift in August 1978 brought new seats for the mainstream Golfs—still tartan in the GTI—sturdier plastic-coated bumpers that wrapped around the corners, and on the dashboard an "econometer" that told you when to change gear for the best fuel economy.

The 1979 Golf Cabriolet

In 1979 Golf body styles blossomed in two directions. First, the Geneva Motor Show in March 1979 saw the first-ever Golf Cabriolet (named Cabriolet in Europe, convertible in the US).

An open-topped Golf was not part of the initial plan, but there would be a gap when the beloved Karmann-built Beetle convertible finished in 1978. Uncertainty over whether American roll over legislation was about to ban soft-tops fed into this and put the brakes on convertible development by some European carmakers even though it didn't come to pass.

Anxious not to lose work, Karmann had tried developing a Scirocco convertible but abandoned it as too cramped. Nobody had thought about chopping the top off a hatchback, but after having shown a taped-up Golf three-door, Karmann's engineers got the go-ahead from Volkswagen and in early 1977 the top was cut off a Golf hatch. Unlike the Beetle, the Golf had a stressed unitary bodyshell, so this robbed it of about 80 percent of its torsional rigidity. Strengthening beams went in across the shell and between the front and rear wheel wells.

The ultimate solution to a floppy Golf was a masterstroke. Although not required by law at the time, a rollover bar was added behind the front seats. It calmed the shaking over rough roads, gave seat belt anchorage points, helped locate the roof, and could bear the weight of the car in a rollover. It earned the Golf Cabriolet the nickname, *Erdbeerkörbchen*, or strawberry basket.

The production Cabriolet was developed over more than two years. To restore structural rigidity, the top extra inner wing, scuttle, sill door, floor, and tail section reinforcement added up to some 90 kg of extra metal. The top-quality five-layer folding top weighed 40 kg more than the steel roof of the original Golf.

The Golf Cabriolet was launched in two versions for Europe: GLS and GLI. Given the extra weight it was carrying, the 1.1-liter engine was only reserved for markets where it would have a tax advantage. Otherwise, the GLS was equipped with the 70 bhp 1.5-liter engine and the GLI received the injected 110 bhp 1.6-liter of the Golf GTI. Factory claimed performance for the GLI was still 0–60 mph in under 10 seconds. The Rabbit convertible was only offered with a 76 bhp fuel-injected 1.6-liter engine.

Production of the Golf Cabriolet settled to 2,000 a year, all that Karmann at Osnabrük could manage. It was to be an exceptional production run, lasting until 1993, still based on the Mk1 Golf.

Jetta: More Golf

In summer 1979, the Volkswagen Jetta (another wind-like name) blew in, a Golf sedan 40 cm longer than the hatch, endowed with a trunk grafted to the rear of the Golf behind the rear doors of the five-door hatch. The grille had rectangular headlamps to distinguish it from the front. A two-door version was available in some markets. While Britain and France had embraced the hatchback, Spanish buyers preferred sedans, perceiving them as more prestigious, as did Finland, but it was America above all that preferred sedans.

The Jetta was engineered with only a small weight penalty of about 30 kg (dry) over a Golf 1100 and in Europe was offered with 1.3- and 1.5-liter engines and with the 110 bhp injected 1.6-liter of the Golf GTI/Scirocco. For 1980, America had an injected and three-way catalyst 1.6-liter Jetta with 76 bhp.

Over 100,000 Golf GTIs had been sold in continental Europe by July 1979, when UK fans rejoiced that they could finally order a right-hand GTI (along with the Scirocco GLI). The suspension was now lowered slightly to the same height as the Scirocco. By 1980, there was a four-month waiting list. Cashing in on GTI fever, Volkswagen UK brought out the 1.3-liter Golf Driver with GTI looks but none of the performance.

The only bugbear of the GTI's conversion to right-hand drive was mushy brake pedal feel from the longer linkage. For a fee, specialists like GTi Engineering would change the brake pads for better specification Mintex items and adjust the linkage.

ABOVE: The first-generation Jetta came with two or four doors but the same generous trunk space. The four-door became the best seller. *(Volkswagen UK)*
OPPOSITE: Nothing changed on the outside with the new 1.8-liter GTI in 1982, but the much appreciated new engine was ready to power the Mk2 GTI when it arrived in 1984 and have a long career. *(Author)*

A five-speed gearbox (still a rarity on small cars) was introduced on European GTIs in July 1979 and came to the UK at the end the year. This might have irked those who had ordered the first right-hand drivers as the new 'box was much appreciated by magazines such as *Motorsport*, as it only added to the sportiness. Rather than a fifth ratio added for economy, it was a set of closer ratios allied to a lower final drive ratio, apart from fifth, which was a little taller than the old fourth and improved fuel economy. "Now that so smooth and extraordinarily efficient engine simply sings through the gears in one of the happiest engine/gearbox combinations on the market" (Clive Richardson, March 1980).

1980–1981

There was a further facelift for all 1980 Golfs, of larger headlamps and wider taillight clusters that included the fog light. The new dashboard included a large lockable glove box, and for 1981 the GTI gained new seats and trims, losing the tartan pattern in favor of stripes.

In 1981 Germany and Belgium gained the choice of a five-door Golf GTI, with a less sporty interior, as did South Africa. A market that always favored sporty Golfs, Volkswagen of South Africa (VWSA) had been producing ever speedier Golfs since 1978 at its Uitenhage assembly site near Port Elizabeth. Although the GTI didn't arrive in South Africa until the 1983 model year, it produced a GT, a GTS, and a GTX.

1982: A Sporty Diesel and the GTI 1.8

Through the 1970s Volkswagen engineers steered clear of the turbocharger for gas engines, citing an increased likelihood of engine wear and turbo lag, but a turbo worked very well bolted to the tougher diesel engine.

Launched for the 1982 model year but in development since 1978, adding a turbocharger to the 1.6-liter diesel produced gas engined levels of performance—70 bhp to match the 1.5-liter gas. With engine mods including a larger oil circuit with an oil cooler, a Garrett or KKK turbocharger was used and maximum torque was developed at 2,000 rpm compared with the 2,500 of the 1.5 gas. A 96 mph top speed and up to 42.5 mpg were both possible. Volkswagen created the world's first sports diesel, the Golf GTD, and dressed it in some of the GTI's details, such as wider wheels with wheel arch extensions and interior trim, but the UK opted not to sell it alongside gas GTIs.

In late 1982 and faced with a growing crowd of more powerful wannabe GTIs, some turbocharged, Volkswagen introduced a bigger-engined GTI, increasing the bore and stroke of the 1.6-liter engine to 1.8-liter.

Added refinements included improved balancing and a torsional vibration damper. There was a revised (lighter) camshaft, new combustion chamber pattern, and a 10:1 compression ratio (up from 9.5:1).

While this only brought an increase of two brake horsepower to 112 bhp, the engine was, as intended, much more flexible and efficient coupled with new taller ratios in the five-speed gearbox allowing 19.7 mph per 1,000 rpm compared with 18.4 of the 1.6. The official British combined fuel consumption of 36.7 mpg at 75 mph compared with 32.5 in the old car.

In the UK there was no price increase over the outgoing 1.6, but the new equipment was a multi-function trip computer, considered a great novelty in the early 1980s. Controlled by a button on the end of the wiper stalk, it could display six things and had two memory settings. The interior was unchanged with black trim, painted metal door tops, and sports seats.

THE FIRST GTIs IN MOTORSPORT

The Golf GTI started as wheels for weekend racers, and pretty soon after launch it was on the tracks. It was sold in a "basic configuration" for racing, which cost around DM 30,000.

In 1977 the Golf Cup racing series followed the example of the Scirocco Cup in Germany and was immediately popular, running until 1982. In the United States, although it was denied the GTI, VWoA supported the Rabbit Bilstein Cup from 1978 to 1982.

The Golf Cup GTIs (near standard) could compete in Group 1 Touring cars races, and according to the regulations came with 138 bhp. For Group 2 more modifications were allowed within rules that governed tires and dimensions, as well as how far the wheel arches could be extended. Group 1 and 2 GTIs were eligible to take part in the World Rally Championship.

Volkswagen left the engine preparation of the cars it backed to specialists and the Hannover University science department. In 1978 a Group 2 GTI with a special cylinder head and Zenith fuel injection produced 180 bhp. Jochi Kleint—the first rally driver with an official Volkswagen contract—took it to second in the opening stages of the 1978 Hunsrück Rallye.

In the UK, Richard Lloyd took the first GTI to the tracks in 1977, as he started his tuning business GTi Engineering. He fitted a left-hand drive GTI with safety kit and racing tires and came second in class first time out at Silverstone with a standard engine. With help from VW Great Britain and some work on the engine, seven wins followed.

For 1978 Lloyd used a left-hand drive UK press car, converted it to right-hand drive, and stormed his way to second overall in the Tricentrol British Sedan Car Championship.

Modifications were few; there was a limited-slip differential, but brakes were standard apart from racing linings and the smaller Golf 1100 brake servo. Much effort was put into the suspension, but while the engine was completely reliable, no more power than the normal 110 bhp could be extracted if the Bosch fuel injection was retained.

In France, proving how lively the Golf diesel engine was, Jochi Kleint and Andreas Hansch competed in the 1978 Monte Carlo Rally on a trial basis with a turbo diesel and caused a sensation when they finished in 13th place—out of 270 participants. On the 1979 Monte Carlo Rally entry list of 253 cars, there were no less than 15 Golf GTIs and four Golf diesels. Nine of the GTIs finished, the highest placed 13th (of 154).

The Golf GTI's first outright rally win was the September 1979 Sachs Rally Baltic, where a Group 2 version was driven by Swedish rally star Per Eklund, the famous Saab driver, still weighing only 790 kg with a roll cage and producing around 170 bhp.

ABOVE: Richard Lloyd kicked off the GTI's UK racing career in 1977 driving what he was told was the first left-hand drive car imported into the UK, with nothing added beyond a roll cage. *(Volkswagen UK)*

A works-backed GTI was then entered for the 1980 Monte Carlo Rally fitted with a Zenith-Pierburg CS racing fuel-injection system and painted yellow, the color of its sponsors. Eklund and co-driver Hans Sylvan were at one point in second place until a half shaft broke but fought their way up to an impressive fifth (of 126) despite particularly icy conditions.

The team color changed from yellow to green between 1981 and 1982 when throat lozenge manufacturer Rheila became an additional sponsor. The green Golf became known as the *Rheila-Frosch* (from the saying, *Gegen Frosch im Hals* "I have a frog in my throat"), and despite a notable write-off when their car landed in a tree, Alfons Stock and Paul Schmuck were crowned German Rally champions in 1981.

In the 1982 Monte Carlo Rally, French driver Francis Bondil with Alain Brunel were first in Group A (the new title for Group 2 from 1982). Per Eklund once more drove for Volkswagen in the 1982 San Remo Rally with its Group B (former Group 4) specification GTI. Its 16-valve Oettinger engine was now giving 193 bhp and was in the top ten before clutch failure. Private GTIs continued to figure in many 1983 European rallies, but Volkswagen did not return to factory rally GTIs until the Mk2 GTI.

LEFT: Swedish duo Per Eklund and Ragnar Spluth on the 1981 Monte Carlo Rally. Champions in front-wheel-drive Saabs, making GTIs perform well in snow came naturally, but they were put out by engine failure. *(Girardo Archive/Alamy Stock Photo)*
BELOW: Peter Diekmann and Holger Bohne at the 1979 Hunsrück Rallye in the works GTI, a two-day event on gravel tracks. There's no GTI badging, but GTI alloys are fitted. *(Volkswagen AG)*

Seen here in the 1982 San Remo Rally, WOB VZ8 was the second "Rheila Golf GTI" rally car built. It had an Oettinger 16-valve cylinder head and found a permanent home in the Volkswagen museum. *(Volkswagen Motorsport)*

LEFT: The Rabbit GTI took the sporty trim of the Rabbit S, which added a front spoiler, before getting to work on the mechanical and suspension upgrades. (*VWoA*)

BELOW: The highly prized Pirelli edition of 1983 was easy to identify by the "P" for Pirelli cut outs in the alloy wheels and Pirelli P6 tires. A four-lamp grille was now fitted across the Golf range to help end-of-run sales. (*Magiccarpix*)

Rabbit GTI

The US-built Rabbit had performed well in its early days, but along with all carmakers, sales of all Volkswagen models nose-dived in the face of Japanese imports. With cheaper gas prices, the Rabbit diesel boom had been short-lived but it had accounted for 70 percent of production. The Jetta was more stable, running at about 20,000 cars a year at the start of the '80s.

Buyers had found the American Golf to be badly built and the Rabbit was judged a little too American by the magazines and enthusiast buyers, with its soft seats and soft suspension. Even Volkswagen chief Carl Hahn (from 1982) admitted in a 1983 interview with *Autocar*, "A European driver used to the Golf could fly off the road in the first turn with a Rabbit . . . we discovered that Americans now want a car with European qualities when they buy a European car." The Rabbit S had some sporty features but no extra power.

America had been denied the GTI because it wasn't considered to be a big seller and required extra detoxing, but now some of its magic was needed as an image booster for the Rabbit. In 1981 Jim Fuller was moved from vice president of Porsche and Audi in America to troubleshoot Volkswagen's problems. An internal corporate campaign called "Roots" was initiated to "Germanise" the cars with firmer suspension, better seats, and more understated trim: "We're through Malibuing these cars around!" Fuller notably said in a reference to the pillowy Chevrolet of the day.

In November 1981 *MotorTrend* wrote an open letter to VWoA stating that all the parts necessary to turn the Rabbit S were available off the shelf and the $250,000 cost of certifying a new engine for a Westmoreland-built GTI would soon be recouped.

The US Rabbit GTI team was headed by VWoA vice president of engineering Duane Miller. He told *Road & Track* that it became possible with the 1981 decisions in Germany to give it the Quantum (Passat) 14-inch alloy wheels and to federalize the new 1.8-liter unit for the European Golf GTI. This was enough for an American GTI. However, rather than import the German 1.8, it bored out the stock 1982 Rabbit 1.7-liter to 1.8-liter to closely match the European Golf—with a compression ratio raised from 8.21:1 to 8.5:1. Larger valves were fitted with a lower restriction exhaust system allied to a re-engineered catalytic converter to reduce back pressure. The five-speed gearbox was imported from Germany with the European GTI's close-ratio gearbox. The Rabbit GTI produced 90 bhp at 5,500 rpm.

30 THE COMPLETE BOOK OF VOLKSWAGEN GTI

This was 22 bhp down on the 1982 Golf GTI 1.8, but the US engine increased flexibility and refinement, with a top speed of 104 mph and 0–60 mph in 9.7 seconds. Crucially, this was a second quicker than the five-liter four-speed Pontiac Trans-Am.

It was 63 kg heavier than the Euro-GTI, and the suspension was made 22 percent stiffer than the standard Rabbit, with added anti-roll bars front and rear and the same German Sachs rear shock absorbers. The new alloy wheels were cloaked with P185/60HR-14 Pirelli P6 tires.

Outside, the first Rabbit GTI had the sporty cues of the German GTI with blacked-out trim highlighted with red and a new front spoiler. Inside, the entire Rabbit range had received more toned-down and European-looking interiors, and the GTI's red-striped seats were relatively subtle.

The Rabbit GTI was previewed in November 1982 for the 1983 model year, while in Germany, the Golf was about to be replaced. *Car & Driver* called it "the most exciting automotive news of the year." Even if it only lasted for two seasons, the first Rabbit GTI was a great image booster.

1983 Mk1 Specials

After the Mk2 Scirocco, the second-generation Golf launched in autumn 1983. The next GTI would not be on stream until 1984, so for the last year the Mk1 GTIs ran-out with special editions.

In Germany the Pirelli Special Edition was marked out by a double-lamp grille (head and fog) and available with three special colors: Helios Blue Metallic, Mars Red, and Lhasa Green Metallic. It rode on distinctive alloy wheels with holes cut in the shape of "P" for Pirelli and 185/60 HR 14 tires of the same name. Planned production of 10,500 units sold out in six months. Similar models were the Trophy for Switzerland, GTI Plus for France, and 1,000 "Campaigns" for the UK. There was a debate among enthusiasts as to what constituted a genuine GTI Campaign. The July 1983 UK brochure just termed it "an extra special GTi" with no mention of the word "Campaign," but it had the Pirelli wheels, a sliding steel sunroof (which was optional in Germany), and came in six colors.

For a car only predicted to be good for 5,000 sales a year, the first Golf GTI sold 461,690 between 1976 and 1983, about 8 percent of first-generation Golf production. There was no question that there would be another GTI in the new generation.

TOP: None of the black austerity of a Euro-GTI; the Westmoreland-built Rabbit GTI stuck with color-matched velour seat trim for close copies of the German seats. *(VWoA)*
ABOVE: From 1980, tartan seats had given way to gray or red striping. Four-spoke steering wheel was leather-wrapped in this Pirelli edition. Small multi-function computer screen is in the center of the instruments. *(Volkswagen UK)*

WÖRTHERSEE, THE FESTIVAL OF GTI

In 1982, what would become the world's biggest annual gathering of GTIs began modestly in the village of Maria Wörth around the beautiful lake Wörthersee in southern Austria.

Passionate GTI owner Erwin Neuwirth decided to organize a meeting, or *treffen*, just for fellow GTI fans and about 80 turned up. The following year Volkswagen itself helped send the invitations out and 754 GTIs appeared. Becoming too big for the local clubs to handle, Volkswagen joined forces with the local tourist board and by 1985 1,160 GTIs and over 3,000 people made it to the lakeside.

By 2013 around 150,000 Volkswagen groupies from all over Europe were converging on the two villages of Maria Wörth and Reifnitz for cars, beer, and mayhem punctuated by exhibitions, talks and film shows, treasure hunt rallies, and driving slaloms. Each event lasted four days, from the Wednesday before Ascension to the following weekend.

Officially sponsored by Volkswagen since 2000, it became a mini motor show. Škoda, Seat, Audi, and Volkswagen showed off modified versions of their sporting cars and began to create concept cars and launch special editions just at the event.

At its peak, 200,000 people showed up to Wörthersee. Although it brought a lot of money into town, the locals eventually grew tired of the upheaval. It was held every year until 2019, but then COVID-19 hit and it didn't restart. In February 2023 the municipality of Reifnitz/Maria Wörth announced that it wouldn't be hosting any more auto shows, not sitting well with sustainability or its climate change policies. Volkswagen swiftly announced it would be hosting the party in Wolfsburg in July 2024.

TOP LEFT: The invitation to the first Austrian GTI gathering was "in the interests of active road safety" but became so much more than a weekend of driving tests. *(Volkswagen AG)*

TOP RIGHT: A Kamei customized GTI leads the lakeside traffic on a sunny 1980s Wörthersee weekend. Modified cars became a big part of the show. *(Volkswagen AG)*

ABOVE: In 2016, the 35th anniversary Wörthersee was a celebration of 40 years of the Golf GTI, with the now customary unique car built by trainees. To the right is a GTI made in granite, which lived in the town. *(Volkswagen AG)*

Golf GTI Mk1

Model	GTI 1.6	GTI 1.8	Rabbit GTI
Engine type/capacity	4-cyls inline 1,588 cc Bosch K-Jetronic fuel injection	4-cyls inline 1,781 cc Bosch K-Jetronic fuel injection	4-cyls inline 1,780 cc CIS fuel injection
Gearbox	4-speed manual (5 from 1979)	5-speed manual	5-speed manual
Maximum power/at rpm	110 bhp@6,100 rpm	112 bhp@5,800 rpm	90 bhp@5,500 rpm
Maximum torque/at rpm	101 lb ft@5,000 rpm	109 lb ft@3,500 rpm	105 lb ft@3,250 rpm
Acceleration 0–62 mph	9 seconds	8.2 seconds	9.7 seconds (0–60 mph)
Maximum speed	113mph (claimed)	113 mph (claimed)	104 mph (*Car & Driver* 1982)
Suspension front/rear	Strut and coil springs, wishbone, anti-roll bar/trailing arms, coil springs, torsion beam axle, anti-roll bar	Strut and coil springs, wishbone, anti-roll bar/trailing arms, coil springs, torsion beam axle, anti-roll bar	Strut and coil springs, wishbone, anti-roll bar/trailing arms, coil springs, torsion beam axle, anti-roll bar
Wheels/tires	5.5J x 13 in alloys (UK) 175 x 70 HR 13 Continental	5.5J x 13 in alloys (UK) 175 x 70 HR 13 Michelin XVS	6J x 14 in alloys 185 x 60 R 14 Pirelli P6
Brakes front/rear	Ventilated disc/drum	Ventilated disc/drum	Ventilated disc/drum
Length	3,705 mm	3,815 mm	3,940 mm
Wheelbase	2,400 mm	2,400 mm	2,400 mm
Width	1,610 mm	1,610 mm	1,610 mm
Height	1,400 mm	1,400 mm	1,400 mm
Kerb weight (kg)	810	871	952
Years produced	1976-1982	1982-1983	1983-1984
Overall production number	462,000 (1976-1983)	n/a	Believed 30,000

2.
GOLF GTI MK2 1984–1992

More of the Same, Please

Volkswagen played it safe with its new Golf for the 1980s. The family hatchback now made up 40 percent of company sales, and the market was awash with similar cars from manufacturers trying to emulate its success with an identical mechanical layout.

The decision to go ahead with a new model was made in 1978, when the original was still selling strongly but pressure to reduce production costs was growing from Japanese carmakers with more efficient manufacturing capabilities. The new Golf not only had to be a better-built car (the first had rusted alarmingly early) but quicker and easier to build, ushering in the use of robots.

Ten different styles were considered (including one from Giugiaro) but the result was an in-house design by Herbert Schäfer, who also designed the new Scirocco and Passat. The new Golf needed

RIGHT: This summer 1983 launch photo of the Mk2 Golf GTI shows the rounded contours are a clear evolution of the Italian-styled original. This GTI is wearing optional alloys wheels. *(Volkswagen UK)*

to be roomier for five adults and their luggage, safer in a crash, and have more room under the hood for extras such as power steering and air-conditioning.

Launched in summer 1983 and offered with three and five doors as before, at 3.98 m long the Mk2 Golf was 27 mm longer than the first, with an extra 75 mm added to the wheelbase at 2,475 mm. It was 55 mm wider but at 1,415 mm high only 5 mm taller. The front track (distance between the wheels) on a standard Golf was 23 mm wider, the rear 50 mm wider.

The look was very Golf-like but without the sharp edges of the Italian original. Extensive wind tunnel work reduced the drag coefficient from 0.42 to 0.34 Cd. The absence of protruding rain gutters along the roof was claimed to control both rain and wind flow along the roof, and the front three quarter windows were flush with the front of the door pillar. The underside was fitted with an air deflector, and the sealing between the hood and radiator was designed to help air flow through the engine bay and keep turbulence to a minimum.

The previous generation's engines were carried over, albeit heavily revised. The base engine was now a 55 bhp 1.3-liter unit over the old 1100 (although Italy got a tax-friendly but feeble 45 bhp Polo 1.1 at first). The next gas engine was the 75 bhp 1.6-liter, later joined by a carbureted 90 bhp 1.8-liter available for the first time in a standard Golf rather than the GTI. The new range-topping 1.8 GLX featured such luxuries as central locking, electric front windows, and power steering plus the trip computer from the GTI. Although not immediately in the showrooms, the GTI's specification was previewed in August 1983 and it carried over the 112 bhp 1.8-liter unit of the last car, with a 130 bhp 16-valve promised later. The 1.6-liter diesel choice continued to be a normally aspirated 54 bhp or 70 bhp turbo diesel.

Weight was up. While a 1974 three-door Golf 1100 came in at 750 kg with no fuel on board, the new 1300 three-door was 845 kg. The increased glass area and the fuel tank alone added an extra 15 kg, but the improved aerodynamics were claimed to largely take care of the extra mass in fuel consumption and performance terms.

ABOVE: Volkswagen designers work on a clay model of the second Golf in the early 1980s. Daring rear styling with a split window was abandoned for a softer-edged resemblance to the groundbreaking original. *(Volkswagen UK)*
OPPOSITE TOP: "How to make a best seller even better?" asks the German brochure for the second Golf. There's a hint of a racier side, as well. *(Author)*
OPPOSITE BOTTOM: Here's the 1983-flavor GTI in an Italian brochure. The badge and the black side trim are there, but with single front lamps, it was hard to make out a GTI from a GTD or a GLX. *(Author)*

The successful philosophy of MacPherson strut front suspension and twist beam rear continued but with a number of changes aimed at improving ride and handling. Although power steering was an uncommon option on the last of the Volkswagen Rabbits, it was now standard on the Golf GL and would be increasingly offered in future, then become standard. All Golfs now had front disc brakes, and the braking system was designed so that in both left- and right-hand drive versions the brake pedal acted directly on the servo rather than by a rod.

While it was anticipated, there would be no second-generation Golf Cabriolet. The original was still only four years old (even less time on the US market) and selling a healthy 2,000 units a year despite newer opposition from the Ford Escort convertible (also Karmann-built). Volkswagen UK's 1983 allocation was sold out before it arrived. To save corporate costs, there was a pragmatic decision not to spend resources developing a new one, and the range-topping GLI/GTI continued to use the 112 bhp 1.8-liter engine, but the US Volkswagen Cabriolet was 90 bhp.

A new Jetta arrived quickly in February 1984, having been designed alongside the Golf hatch. In the UK, Volkswagen opted not to take the 112 bhp 1.8 GTI engine, staying with the carburetor version with 90 bhp for the range-topping GLX. In the United States the first-generation Jetta GLI was sold only for the 1983–1984 model year with GTI-style trim with an injected and catalyzed 90 bhp 1.8, close-ratio five-speed manual transmission and sports suspension.

The Ultimate hatchback.
The Golf GTi has been described by motoring writers as the "ultimate hatchback". It is powered by the renowned 1800 cc fuel injection engine producing 112 bhp.
Combine this with a 5 speed close ratio sports gearbox, more aerodynamic body, improved suspension, disc brakes all round, low profile tyres and the new Golf GTi is all set for supremacy on the road. Top speed is 119 mph and 0–60 is reached in a rapid 8.3 seconds.
The GTi, now available with 3 and 5 doors, is immediately recognised by its red trimmed, twin headlamp grille, large wheel arches and black surround to the rear window — all features that have become synonymous with fast living.
New for 1985 is the addition of twin exhaust pipes, red trim strips for the bumpers, a wide side moulding, steel sliding sunroof and sporty striped upholstery. An attractive 6 J x 14 steel wheel is now offered as standard on the 3 door model with the option of specifying the Pirelli-styled alloy road wheels. The alloy wheels are standard on the 5 door model.

GTi dashboard.

GTi front sports seats.

Golf GTI 1984— Not Quite Right Yet

A GTI in the new body shape didn't go into production until January 1984. Although the 16-valve engine was eagerly awaited, the eight-valve 1.8-liter 112 bhp engine and gearbox had been redeveloped for flexibility, achieving maximum power at 5,000 rpm instead of 5,800 rpm and torque was increased by 5 percent and developed at a lower engine speed of 3,100 rpm. The final drive and the fifth-gear ratios were altered to increase the spacing between fifth and the intermediate gear ratios.

The Mk2 GTI's suspension was set 10 mm lower than lesser Golfs and had stiffer springs and shock absorbers with front and rear anti-roll bars. The wheels were now 14-inch rather than 13 in items, steel in standard specification with an option of the Pirelli P pattern alloys and fitted with 185/60SR-14 P6 tires. Disc brakes were fitted front and rear for the first time, 9.4-inch ventilated at the front.

The red striping was there on the grille, and the black cladding, but the 1984 Euro-flavor GTI looked a little dull to many eyes because it had single headlamps and plain black bumpers. Perhaps customers were used to four-lamped Golf GTIs in bright colors with the highly successful run-out special editions of the last model, but the proportion of GTI to total Golf sales fell from 30 to 13 percent with big GTI markets France and Italy distinctly underwhelmed.

TOP: That's better! This 1985 British brochure shows the new four-lamped face of the GTI with added red piping on the bumpers. A five-door GTI was a new addition for Europe. *(Author)*
ABOVE: The sports seats of the 1983 European GTI brought an individual splash of color—regular Golf had plain tweed-like material. *(Phil Talbot/Alamy Stock Photo)*

TOP: The 112 bhp eight-valve 1.8 had already proven itself in the previous car. The engine bay looked much the same but with more space around the engine and a giant washer bottle for front and rear screens. *(Phil Talbot/Alamy Stock Photo)*
ABOVE: The 1984 Jetta GT was the European sports Jetta, taking the 112 bhp GTI engine also used for some markets in the two-door Audi GTE. It came to the UK in 1986. *(Volkswagen UK)*

Volkswagen UK made sure all its spring 1984 press cars had four lamps, and toward the end of 1984—less than a year after its German launch and less than six months after it had gone on sale in the UK—the GTI received a premature facelift for the 1985 model year. A twin headlamp grille was added with additional red lines to the bumpers and side trim, black door sills, twin exhaust tailpipes, new sports seat upholstery and door trims, plus new steel sports wheels in addition to optional alloys.

On its paper specification, the new GTI was not expected to be startlingly different from its predecessor, especially as it carried over what was essentially the same engine. Would the better aerodynamics cancel out the weight gain? *Autocar* (May 12, 1984) measured a best top speed of 114 mph over the previous 113 mph and 8.6 seconds needed to cover 0–60 mph compared with the prior 8.3 seconds. However, there were gains in suspension and braking. With the larger wheels and tires the ride was slightly harsher, but grip and traction were "superb," while the foot pressure needed for lower speed braking had lessened. The clutch and steering were heavy (no assistance offered on European GTIs) and the engine was found to be boomy at motorway speeds. The windshield wipers were still set for left-hand drive. At £7,867, the new GTI was over £1,000 more than the old car. Was it still the hot hatchback king? "In its latest guise, the Golf GTi certainly remains a tough competitor in the hot hatchback stakes; whether it is good enough to retain its position in the face of ever-stronger opposition is not quite such a certainty."

Buyers still had no doubts about the desirability of the Golf Cabriolet, facelifted in 1983 with body-colored bumpers and given a larger fuel tank. In 1984 the "All White" Golf Cabriolet special launched in the UK with the GTI's 112 bhp engine. US Cabriolets were up-engined from 1.6 to 1.8 liters and 90 bhp, and for 1985 were available in limited-edition Wolfsburg trim with power steering, leather interior, and alloy wheels as standard.

1985—The Rabbit Hops Away

The new Golf reached the American market at the start of 1985 badged as a Golf, rather than a Rabbit. The last Rabbit left the Westmoreland line in June 1984. The new American-built Golf was once more easily distinguishable by its rectangular headlamps, and under the skin the suspension setting changes were minimal, to account for the extra weight of emissions equipment. The base 1.8-liter engine with Bosch fuel injection and a three-way catalytic converter gave 85 bhp, almost equal to the short-lived Rabbit GTI.

Enthusiasts were delighted that the Volkswagen GTI followed the Golf the same year, 1985, now just called the Volkswagen GTI, a line on its own. With a three-way catalytic converter, power was not so far from the European car, at 100 bhp, and 10 bhp better than the Rabbit GTI. Compared with the regular US Golfs it had larger flush-fitting rectangular headlamps, a small spoiler at the top of the rear hatchback, black wheel arch trims, black bumpers, and side strips with red accents. There were sports seats and a leather-topped Scirocco steering wheel. The wheels were 14-inch as on European Golfs, but with Goodyear Eagle GT tires instead of Pirelli P6. Tested by *Car and Driver* (March 1985) as with the British magazines, it found acceleration down, top speed up (114 mph), and great adhesion from the Goodyear tires. The test car had the optional power steering ($230 onto a base of $8,990, which the testers found to be high precision, and with the improved cornering and braking, "the GTI is a car that practically drives itself. On a difficult road it feels almost programmed." Complaints were minor, such as the heater making the center console very hot to the touch and unexciting looks.

TOP: The 1985 US-built Volkswagen GTI could be marked out from lesser versions by large rectangular headlamps. Side marker lamps were not required in Europe. *(VWoA)*
MIDDLE: Rabbit no more, this was just the Volkswagen GTI. Only offered as a three-door, the fact that it looked much like slower Golfs was seen as an added attraction. *(VWoA)*
BOTTOM: The interior was much the same as the German-built GTI, minus the golf ball gearknob. The thinly striped seat pattern was the other difference. *(VWoA)*

BELOW: Small square headlamps marked out a regular 1985 US Golf from a GTI. A Jetta GLI is in the background and would become a big hit with American buyers. *(VWoA)*

Bodykits for GTIs were such big business that Volkswagen offered its own in 1985—the "BBS" Golf GTI with spoilers, skirts, and RS three-piece modular racing wheels. *(Author)*

SCIROCCO GROWS UP: 1981–1992

Work on a successor to the original Scirocco had started in 1977, code-named EA491. It had a new body and new dashboard, but used a developed version of the first Golf's chassis. It was originally due for launch in 1980 but was postponed for cost reasons until the following year.

Once more built by Karmann, like the Mk2 Golf, Volkswagen chose not to go the Italian styling route but opt for an in-house design from Herbert Schäfer. The square edges of the 1970s were replaced by wind-tunnel smoothness to give a CD value of 0.38 instead of 0.42, and slightly above that of the new Golf (0.34).

With more window glass, thinner rear pillars, and more interior space (although the rear seats were best for children), the second Scirocco grew from 3.85 to 4.05 meters long, but it retained the 2.4 m wheelbase of the earlier cars on which it was based. It had no rain gutters but featured a distinctive polyurethane rear spoiler that sat just above the glass of the hatchback window. It was claimed to increase downforce on the rear axle by 60 percent and prevent dirt getting onto the rear window, making a rear wiper unnecessary (although higher specification cars had one). The new front spoiler was claimed to reduce frontal lift by 30 percent.

The press sampled the first new-generation Sciroccos in the South of France in spring 1981 and found it a little more grown up, more solid than before, because, with the extra size and to satisfy the latest crash tests, it was heavier by almost 100 kg.

Mechanically, the Mk2 Scirocco was unchanged from the outgoing car apart from the availability of higher fourth and fifth Formel E (economy) gears for some versions. In showrooms in May 1981, Germany had the 1.3-liter (60 bhp), 1.5-liter (70 bhp), and 1.6-liter (85 bhp) engines, and a 1.6-liter injected GTI/GLI engine (110 bhp).

The new Volkswagen coupé now faced strong internal competition from the cheaper Golf GTI on the one hand and the new Audi coupé on the other, and as detailed in *Golf Story, VW Golf Story,* and *Alle Generation Seit 1974*, special editions began early in Germany. Following the previous (and future) Golf GTI, from January 1983 it gained the 1.8-liter 112 bhp unit, which brought a small power boost but useful extra torque.

When it assessed a (947 kg) 1.8-liter Scirocco GTI in July 1983, *Autocar* found that the (871 kg) Golf GTI 1.8 it tested in December 1982 was much quicker from a standing start, the greatest gaps found at 0–90mph and 0–100mph. That Golf's best top speed was 112 mph, but the Scirocco's was 116 mph, which made it the fastest in coupé company that included the Renault Fuego, Toyota Celica, Opel Manta, and aging Ford Capri. The chic styling of the Scirocco attracted a £1,197 premium over the £6,808 Golf GTI three-door.

German tuners got to work on the Scirocco GTI as they continued with the Golf. In 1982 Zender showed the ultimate Scirocco GTI with unmissable flared bumpers, bigger front and rear spoilers, and wheel arches. The engine was turbocharged and the interior custom made. From 1983 GMP in North Carolina began importing finished bodies from Zender, adding the mechanical and suspension parts and the interior. Rather than a turbocharger, the engine was bored out to 1.8 liters and with a high-lift camshaft, the GTI cylinder head with larger valves made the same 140 bhp.

In Old Lyme, Connecticut, Reeves Callaway continued with turbo conversions, adding in the new Scirocco in 1983. The conversion boosted horsepower from 74 to 117. Water injection and premium-unleaded fuel were needed to prevent ignition problems and there was a thermostatically controlled oil cooler. Callaway turbo graphics featured on the body stripes and the seats, and there were 5.5-inch-wide Centra or ATS alloy wheels, Bilstein shock absorbers, stiffer springs, and a 19 mm rear anti-roll bar.

In autumn 1984 European Scirocco badges had a shake-up, with CL, GL, and GTI giving way to GT, GTL, and GTX, which all had varying amounts of sporty details and could be mixed and matched with different engines. The GTX started as a special edition with a Kamei spoiler set, but this was such a hit it became the GTI replacement. British buyers happily greeted another edition of the Scirocco Storm with a leather interior and every extra on the list.

WINNING THE POWER GAME— SCIROCCO 16-VALVE

Since its launch, the second Scirocco gradually lost the power game to newer rivals,

OPPOSITE: The new Scirocco GTI had GTI badging and spelled its name out in large letters below the effective rear spoiler. *(Author)*

RIGHT: All versions of the second-generation Scirocco had the same double headlamp style. Volkswagen's American advertising was as inventive as ever in the face of hard times for fast cars. *(Motorbooks)*

so it received a major boost when the GTX went on German sale with the new 1.8-liter 16-valve engine in August 1985, well ahead of the Golf GTI 16-valve (see page 48), to allow engine production to ramp up in the same way as 1974. A red 16V badge on the front grille was a very desirable addition.

Coupled to the three-way catalytic converter, mandatory at that time, it developed 127 bhp, and for markets without this (such as the UK) 137 bhp. Tested by *Autocar*, the mean maximum speed was 130 mph to the 117 mph of the eight-valve GTX.

Rear brakes were now discs instead of drums; the front discs were enlarged, and there were stiffer front springs. The rear anti-roll bar's diameter went from 20.5 mm to 24 mm, and the driveshafts were reinforced. For the first time, a European Scirocco could be ordered with power steering. The British press was annoyed to be told that the GTX 16-valve could not be engineered for right-hand drive because redesigning the brake pedal linkage for right-hand drive production was judged too difficult as it was still based on the first Golf floorpan. VW UK offered left-hand drive imports but no more.

The speedier Scirocco arrived in the US in summer 1986 badged simply as the Scirocco 16V but with all the styling mods of the GTX. "With one fell swoop, the wizards of Wolfsburg have transformed the ho-hum VW Scirocco from an also-ran into a supercoupe to be reckoned with," said the August 1986 issue of *Car and Driver*. Power was down to 123 bhp with US emissions equipment, but that was a sizable 33 bhp more than 1985. At 8.5 seconds, it was faster from 0–60 mph than a Porsche 944. A four-wheel-drive Scirocco was said to be in the pipeline but never arrived.

Back in regular Scirocco-land, new special editions continued to prop up sales in the fashion-led coupé market. The 1985 German White Cat was only available in Alpine White, and the 1986 Tropic came in Madison Turquoise and Kiwi Brown. The 1986 (1987 UK) Scala had its all-around spoiler/bodykit painted in car color, new alloy wheels, and offered the new combination of five gears and 90 bhp priced less than the 112 bhp 1.6 GTX.

With the advent of the 1988 Karmann-built Volkswagen Corrado coupé (see page 64), the Scirocco Mk2 began a gentle run toward retirement, kept on in Europe as a lower-priced alternative to the car designed to replace it and to help Volkswagen out of another financial crisis. From 1987 to 1989 Scirocco production dropped from 23,013 to 8,865.

The engine choice was slimmed down to a 1.6-liter 72 PS with an unregulated catalytic converter and carburetor and a 1.8-liter 95 PS, fuel injection with closed-loop catalytic converter. At the beginning of the 1990s, it was dropped in the US in favor of the Corrado, and in Europe was only offered as the Scala and GT II; from 1991 onward, the 129 PS 16-valve engine returned to the range. The last second-generation Scirocco of 291,497 was built on September 7, 1992. There would be a long break until the name returned.

ABOVE: A 1991 UK example of the Scirocco GT II, which had a sporty bodykit but a modest 90 bhp. By now, the Corrado was Volkswagen's performance coupé. (*Magiccarpics*)

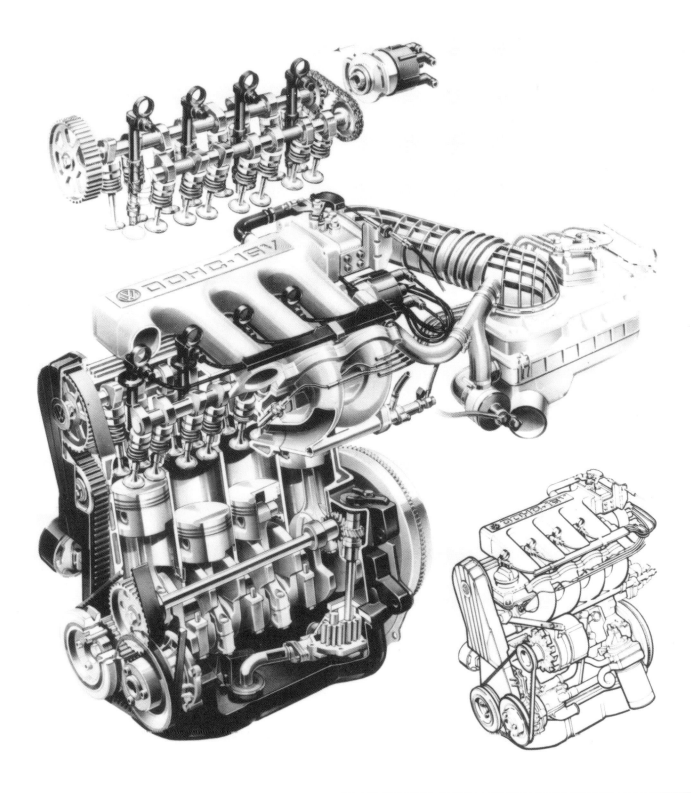

The 1985 Jetta GLI

Looking unexciting yet being a great drive was soon found to be the big attraction for the second-generation Jetta GLI. Imported from Germany, it was introduced to North America in late 1984 for 1985, its Bosch KE-Jetronic injected 1.8-liter producing 100 bhp. Volkswagen liked to claim it had more room inside than the prestigious BMW 3-Series or Mercedes 190E. The trunk was, as expected, vast. With its test weight of 1,189 kg, *Road & Track* posted an estimated top speed of 115 mph, and once drivers were used to the quick steering reaction, "they took delight in flinging the GLI around every corner in sight." The 112 bhp Jetta GLI was on sale in mainland Europe from spring 1985. For the 1986 model year the US GLI got the extra two horsepower.

ABOVE: Long in development, Volkswagen's first 16-valve engine was an instant GTI performance boost. This cutaway shows how a single belt drives one camshaft, which then takes drive via two smaller cogs to the other one. *(Volkswagen UK)*

GTI 16-Valve 1985–1986

Late in 1985, the long-awaited Golf GTI 16-valve arrived. In the 1980s, putting "16-valve" by a car's name was just as exciting as "turbo." Using an existing engine block, power and efficiency were boosted by having four overhead valves per cylinder (two intake and two exhaust) driven by twin overhead camshafts. With a four-cylinder engine, that equaled 16 valves.

While turbo conversions for Golfs and Sciroccos abounded, the engineers of Wolfsburg were not fans, equating turbocharging with poor low-speed torque and high fuel consumption (the slower-revving diesel was a better candidate). "Blown" engines had been considered for all the Volkswagen GTIs and tests dated back to 1981, but heat and fuel consumption were both excessive. Supercharging was in the Golf's future (see page 60).

Volkswagen started development of a 16-valve cylinder head for the 1.8 in 1981 alongside the 1.8-liter version of the GTI. Initially, the new unit was to power versions of the Golf and the Scirocco but later other models. Informed by its experience of the Oettinger 16S (see chapter 1) and reportedly with pressure from Volkswagen's French sales organization, an official 16-valve program was developed by Audi on the basis of the trusty EA827 unit. A prototype was shown to the press in September 1983 but delayed going into production as Audi engineers were reportedly not happy with its refinement. Two versions were developed: one for premium grade leaded gas and another for the unleaded fuel demanded by a catalytic converter.

Keeping the European standard GTI's Bosch KA-Jetronic mechanical fuel injection and 10:1 compression ratio, the fuel and air mixture was fed into a bigger plenum chamber above the new cylinder head. To accommodate the higher temperatures, the exhaust valves were filled with sodium while the undersides of the piston crowns were cooled by jets of oil from the crankcase when pressure exceeded 28 psi, and the engine was fitted with the larger-capacity oil pump from the Golf diesel.

BELOW: The Scirocco 16V was a virtual twin of the Golf in terms of its bodykit and wheels, but badged GTX rather than GTI. *(Author)*

OPPOSITE: The Golf GTI 16-valve was the dream of many dynamic young men in suits (aka yuppies). Playful ads reinforced the value of investing more in a Golf. *(Author)*

Because the new 16-valve cylinder head had to bolt on to a block designed for a narrower unit, the valve layout was not symmetrical, with the exhaust valves placed vertically and the inlet valves inclined by 25 degrees to save space. To aid refinement and reduce maintenance, the valves were activated by hydraulic tappets, a feature that soon found its way onto lesser Golf engines.

It was usual practice for a chain or toothed belt to drive both overhead camshafts, but to save space in this transverse installation, Volkswagen followed Porsche and designed the exhaust cam to be belt driven in the conventional way, but drive to the other cam was by a small chain taken off the drive at the opposite end of the cylinder head. In pre-production the drive was by gearwheels, but this was changed to chain drive for quieter running. The bottom half of the 1.8-liter engine block was largely unchanged, but the crankshaft was reshaped to cope with the extra stresses and both it and the pistons were lightened. It gained a reputation as a very tough engine.

In its final form, peak power compared with the eight-valve was up from 112 bhp to 139 bhp developed at 6,100 rpm. In development it had been safe at speeds in excess of 7,000 rpm but when released a rev limiter was set at 7,200 rpm. The performance improvements over the standard GTI were decisive, with power up by 24 percent and torque up by 9 percent. The GTI 16V had a slightly shorter fifth gear ratio than the eight.

Following the Scirocco 16V, the Golf GTI 16V went on German sale in November 1985, reaching the UK in late 1986. A catalyzed version for other markets was introduced with a 10 bhp loss of power, considered low at the time. The 16V was an additional model to the eight-valve, rather than replacing it.

Outside, it resembled the eight-valve GTI apart from discreet badging, slightly bigger front and rear spoilers, and a ride height further lowered by 10 mm. The suspension was stiffened by 10 percent front and 19 percent rear, and the disc brakes had larger pistons and extra venting for the front pair.

Tested by Britain's *Motor* magazine (December 13, 1986) it was the fastest factory Golf to date with a 124.6 mph top speed (VW had claimed 130 mph possible) and 0–60 in 7.5 seconds with an overall fuel consumption of 28.1 mpg. This put it comfortably back in contention with its direct turbocharged rivals. "The extra power is there, all right," said the test, "but the engine has to be revved hard to unleash it . . . so long as the full rev range is used, the Golf's acceleration is stunning."

All the action happened higher in the speed range. The 16V reached 100 mph in 21.6 seconds, which was 2.1 seconds faster than the Ford Escort RS Turbo and five seconds before the eight-valve GTI. At £10,849, this was considered expensive even for a Golf, and with a £1,900 premium over the eight-valve. However, in addition to the extra performance, the 16V added alloy wheels, tinted glass, electric front windows, and central locking. But in the UK the economy was booming, and some young professionals wanted a Golf GTI almost just because it was expensive—and rare. In 1984, 19,772 Ford XR3is and 3,885 Golf GTIs were sold in the UK.

The 112 bhp fuel-injected 1.8 was available in the European Jetta since the spring of 1985, but due to engine supply limitations, UK customers had to wait until April 1986 for the new sporty Jetta that was badged as the Jetta GT (across Europe) with GTI touches, such as red bumper stripes and black side cladding. To keep costs down, the low-profile tires were on 14-inch wheels, but the suspension set-up was as sporting as a GTI. It was no slouch, and *Autocar* bettered the GTI's top speed in its GT at 117 mph.

THE MK2 GTI IN MOTORSPORT

With the rally success of the first-generation Golf behind it, Volkswagen Motorsport in Hannover committed to an international rally career for the second GTI.

By then the rally playing field had split in a new direction. In 1982 the classes in the World Rally Championship (WRC) became Group A for fairly standard road cars and Group B for specials with few limits, which led to a short era of super-powerful four-wheel-drive turbo monsters, such as the Peugeot 205 Turbo 16 and Lancia Delta S4.

Audi was enjoying the golden years of the rally Quattros, winning the WRC in 1981 and 1984—the year of the astonishing 302 bhp Group B Sport Quattro S1, which was followed by the 473 bhp S2 a year later.

Somewhat in the shadow of Audi's crushing success, Volkswagen Motorsport stuck with a low-budget entry into WRC Group A for the new GTI, which drivers found a more forgiving car than the Mk1 thanks to its longer wheelbase and longer suspension travel. It was first given to the skilled hands of Swedish driver Kalle Grundel, who had driven works GTIs in Swedish and German championships since switching to Volkswagen from Saab in 1982.

Grundel drove selected rounds of the 1984 WRC season with co-driver Peter Diekmann. The 160 bhp GTI Mk2 made its debut at January's Monte Carlo Rally and came in ninth overall, after a battle with the Group A Quattro of Bernard Darniche. The pair alternated between an Mk1 and Mk2 GTI for the rest of the season, the best Mk2 GTI result a category A win in October's San Remo Rally (sixth overall).

In 1985 European Volkswagen importers backed Volkswagen Junior Rally teams for rising rally stars. For example, four UK drivers were given 170 bhp eight-valve GTIs until the 16-valve was homologated in the middle of 1986. Each had use of a service van, spare parts, and the services of new factory driver Jochi Kleint, who ran in selected rounds of the 1985 WRC in an

eight-valve GTI. Kleint and Werner Hohenadel began with the March 1985 Portugal rally (gearbox failure), then the 1000 Lakes joined by Franz Wittmann and Ferdinand Hinterleitner in the first outing for the 16V. The cars finished 11th and 12th, respectively, then ninth for the 16V in San Remo.

For 1986 Volkswagen Motorsport entered its first full WRC season with a 212 bhp (215 PS) GTI 16-valve driven by Kenneth Eriksson (who went on to great things with Toyota and Subaru) and now 1985 German rally champion Peter Diekmann as co-driver. Volkswagen Motorsport's team was tiny compared with the likes of Toyota, and in 1986 it had just 15 mechanics compared with about 100 for the big names. In ten events Eriksson and Diekmann scored five class wins, enough to secure the Golf's only WRC win for Group A.

Group B rally cars were now reaching 500–650 bhp, until a series of tragic accidents in which spectators were killed called for the cars to be banned, and a series of restrictions that year canceled them after the 1986 season. Audi shocked the rally world by abruptly withdrawing its team in May 1986 to concentrate on a different image for the brand, and a move toward circuit racing. Eriksson was the 1986 winner of the FIA World Championship for drivers of Group A cars (the only year it was awarded).

Eriksson and Diekmann continued to drive for Volkswagen in the 1987 WRC, their best result a win in the extremely tough Ivory Coast Rally. For six events they were joined by Erwin Weber and Matthias Feltz in another Volkswagen Motorsport 16V. Meanwhile on American racing circuits, 1987 was the GTI's—and VWoA's—most successful season, winning four national championships with the 16V.

In 1988 Audi ran three Group A production cars to Volkswagen's single GTI 16V and Weber/Feltz had a WRC class win (A7) in Portugal, Konstantinos Apostolou and Mihalis Kriadis another on the Acropolis in Greece. The Vredestein tires GTI 16V had a class win at San Remo.

After several low-key years with the GTI, in 1989 Volkswagen resolved to take on the all-conquering four-wheel-drive Lancia Delta Integrale in Group A. Launching the 280 bhp supercharged Golf Rallye G60 that summer (see page 60) it bullishly claimed that it was designed to win the WRC, even though it was about 20 bhp down on the top cars.

Entrusted to Erwin Weber, the Rallye G60 failed to shine, a water pump failure putting it out of its debut at the Acropolis

OPPOSITE: Lars Erik Torph and Jan Svanström provide spectator thrills on the Swedish Rally of the 1,000 Lakes, August 1985. They came in ninth of 81 finishers. *(James Claydon/Alamy Stock Photo)*
ABOVE: Kenneth Eriksson and Peter Diekmann in their Group A GTI 16V on the 1986 Rally of New Zealand, part of the WRC championship. TA stands for computer company Triumph Adler, which Volkswagen then owned. *(Volkswagen AG)*

Rally and the only notable result a third place in the New Zealand Rally. Volkswagen withdrew from rallying after 1990 and did not re-enter until 2011. Lancia and Toyota's faster cars, more advanced four-wheel-drive systems, and greater World Rally experience all conspired against the Golf. However, Weber and the Rallye G60 did win the German Rally Championship in 1991.

THE PIKES PEAK TWIN GOLF

Following Audi's success, and to promote the Golf in the US, Volkswagen expended a lot of effort on the historic Pikes Peak International Hill Climb in Colorado. Held in the Rocky Mountains, the 12.4-mile course with 156 turns started at an altitude of 2,865 meters and finished approximately 1,440 meters higher.

Want more power? Try two engines. Having built one Jetta and two Sciroccos with double powerplants and therefore four-wheel-drive, in 1985 Volkswagen Motorsport took a Golf bodyshell, flared the wheel arches, and let two ventilation grilles into the roof but it still resembled a regular GTI, retaining the rear hatchback.

Two 1.8-liter GTI engines were fitted longitudinally, with Oettinger 16-valve cylinder heads (Volkswagen's own design not ready yet) for a combined output of 390 bhp. It had a custom-designed dashboard with two sets of accelerator and clutch cables that could be adjusted from inside the cockpit.

Volkswagen's WRC driver Jochi Kleint drove the twin-engined Golf at the July 13 event and finished sixth overall, while Michèle Mouton won in a record time of 11 minutes 25.39 seconds in an Audi Sport Quattro. Before the start, Kleint gave the amusing accidental spectacle of all four wheels spinning on a stationary car by somehow selecting first gear for the front engine and reverse for the rear.

In the 1987 version the twin Golf returned with both engines turbocharged for a combined 644 bhp (652 PS) and completely removable front and rear bodywork. Kleint was on course for the best time but had to give up shortly before the finish due to a defect in the suspension.

ABOVE: The second Pikes Peaks GTI build was far more extreme than the first and weighed just 1,040 kg. The two large holes are cooling inlets for twin radiators. *(Volkswagen AG)*
OPPOSITE TOP: The entire front and rear sections of the 1987 car could be unbolted—fiberglass at the rear—here showing one of the two 1.8-liter turbo engines. The standard doors were retained, minus glass. *(Volkswagen AG)*
OPPOSITE BOTTOM: Maintained by Volkswagen Classic, the 1987 Pikes Peak Golf toured the world, here driven by Jochi Kleint at the 2018 Goodwood Festival of Speed in England. Rear engine was fed by huge roof scoop and vents in rear windows. *(pbpgalleries/Alamy Stock Photo)*

1987 and an American Reshuffle

Summer 1987 saw the first US-specification GTI 16Vs put to the test by enthusiast magazines. VWoA downgraded the eight-valve GTI to GT status, resorting to rear drum brakes and plainer seats, but a lower price.

Now keeping to the mantra of staying as close to the German original as possible, the US-specification GTI 16V offered 123 bhp with a three-way catalytic converter—virtually the same as the catalyzed engine sold to some European buyers. Rich Ceppos reviewed it for *Car and Driver*'s August 1987 edition, "The new powerplant does what it's supposed to, transforming the GTI from a lively car to a quick one (117mph)."

Whereas some European markets could choose steel wheels for their GTI 16Vs, American buyers had standard Scirocco alloys and 205/55VE-14 Pirelli P600s, which the magazine felt were for the sake of appearances as they did not improve grip on the skidpan.

The verdict was not quite as fulsome as the British tests, given that with extras such as air-conditioning and metallic paint (power steering standard) the test car's $14,410 price tag would buy you a lot of other drivers' cars from four-cylinders to V8s. "The little sedan that fights the good fight just doesn't stand out like it used to."

As ever, other markets could mix and match trims with GTI engines. From 1987 Volkswagen South Africa (which had kept building the Mk1 Golf as the low-priced CitiGolf) sold a five-door version with power steering, leather seats, and air-conditioning called the Executive, which kept the suspension settings of the regular GTI.

For 1987 European Golfs had a new grille with wider slats, wider side rubbing strips, and a bigger VW logo. The front quarterlights were removed to give larger opening front windows, and the wing mirrors moved further forward, countering criticism that they were fitted too far back for some drivers.

In 1986 the European Jetta was given the 16V engine and became a GTI. For 1987 Volkswagen UK decided the Jetta image needed a little more zing and renamed the previous eight-valve GT as the GTI. The Jetta GTI 16V had the same suspension settings as the hatch, notably sitting 10 mm lower than the eight-valve car on Pirelli or Continental tires. A top speed of 127 mph was claimed, and Volkswagen UK later began offering low-cost performance driving coaching to buyers of this very discreet 139 bhp sports sedan with its slim black trunk lid spoiler.

The Golf Cabriolet had a major facelift in 1987 for the 1988 model year, with bigger bumpers and plastic cladding around the lower half of the bodywork that made it look wider than the skinny original and allowed wider wheels. Now outdated, heavy to drive, and wobblier than newer soft tops, the Golf won out as a fashion accessory, with ever-changing colors and special editions to give buyers reasons to want one. Because it was based on the Mk1 Golf, the GTI Cabriolet wasn't given the 16-valve engine.

From 1987 all European Golfs ran with Digifant fuel injection, rather than the famous Bosch K-Jetronic system. This was developed in-house by Volkswagen, which by November 1987 had com-

---

BELOW: In 1987 with the arrival of the GTI 16V in America, the previous GTI was downgraded to GT status, with the same 102 bhp engine. (*VWoA*)

OPPOSITE: The 1987 North American GTI 16-valve was a shot in the arm for the GTI's image in the face of faster and cheaper competition. (*Author*)

Follow the leader just became a little harder to play.

When Volkswagen first introduced the GTI, we did more than just create a new car. We created a new class of car. But it didn't take long before we noticed something vaguely familiar in the rear-view mirror. The competition.

Well now, we have some disheartening news. To those cars that try to perform like a GTI. To those that try to handle like a GTI. And to those that try to be as much fun. Here comes the new 16-Valve Volkswagen GTI. Faster. More powerful. And according to *AutoWeek*, "still the best enthusiast three-door around."

And where will the competition be? Well once again, we expect them to be behind us all the way.

Introducing the GTI 16V.

©1987 Volkswagen Seatbelts save lives.

pleted the changeover of its production to catalytic converter technology—it became mandatory for the German market in 1989 (for cars over 2.0-liters) but it was not a legal requirement for British registered cars to have closed loop catalysts until 1992, by which time the GTI Mk3 had arrived.

1988–1991 Chop and Change

The late 1980s saw a slump suffered across the US industry in the face of Japanese competition. The Jetta was proving the better seller at around 60,000 cars a year, and the plant at Westmoreland was no longer profitable, so it was closed in 1988. While GTIs continued to come from Germany, production of regular Golfs and Jettas for the US market moved to the modernized Volkswagen plant in Puebla, Mexico.

ABOVE: The Mk1 Golf Cabriolet lived very profitably from the late 1970s to the 1990s. This 1987 facelift brought a bodykit that attempted to make it look wider. *(Volkswagen UK)*
OPPOSITE TOP LEFT & RIGHT:: For 1990 the Jetta GLI became the "stealth" sedan of choice with a 134 bhp 2.0-liter 16-valve engine. Jettas were facelifted with bigger bumpers. *(VWoA)*
OPPOSITE BOTTOM: British buyers preferred hatchbacks, so Volkswagen UK hoped the Jetta 16V would add a dash of sports appeal to its sedan cars. *(Volkswagen UK)*

A final facelift came for Golf GL and GTI models in August 1989, with bulkier bumpers and small changes to the interior. With the Golf-based Corrado coupé coming into full production, there was more internal competition for the GTI, and the final evolutions of the Mk2 were the supercharged, super-rare, and super-expensive Golf Rallye, G60 Limited, and GTI G60 (page 60). For the Australian market, 1989 was the first year the Mk2 GTI was imported, the only Mk2 Golf sold there until 1992.

The Berlin Wall fell in November 1989 and suddenly opened up new sales and the prospect of new factories in Eastern Europe for all carmakers. As the second Golf headed into its final years (the millionth GTI was built in 1990), even the fashionable GTI needed some sales incentives, so from 1990 BBS alloy wheels became standard on the 16V for UK buyers, then the regular car. Smoked plastic lenses for the rear lights were also added. Volkswagen UK also found that the quickest way to sell basic Golfs was to give them a GTI-like four-headlamp grille and speedy-sounding names such as the Driver and Ryder.

For 1990 the Jetta GLI gained the 134 hp 2.0-liter 16-valve engine. Opting for the Wolfsburg Edition added 15-inch BBS alloy wheels, velour Recaro seats, and special exterior badging.

The North American Golf GTI dropped the "Golf" in 1990 (not to return until 2014) and the GTI 16V was quietly dropped from 1990 sale. The eight-valve GT was promoted back to the rank of GTI and came in at low base price of $9,950, which helped it compete with rivals such as the Honda Civic EX.

Power was 105 bhp for 49 of the US states, except California, where it lost five of those horses. Even the brakes were downgraded compared with the previous GTI to solid front discs and rear drums. But compared with the GTI 16V, the 25 percent power loss seemed the most bizarre change. "Why did VW take a successful car like the GTI and put a castrated motor in it?" asked Peter Albrecht in *Sports Car International* (July 1990). Perhaps there was an engine production capacity problem, he wondered, as the Jetta GLI received a new 2.0-liter (2.0-liter) version of the 16-valve engine, giving 134 bhp at 5,800 rpm.

It turned out that the American GTI 16V had been the victim of demand for the 2.0-liter 16V for both the Jetta GLI and the new Passat, so in 1991, the only 2.0-liter Mk2 Golf GTI 16V appeared just for this market. Unlike 1.8-liter European GTIs, it stuck with Bosch fuel injection—KE Motronic, rather than Volkswagen's Digifant. *Sports Car International* (April 1991) was jubilant. "After a false start with the GTI 8V, the 2.0-liter 16V showed that our guess was right. The Corrado's looks may win some buyers, but in performance the Golf GTI 16V wins, hands down."

The European 2.0-liter GTI 16V would appear in the third-generation Golf in 1992. Ahead of it, the regular flavor Golf Mk3 was presented in July 1991 but with the VR6 engine to the fore (chapter three). Meanwhile, the Mk1 Golf Cabrio motored breezily onward, with 1993 the last year of production as it gave way to an all-new Cabriolet. Karmann was now building Ford Escort and Opel/Vauxhall Astra convertibles. Germany kept Golf interest going with a raft of special editions, as did the UK, in 1991, replacing the GTI Cabriolet with the GTI Sportline, GTI Rivage five-speed, and GTI Rivage Leather. VWoA offered the Cabriolet through most years of the 1980s as the extra equipment Wolfsburg Edition (along with other VWs).

Reflecting the booming car market created by German re-unification, the second-generation Golf overlapped, continuing in production into 1992 in the new factory in Mosel (near the old Trabant factory) to meet demand from the re-unified Eastern Europe. The last European GTIs made way for the Mk3 in February 1992.

OPPOSITE: This "big bumper" 1992 GTI 16V is one of the last of the Mk2 series, with the third-gen Golf already launched. The 1988 facelift brought integrated fog lights in the front spoiler. *(Magiccaropix)*

BELOW: Aboard a 1992 16V, the only marker is a badge on the glove box. Seat stripes are now more subdued, and it has the latest Volkswagen corporate steering wheel. *(Magiccarpix)*

CHAPTER 2. GTI MK2 1984–1992

THE SUPER GTIs: GOLF RALLYE, GTI G60 LIMITED, AND GTI G60

For a quicker GTI, the 1980s default option was bolting on a turbo. In America, having turbocharged the new Scirocco, Reeves Callaway turned his attention to the second-generation Golf in 1985. The standard Bosch KA fuel injection was swapped for the higher delivery KE-Jetronic system, a Japanese IHI RHB5 turbocharger boosted at 10 psi to give up to 150 bhp and a top speed of 122 mph over 114 mph. A full BBS bodykit was standard, with a Nissan 300ZX air scoop on the hood to feed the newly relocated air-to-air intercooler. The fat Goodyear Eagle 205/50VR-15 tires worked with Volkswagen's standard suspension set, up. It was, as *Car and Driver* put it in July 1985, the "Bullet of the byways."

In Britain, while companies such as Janspeed continued to turbocharge, GTi Engineering avoided it, preferring to go through engines in great detail and enlarge their capacities for a reliable conversion. In 1986 the "Plus Pac" power conversion would raise power from 112 bhp to 135 bhp, then there was a 2.0-liter eight-valve 152 bhp conversion and a 2.0-liter 16-valve 170 bhp Oettinger conversion that cost over £4,000 (a regular GTI was about £8,000 then).

Once the official GTI 16-valve was in prospect, GTi Engineering boss Richard Lloyd produced the 1900RE, which kept the eight-valve engine but enlarged the valves and cylinder capacity to 1,870 cc rather than 1.8-liter. Power was a claimed 142 bhp.

There was a brief flirtation with supercharging ahead of Volkswagen, in 1985 plumbing an American Magnacharger supercharger onto the development car for the 1.8-liter conversion and touting it around the car mags with a claimed 165 bhp.

THE SUPERCHARGED GOLFS

From 1978, Volkswagen had been experimenting with the supercharger, a device used on high-performance cars in the 1920s and '30s. The most famous supercharger, or "blower," of that time was the Roots type, which introduced compressed air into the engine for better ignition, having squeezed it between two rotors. The Volkswagen version was based on a 1905 design that squeezed the air through metal scrolls, although at that time the technology to machine the parts with sufficient accuracy had not been available. Over 400 variations were said to have been tried.

Turbochargers and superchargers are both forced-induction devices, but while a turbocharger works from waste gases in the exhaust system, a supercharger is driven by a belt from the crankshaft. A supercharger spins all the time and boosts in proportion to engine speed, not load, as a turbocharger does, and early turbochargers suffered from "lag"—a gap under acceleration where nothing happened until the engine boosted in a surge.

Volkswagen considered the supercharger superior because it produced boost from much lower speeds and developed torque or engine pulling power across a broader rev range. The supercharger also did not generate as much heat as a turbo, which demanded special materials for exhaust manifolds and pipes. It was potentially quieter and demanded no special lubrication. Before entering the engine, the compressed air was cooled by passing through an intercooler for better ignition.

The first supercharged Volkswagen recipient was the second-generation Polo. The 1985 Polo G40 had similar power to the eight-valve Golf GTI, its 1.3-liter four-cylinder engine boosted to 115 bhp thanks to what Volkswagen called a G-Lader (G-Charger) after the G-shaped spirals inside the supercharger unit. The "40" stood for the height of the spiral walls in millimeters.

GOLF RALLYE G60

The G60 was the supercharged version of the group eight-valve 1.8-liter four-cylinder announced in June 1988 with the first pictures of the Corrado G60 coupé but was seen just before in a pumped-up Golf.

At the start of June 1988, a pair of 160 bhp supercharged "Super Golfs" called the G60 Rallye made a surprise appearance at the Acropolis Rally, one as a "sweeper" reconnaissance car and one in road trim as the official pursuit car. Both had been built by the competitions department and combined the G60 with the Syncro four-wheel-drive system available on non-GTI Golfs since 1985. A new housing was bolted to the gear/differential casing, and a short drive-shaft took the drive to an angled bevel gear set mounted in line with the center of the car. The drive was taken to an all-new rear axle via a three-piece propeller shaft and the viscous coupling. Most of the time all but 5 percent of drive went through the front wheels, but as the system kicked in when the wheels started to slip, all the power could be transferred to the rear.

The three-door Rallye had slim rectangular headlamps, a wide grille covering an intercooler, and Lanica Delta Integrale-style wheel arches. It was ready for production, the company claimed, depending on the reaction in a series of customer clinics and could be built the following year—and the implication was that an assault on the 1989 World Rally Championship was likely.

For the 1990 season, Group A homologation rules required at least 5,000 road cars be built in a year. The best way to ensure these would sell was to drum up excitement by testing the water with the "Super Golf," and orders flooded in. This highly specialized project was transferred from Wolfsburg to Volkswagen Brussels, which was equipped for very small production runs.

The Golf Rallye G60's engine was downsized slightly to 1,763 cc from 1.8-liter so that when it was multiplied by the forced-induction conversion factor of 1.4 demanded for the World Rally Championship it came in under the equivalent 2.5-liter class limit. The compression ratio was lowered from 10.0:1 to 8.0:1. Spinning at 1.7 times engine speed, it delivered a maximum boost of 0.65 bar (9.4 psi), and the intercooled air temperature was reduced by up to 55 degrees. In competition trim Rallyes it developed up to 282 PS (278 bhp).

Twin catalysts were fitted as standard to the 160 bhp roadgoing Rallye, and although it was the most powerful factory-produced Golf to date, with the weight of the Syncro system (230 kg more than the 139 bhp GTI 16V), on paper it didn't produce performance figures very much different than its cheaper relative with a top speed of 130 mph as opposed to 127 mph and a 0–100 kph (62 mph) time of 8.6 seconds. It did gain by having superior torque and the ability to safely put all that power through four wheels. As well as the mechanical package and the unique styling, equipment included leather seats, power steering, and improved anti-lock brakes. Between 1990 and 1991, 5,600 were eventually built, with 2,000 of the left-hand drive only model staying in Germany.

OPPOSITE: Officially backed by Volkswagen UK, GTi Engineering was thriving when this 1986 ad appeared. Engine enlargements went as high as 2.5-liters for both VWs and Audis. *(Author)*
ABOVE: The rare 1988–1991 Golf G60 Rallye kicked off a line of superfast supercharged Golfs. An extra air intake was needed below the bumper for the heat of the supercharger. *(Volkswagen UK)*

GOLF G60 LIMITED

How about a Golf GTI 16-valve with 210 bhp and all the Rallye goodies hiding discreetly undercover? Meet the ultra-rare Golf G60 Limited. When it was announced in 1990, over 1,000 inquiries came into dealers but just 70 would be hand-built at the rate of one a week from 1989 to 1991 at Volkswagen Motorsport in Hannover. The price of this GTI unicorn was DM 68,500, about £23,000 at the time.

Volkswagen Motorsport took the regular five-door GTI bodyshell but grafted on the inner wheel arches and suspension of the Rallye. It was only ever built as a five-door, although one three-door was made and retained by Volkswagen. Not fitted with the larger bumpers of the 1989 facelift, the only way quick way to distinguish it was by the VW Motorsport badges and a blue line around the front grille.

The 1.8 16V engine had special pistons and different camshaft profiles giving increased lift. The compression ratio was reduced to 8.8:1, and again twin catalysts were used. Maximum power was produced at 6,500 rpm but the driver could floor the throttle in fifth gear from 1,000 rpm and be rewarded with a relentless surge of power. Although the G60 Limited had four-wheel-drive, Volkswagen added what it called an Electronic Differential Lock (EDL) as standard, an early type of stability/traction control that would attempt to apply brake restraint to the spinning wheel.

When *Autocar* tested Volkswagen UK's press demonstrator in March 1991, it recorded a top speed of 140 mph and in gear acceleration from 30 to 50 mph in 6.5 seconds, drawing comparisons with the Ford Sierra Cosworth and the BMW M5.

GTI G60

With the Opel/Vauxhall Astra GTE 16V becoming a serious threat, the Mk2 Golf GTI ushered out the 1980s with one final power bid, announced at the 1989 Frankfurt Motor Show. The Golf GTI G60 had the same eight-valve 1.8-liter engine of the Corrado, developing 160 bhp at 5,800 rpm. It lasted less than two years. The quoted performance figures were a 134 mph top speed and a 0–62 mph (100 kph) figure of 8.3 seconds.

The GTI G60 came onto the German market in March 1990 and was only available as a left-hand drive import in the UK. Right-hand drive was not contemplated because, Volkswagen said, the MQ gearbox from the Passat was so large that a steering wheel on the right-hand side precluded the fitment of the anti-lock brake unit and master cylinder. However, *Autocar*'s Peter Robinson (March 19, 1990) wrote that, "Insiders admit it's an excuse based on economies of scale.

BELOW: The 1990 Golf G60 Limited was an instant sell-out because it looked so discreet. The blue VW logo is from Volkswagen Motorsport, where it was built. *(Volkswagen UK)*

While Volkswagen concedes that all future major new model programs will embody rhd engineering from the drawing board, market for the Golf has grown." In 1989 the Golf GTI had outsold even Germany in the UK, at 16,058 cars.

GTI G60 chassis changes included 15-inch wheels to accommodate Corrado-sized brakes with anti-lock fitted as standard, as was power steering that gave only a little assistance. It had thicker anti-roll bars and 185/55SR 15 tires as standard. The suspension was lowered by 10 mm at the rear, 20 mm at the front.

Putting 160 bhp through only the front wheels could provoke furious wheelspin and torque steer (trying to steer itself sideways out of junctions and bends), but the Electronic Differential Lock (EDL) of the G60 Limited was only offered as an option.

The GTI G60 lasted until late 1991 and the third-generation Golf. A four-wheel-drive Syncro version was added for the final year. There was also a special edition, the Fire and Ice (named after a film), with special paint and badging. The G60 was regarded as the pinnacle of the second GTI's career.

ABOVE: On the equally discreet GTI G60, the 16V's badge gave way to a red G60 against a grille with four thick bars. The Volkswagen logo was black. *(Volkswagen UK)*

THE VOLKSWAGEN CORRADOS

In early 1981, with the new Scirocco about to launch, Volkswagen was wavering on how to make the third generation. A tough economic climate and the heavy losses Volkswagen suffered through the bankruptcy of the Triumph-Adler group saw product planners wavering between a low-cost high-volume coupé and a higher-profit car produced in lower numbers. They opted for the latter.

By 1983, the style of EA494 was fixed (again in-house), but production costs were escalating. Logically, for budget reasons, the new coupé would be based on the floorpan and engines of the Mk2 Golf. Also, for cost reasons the dashboard was Passat-derived, but the headlamps were expensively unique.

The Golf GTI was steadily outselling the Scirocco—hot hatches were generally usurping coupés in the desirability stakes, so in Europe the Corrado was pushed upmarket as a kind of super-Golf or even a lesser Porsche, leaving the current Scirocco to continue with a reduced range of engines.

There was very little difference in dimensions between Corrado and Scirocco. The new car was fractionally shorter at 4.48 m compared with 4.05 m, a little lower and a little wider at 1.67 m. However, thanks to the longer second-generation Golf wheelbase (listed as 4,470 mm, however, not 4,475 mm) and shorter front and rear overhangs, there was more interior space.

The Corrado had a lower drag factor than the Golf Mk2 and a novel application of active aerodynamics. To aid high-speed stability, a spoiler at the bottom of the rear window automatically extended at speeds above 120 kph/75 mph, but since this was above the UK speed limit, it was reduced to 45 mph for this and the US market, retracting below 12 mph. According to contemporary tests, it worked.

Revealed in June 1988 and launched to the press in August, two well-equipped versions of the Corrado were offered in Europe with the 1.8-liter 16-valve 136 bhp (139 PS) non-catalyst version of the Golf GTI's four-cylinder, and, more interestingly, it was the second recipient of the eight-valve 1.8-liter four-cylinder supercharged G60 (G-lader) engine, giving 162 PS (160 bhp) coupled to the same five-speed manual gearbox and twin cable shift mechanism developed for the new Passat to cope with the increased torque.

The Corrado G60 was over a year ahead of the Golf GTI G60 but unveiled at the same time as the Golf Rallye (see page 66). At the time, Volkswagen preferred these supercharged engines to turbocharging, and they built up speed deceptively quickly. The company compared its power and torque to a 2.6-liter six. While the Corrado was some 150 kg heavier than a GTI 16V, 8.3 seconds to 100 kph (62 mph) was good and the 140 mph top speed easily attainable thanks to the lower CD and reduced frontal area.

Volkswagen hoped it would slot into the higher-priced Japanese coupé and sub Porsche market, even though this was in decline, but helpfully, the Porsche 924 had just ended production in favor of the more expensive larger-engined 944 (Volkswagen did not fully own Porsche until 2012). Nonetheless, sales projections were cautious. Reaching full production in 1990, it was not expected to be produced at more than 20,000 a year. It went on US sale in 1990, a badly needed image-booster for Volkswagen of America's flagging sales, offered only in G60 form with added equipment such as air-conditioning and cruise control. The Scirocco had been dropped and the Corrado's $17,900 ticket price was good value, with anti-lock brakes $834 extra.

OPPOSITE: The 1988 Corrado C60 was aiming to poach coupé sales from Porsche. Its smart—perhaps conservative—styling didn't differ between European and US-market versions. *(Volkswagen UK)*

BELOW: A pop-up rear spoiler was a real talking point on a 1980s Volkswagen. You could do it yourself with a button in the cabin. *(Magiccarpix)*

CHAPTER 2. GTI MK2 1984–1992   **65**

LEFT: The Corrado replaced the Scirocco in America, and it was well priced against the competition but found modest sales. Its best year was 1990, with 5,675 units sold. *(Patti McConville/Alamy Stock Photo)*

SIX IS ALWAYS BETTER THAN FOUR

The only common test gripe was the vague nature of the cable gearshift, but the real crowd-pleasing Corrado was the six-cylinder VR6, which replaced the G60 in autumn 1991. The intriguing narrow-angle transverse-mounted 2.8-liter engine had already been seen in the Golf Mk3 in 2.8-liter form (chapter 3) and in the Corrado developed 192 PS (190 bhp). The Corrado G60 was the last Volkswagen of the 1990s to use the supercharger—which was expensive to machine accurately—and in 1994 Audi applied a turbocharger to its four-cylinder 1.8-liter A4 for an output of 150 bhp.

The VR6 Corrado was good news for the American market (which had the 2.8) and a worry for the six-cylinder BMWs. Tested by *Autocar* in 1992, the Corrado VR6 was a refined 145 mph car, handling well-tamed by standard traction control. The wheel arches were flared, spring and damper rates were adjusted, and BBS alloy wheels included. A four-speed automatic transmission was an option, and a new radiator grille and raised center hood line marked a mild facelift.

Also in 1992, the 16-valve Corrado adopted the 136 bhp 16-valve engine of the current GTI 16V. For 1994 the 115 bhp eight-valve GTI engine provided an entry-level model to the three-car range, and in 1995 the UK-only Corrado Storm limited edition included 15-inch BBS wheels and leather seats. However, this was the last year of production. While the Corrado came to be considered a modern classic, a total of 97,535 units in seven years was less than the modest initial hopes. At the end it was considered too expensive and, in Germany, very hard to insure as according to Joachim Kuch in *Golf Story* as well as being frequently crashed by its owners, the Corrado had become the most stolen car in Germany. With the Scirocco long gone, Volkswagen would be out of the sports coupé market for over twenty years.

Golf GTI Mk2

Model	GTI 1.8 8-valve (Europe)	GTI 1.8 8-valve (US)	GTI 1.8 16-valve (Europe)	GTI G60
Engine type/capacity	4-cyls inline 1,781cc	4-cyls inline 1,781cc	4 cyls inline double overhead cam 1,781cc	4 cyls inline single overhead cam 1,781cc supercharged
Gearbox	5-speed manual	5-speed manual	5-speed manual	5-speed manual
Maximum power/at rpm	112 bhp/5,500 rpm	100 bhp/5,500 rpm	139 bhp@6,100 rpm	160 bhp@6,800 rpm
Maximum torque/at rpm	114 lb ft/3,100 rpm	105 lb ft/n/a	124 lb ft@4,600 rpm	165 lb ft@3,800 rpm
Acceleration 0–60 mph	8.3 seconds	10.1 seconds	7.5 seconds	8.3 seconds
Maximum speed	115.4 mph (*Autocar* 5 May 1984)	114mph (*Car and Driver* March 1985)	124.6 mph (*Motor* 13 December 1986)	1134 mph (claimed)
Suspension front/rear	Strut and coil springs, wishbone, anti-roll bar/trailing arms, coil springs, torsion beam axle, anti-roll bar	Strut and coil springs, wishbone, anti-roll bar/trailing arms, coil springs, torsion beam axle, anti-roll bar	Strut and coil springs, wishbone, anti-roll bar/trailing arms, coil springs, torsion beam axle, anti-roll bar	Strut and coil springs, wishbone, anti-roll bar/trailing arms, coil springs, torsion beam axle, anti-roll bar
Wheels/tires	6J x 14 in alloys 185 60 HR 14 Pirelli P6	6J x 14 in alloys 185 60 HR 14 Goodyear Eagle	6J x 14 in alloys 185 60 VR14 Pirelli P6	6J x 15 in alloys 185 55 RVR15 Pirelli P6
Brakes front/rear	Ventilated disc/disc	Ventilated disc/disc	Ventilated disc/disc	Ventilated disc/disc, anti-lock standard
Length	3,985 mm	4,013 mm	3,985 mm	4,040 mm
Wheelbase	2,475 mm	2,471 mm	2,475 mm	2,475 mm
Width	1,680 mm	1,679 mm	1,680 mm	1,700 mm
Height	1,405 mm	1,415 mm	1,395 mm	1,405 mm
Curb weight (kg)	1,400/1,430 (3/5-door)	1,048 (three-door)	1,430 (3-door)	1,530 (3/5-door)
Years produced	1984-1992	1985-1993	1986-1992	1989-1991

3.
GOLF GTI MK3
1991–1997

Did somebody forget the GTI? At the June 1991 press launch of the third all-new Golf, the legendary hot hatchback had taken a back seat to the world's first Golf with a six-cylinder engine. Packing 174 bhp, the Golf VR6 was a whole lot faster than even the supercharged Mk2s, and it wasn't wearing the GTI badge.

Examples of the new 2.0-liter 115 bhp GTI were available for the launch, but there was no sign of the expected 16-valve version—it was suggested in August 1991 that it had been postponed due to lack of power and refinement. The 115 bhp eight-valve was already fitted to the Passat.

RIGHT: The Mk3 Golf was chunkier-looking and weightier than before. Large one-piece plastic fenders were easier to make and could be entirely finished in the body color or plain gray on a basic Golf. *(Volkswagen UK)*

ABOVE: The European Golf VR6 ran on BBS wheels, but otherwise was hard to tell apart from a four-cylinder Golf GTI, especially in a dark color, but that discretion added to its appeal. *(Volkswagen UK)*

Meanwhile, it was unprecedented for a car in the Golf class to have a six-cylinder engine, let alone one compact enough to mount transversely. The VR6 was technically fascinating because it combined the width of a four-cylinder engine but added two further cylinders by "staggering" them within an aluminum cylinder block that had only one 12-valve cylinder head rather than the normal two of a traditional V6 engine. In the latter the angle at which the two banks of three cylinders opposed each other would be 60 or 90 degrees, but the angle of the VR6's cylinders was only 15 degrees. The initials were explained as being for *Vee Reihenmotor*, which translated to "in-line vee," although it would become simply known as the Volkswagen V6 during its long life. While it had been tested in various capacities, in its first Passat and Golf applications the VR6 was set at 2.8-liter and gave 174 bhp. A 2.9-liter 190 bhp version was reserved for the Corrado later in the year (see sidebar, page 71).

The Golf VR6, Volkswagen explained, was the post-GTI GTI—a family hatchback for grown-ups who had grown out of raucous hot

DEVELOPING THE VR6

The idea of a six-cylinder engine compact enough to fit across the engine bay of a front-wheel-drive Golf-sized car was that of Volkswagen powertrain engineer Peter Hofbauer.

The VR6 was originally called the RV6 for *Reihenmotor* V6, meaning inline V6 as although it was a V6 it had the features of an in-line engine, namely a single cylinder head and fairly compact width/length. However, realizing that in America RV meant recreational vehicle, it was christened the VR6 and eventually just V6.

A 2.0-liter engine producing 100 bhp was built in 1978–1979, and then a 2.2- and a 2.4-liter were tested in first-generation Jettas and Golfs. While the VR6 continued as a research project, there was little appetite for such a production Volkswagen. However, the idea gained new ground with the arrival of Carl Hahn as chairman in 1981. In his autobiography, *Meine Jahre Mit Volkswagen*, he explained, "We needed a credible, competitive six-cylinder program . . . our [Audi] five-cylinder engine was too long, and European and Japanese competitors already had six-cylinder engines from the Passat class upward. For US automobiles a four-cylinder engine from this class was as good as extinct."

With the 1988 Passat due to abandon parts sharing with Audi and become a transverse rather than longitudinal-engined car, it became imperative to develop a compact six-cylinder engine that could be mounted transversely to ensure its place in the American market.

As an illustration of how Audi and Volkswagen were allowed to make independent engineering decisions, Audi was also looking to create a V6 engine that could form the basis of a V8 and its entry into a higher class of the luxury car market. In the latter half of the 1980s Hahn allowed engineers in Wolfsburg and Ingolstadt to develop two different six-cylinder concepts with the view that one would become a group engine for both brands. Hahn said each design was so good that he and the board agreed to release both for development and production.

The first prototype of Audi's V6 ran in 1985. It was more conventional than the narrow-angled vee of Volkswagen, with two cylinder heads in a 90-degree vee, enabling it to be made on the same production line as the new V8 launched in 1988 and some components from the trusty EA827 four-cylinder engines. By being mounted longitudinally in Audi engine bays it could be wider than Volkswagen's VR6.

The VR6's development was played out as on/off in industry gossip in the last few years running up to its 1990 unveiling. In an August 1988 interview with newly appointed Audi chairman Ferdinand Piëch, *Car's* Gavin Green reported, 'It does Audi's up-market drive no good," argued Piëch, 'if it continues to use engines that also find their way into Volkswagens.'"

In October 1988 German magazine *Auto Zeitung* reported that the VR6 had been dropped because of noise and vibration problems and that an Audi-developed V6 would be used instead. Rumors about vibration and overheating problems persisted into the following year.

The VR6 was launched in the Passat at the 1991 Geneva Motor Show and spread across the Volkswagen range. As an aside, an agreement was reached in 1993 for VW to supply VR6 engines and transmissions to Mercedes for its 1996 V-Class people carrier because the Mercedes V6 would not fit under its short hood.

It was widely anticipated that there would be a host of V6 hatchbacks following the Golf's example, but it was to remain unique in its class, with highly developed VR6 Golfs until 2009. However, versions of the VR6/V6 had a very long life, appearing as late as 2023 in the Volkswagen Atlas SUV.

ABOVE: The VR6's compact 15-degree vee layout meant that the inlet tracts were on the front of the engine and the exhaust behind it. The valves were driven by a two-stage chain to reduce the engine height. *(Volkswagen UK)*

hatchbacks and were looking for performance with refinement. It was also an attempt to broaden the European market in the wake of sky-high car theft and insurance premiums for overtly fast family cars.

With three of five doors, there were no sporty stripes for the Golf VR6. It rode 20 mm lower than the standard Golf and had a thicker front anti-roll bar. Its 205/50 Continental tires were fitted to 6.5 x 15-inch BBS cross-spoke alloy wheels. Anti-lock brakes with all-round discs were coupled to standard traction control. Inside there were bolstered sports seats, electric windows, sunroof, and mirrors, plus a leather-trimmed steering wheel handbrake and gear lever gaiter. Leather seats and air-conditioning were optional. At £18,461 in mid-1992 the premium of a five-door Golf VR6 was just over £4,000 for this Golf, and in 1994 for some markets, the Syncro four-wheel-drive system could be ordered attached to the 2.9-liter version of the VR6, which upped power from 174 bhp to 190 bhp to cope with the power losses in the system.

Bigger, Rounder, Safer

The new Golf's exterior design was once more by Herbert Schäfer and followed an evolutionary route; the wide, windowless three-quarter rear pillar was a Golf marker. However, the distinctive twin round front lamps (for Europe) had gone in favor of almost-oval lenses behind which were single or double headlamps. Depending on the version, the lowest drag factor was 0.30 Cd, the highest 0.33 Cd.

The Mk3 Golf's proportions were familiar but gently expanded for passenger comfort, luggage space, and crash safety. It had the same 2,475 mm wheelbase of the previous Golf, was only longer by 25 mm but had a wider stance to convey the very real solidity it was carrying—about 100 kg more on average per version. The front track was widened from 1,413 mm to 1,478 mm and varying offset wheels meant they were always flush with the line of the bodywork no matter how narrow the tire was. One welcome development was a trunk aperture that opened to bumper level.

The lightest Golf now weighed 960 kg against its nearest rival the Opel/Vauxhall Astra's 930 kg. Thanks to crash tests carried out by German car magazines, safety was now a major marketing fac-

ABOVE: The eight-valve 2.0-liter European GTI at launch in 1991. The smooth shape abandoned twin lamps, so the US version would lose its square lights. The traditional black GTI trim continued. *(Volkswagen UK)*

OPPOSITE TOP: Farewell, golf ball gear lever! The GTI had the same comfortable shifter as any other Golf. Driver airbag now standard, and, on this UK car, an alarm (red light center). *(Volkswagen UK)*

OPPOSITE BOTTOM: The roomy rear space for the Mk3 Golf included the new feature of a two-third split rear seat and seatbelts for three adults. *(Volkswagen UK)*

tor, and most of the Mk3 Golf's weight gain was explained by crash reinforcements and extra safety kit. A single safety specification was engineered for both the European and US markets—with doors reinforced by side impact beams ready for the 1994 US 33.5 mph side impact law.

The latest Passat was transverse-engined for the first time, so it could donate engine and suspension components to the 1991 Golf. The rear suspension continued to refine the torsion beam concept, and wedge-shaped track correction mountings from the Corrado and Passat were claimed to give a degree of rear wheel steering to keep the car in line. A rear anti-roll bar was fitted to faster cars that also had the "Plus" front suspension. The distance between the steering axis and the point of wheel contact with the road surface was shortened from 52 mm to 40 mm to improve straight line running and was claimed to virtually eliminate torque steer. The power-assisted steering (standard on all except the base 1.4 Golf) was now firmer.

At launch an early type of traction control system (called TCS) was standard on the Golf VR6 and an option on the eight-valve 2.0-liter GTI. It required anti-lock brakes (optional for all but VR6 Golfs) with four electronic sensors monitoring the speed of each wheel. A computer compared the speed signals with pre-programmed values and could reduce or increase hydraulic pressure between four and ten times a second—as the driver felt the pedal vibrate beneath their foot. TCS would brake the individual wheel that was starting to spin.

The new Golf was fully launched at September's Frankfurt Motor Show. For Europe there were four different capacity gas engines from 1.4 to 2.8 liters and power outputs from 60 to 174 bhp (all fuel injected and catalyzed). Every engine had a 16-valve cylinder head—which made the first eight-valve GTI look even more out of place. Two diesels completed the power choice and there would be a major push on diesel technology ahead.

Four- or five-speed manual gearboxes were offered across the third-generation Golf, with no further use of the Formel E or 4+ E descriptions. A seven-speed automatic gearbox developed between Volkswagen and Renault was reported to have foundered two years before launch, so the Passat's new four-speed became available on the Golf from the 1.8-liter upward, including the VR6.

As well as its spiritual home in Wolfsburg, the Golf was built in Puebla, Mexico (supplying North America); Uitenhage, South Africa; Brussels; and the new Mosel factory near the old Trabant plant at Zwickau in the newly unified Germany. In 1994 Volkswagen Bratislava (Skoda) took over sole production of the Golf Syncro and became a center for the group's four-wheel-drive cars.

ABOVE: The named-for-Europe Vento was pitched as an executive sedan in VR6 form. It retained front and rear Golf doors but had its own front and rear styling. *(Volkswagen UK)*
OPPOSITE: The 2.0-liter 16-valve Golf GTI was delayed on sale because the original planned 143 bhp wasn't going to be enough to match the 150 bhp Opel/Vauxhall Astra GSi. *(Volkswagen UK)*

Some Call It Vento...

Third time 'round, Volkswagen tried to distance the trunk version of the Golf from the hatchback, perhaps seeking more cachet. In February 1992 the new Vento appeared. It was 36 cm longer than a Golf at 4.38 m and had a vast trunk of 550-liter capacity with fold-down rear seats. A rear anti-roll bar was standard to cope with the extra luggage this might encourage.

However, in America the Jetta name stayed as its real estate was too valuable to mess with. Where Golf sales had faltered, the Jetta stayed strong and was credited with having saved Volkswagen from pulling out of the US altogether in the early 1990s. Overall sales went from 49,533 in 1993 to 97,043 the next year, following the third Jetta's introduction, and continued to climb.

Wherefore GTI?

By October 1, 1992, 1.14 million Golf GTIs had been built, but blink and you could let an Mk3 GTI pass you by. As all Golfs now had a single headlamp cover, a twin-lamped GTI couldn't readily be distinguished from any other from the front, apart from the badge and clear indicator lenses. The red piping was absent from the front grille as it was body colored, but there was a large GTI badge. It had sports seats, but the pattern was subtle shades of gray rather than red stripes.

Compared with a regular Golf, this GTI was lowered by 10 mm at the front, 20 mm at the back, with disc brakes all around and alloy wheels with 195/50 R15 tires. Power-assisted steering was standard, but at first anti-lock brakes and traction control were optional.

The new eight-valve 2.0-liter GTI engine was derived from the well-proven E827 iron block/alloy head 1.8 with an increase in stroke from 86.4 mm to 92.8 mm and an increase in bore from 81.0 mm to 82.5 mm for 2.0-liter. The cast-iron cylinder block of the 2.0-liter was 16.5 mm taller with reinforcing ribs and an alloy oil sump.

Digifant, Volkswagen's own version of the Bosch L-Jetronic engine management system, controlled the fuel delivery. The eight-valve GTI's claimed top speed was 123 mph and a 0–62 mph figure fractionally quicker than the old 1.8, from 10.3 to 10.1 seconds. It was treading water in the hot hatch performance wars, but it had improved on the much-appreciated low-down maximum torque—122 lb ft at 3,200 rpm compared with 114 lb ft at 3,100 rpm.

Autocar (March 18, 1992) pitched a five-door GTI against the latest Ford Escort XR3i, the Ford's new 1.8-liter 16-valve "Zeta" engine, gaining 15 bhp over the 2.0-liter GTI. "In a straight fight from rest against the clock, the Escort wipes the floor and several untidy areas of next door's back yard with the Golf," it said. On the figures it was hard to argue that the new, 45 g heavier (at 1,165 kg) eight-valve GTI was a competitive hot hatch with a recorded 9.9 seconds to 60 mph against the Ford's 8.6 and a top speed of 121 mph against 125 mph.

And yet the magazine preferred the way that the Golf delivered its power to the Ford's: "The Golf's engine is no firecracker, but it does strike an intelligent balance between vigour and flexibility . . . you don't have to try too hard to go fast in the Golf and the experience is never wearing."

ABOVE: The rear of a GTI 16V was marked only by an extra badge. A wide rear pillar continued to be a Golf style marker. A small spoiler was integrated into the top of the tailgate, which for the first time on a Golf, opened to bumper level. *(Interfoto/Alamy Stock Photo)*

LEFT: The Mk3 Golf GTI's 16-valve engine was set apart from the eight-valve by its long alloy induction piping. It was designed to maintain the GTI's reputation for flexibility. *(Volkswagen UK)*

OPPOSITE TOP: The six-layer fully insulated fabric roof of the new Cabriolet was up to the expected standards of insulation and folded flatter than before for better rear visibility. *(Volkswagen UK)*

The 1993 GTI 16-Valve

In January 1993 the new 2.0-liter 16-valve GTI appeared, offering 150 bhp, a midway performance point between the eight-valve GTI and the VR6. It was claimed to run more quietly than the old 1.8. The 16-valve aluminum alloy cylinder head was developed by Audi in Ingolstadt, with a chain drive connecting the two camshafts as before.

Outside, the GTI 16V was as subtle as the eight-valve with a GTI 16V badge front and rear plus on the side strips, black wheel arches and sills, and "Le Mans" or "Monte Carlo" alloy wheels, with optional black Recaro sport seats inside. TCS traction control was standard.

In the UK it commanded a healthy premium over the regular GTI; in 1994 £2,000 more at a list price of £15,999 for the three-door, however, with car theft raging, *Autocar and Motor* was baffled at the lack of a standard alarm and immobilizer (added later). It won its October match against an Astra GSi and the Fiat Tipo 16v through its chassis refinement and handling security—plus, a 0–60 time of 8.1 seconds was almost two seconds better than the eight-valve with a top speed of 134 mph. "The good news for all those die-hard fans of the old 16-valve Golf is that the new version goes to the top of the class."

In September 1993 the Frankfurt Motor Show saw the long-awaited Golf Cabriolet, with rollover safety high on the shopping list. It was still the *Erdbeerkörbchen*, or strawberry basket, with a chunky rollover bar midway along the passenger compartment; Herbert Schuster, by then a board member for technology, had insisted on it. New Cabrios were pictured being overturned with crash test dummies snug in their seatbelts. The added benefits of the bar were good hood and window location and the ability to accommodate a roof rack and go through a brush car wash without incident. Electric folding was standard.

As before, built by Karmann in Osnabrück (but also in Puebla for the US from April 1996), to achieve the same claimed level of refinement as the closed Golf, the Cabriolet boasted front and rear "harmonic vibration dampers." This consisted of a 10 kg cast-iron weight mounted on rubber blocks behind the left-hand rear wheel and a specially designed mounting system for the entire mass of the engine and transmission at the front. The floorpan, front and rear structure, and door sills were reinforced.

In Germany and elsewhere in Europe the Mk3 Golf Cabriolet was introduced in top trim form with a Mercedes-like name of Avantgarde with the 115 bhp eight-valve GTI engine and its alloy wheels. There was no GTI badging, but Avantgarde Cabriolets had the same black wheel arch cladding with smaller "Orlando" 14-inch alloy wheels. Regular 1.8- and 1.6-liter engine choices came later as well as the novelty of a diesel Cabriolet, but the VR6 engine was not on offer. Multiple colorful special editions followed.

The same year also saw the arrival of a long-awaited Golf derivative in the shape of an estate, or kombi, that retained the rear doors of the hatchback but was extended behind the rear wheels by an extra 32 cm at 4.34 m long, essentially a Vento/Jetta platform. On sale only in Europe, and perhaps to the detriment of the image of the basic GTI, you could have the same eight-valve 115 bhp engine in the 2.0-liter Golf GL estate.

THE MIGHTY A59

In 1992, as the third Golf was getting into its stride, stories began to circulate that Volkswagen would re-enter the World Rally Championship (WRC) with a new super-Golf, ready to battle with such giants as the Ford Escort RS Cosworth, Lancia Delta HF Integrale, and Toyota Celica ST185.

In its March 18, 1992, issue *Autocar & Motor* reported that the green light had been given to a 200 bhp–plus Golf. Two prototypes with different engine and four-wheel-drive combinations were said to be already under development, and Volkswagen started assembling a team including Audi WRC champion Walter Röhr, with Audi to help with development.

To be ready for the 1994 WRC season, production of 2,500 road cars needed to start in 1993 for the car be homologated. Mindful of the failure of the Golf Rallye G60, the new car was billed to have the maximum permitted 2.0-liter forced induction arrangement to produce well over 300 bhp in rally trim. "We haven't decided on the final specification of the engine yet," said Klaus Rosorius, VW Motorsport's managing director. "We're thinking about a 2.0-liter 16 or even 20-valve four with either turbo or supercharging."

Starting in early 1992, the first A59 prototype (for *Auftragsnummer* 59, order number 59) was built in complete secrecy by tuner Schmidt Motorsport (SMS) in Cadolzburg near Nuremberg, which already made Audi DTM rally cars. Owner Konrad Schmidt recruited three engineers from the Toyota GT4 rally team: Karl-Heinz Goldstein, Eduard Weidl, and Norbert Kreyer, with the aim that it would debut at the 1994 Monte Carlo Rally.

A 20-valve version of the EA827 engine was considered but judged not strong enough to withstand the boost pressures, so the A59 had a bespoke all-aluminum 2.0-liter turbocharged four-cylinder unit (Golfs had an iron block) with 275 bhp in road trim and up to 400 bhp in Group A specification.

It was still mounted transversely to match regular Golf production lines and coupled to a redeveloped version of the Mk3 Golf Syncro system, where a viscous coupling could potentially transfer all the power to the rear wheels when it sensed slippage. The coupling was replaced by an electronically controlled center differential developed by Steyr Puch. The six-speed gearbox was an FF Developments racing unit.

The front suspension used strut-type suspension with Bilstein shock absorbers and front control arms lengthened by three inches compared with the standard car to give better ground clearance. Rear suspension was fully independent multilink—again a legacy of the Syncro axle, which had wishbones and struts. The Brembo brakes featured cross-drilled discs.

The A59 was bodied in steel but with custom-made wheel arch extensions and some panels in Kevlar to keep weight down. As a potential production car was fully trimmed, it had four seats, at the front Recaro A8s with slots for a four-point harness. The dashboard featured a digital display not offered on any other Volkswagen at the time.

By May 1993 the car was almost ready and Volkswagen dealers were calling for a small series, but at a potential price of DM 80,000 (about £35,000) the project was canceled by new Volkswagen boss Ferdinand Piëch. Europe was in recession, Volkswagen was embarking on a multi-million-pound motorsport campaign, and selling a Golf almost three times the price of a GTI was out of the question. The A59 was consigned to the Volkswagen museum in Wolfsburg without having turned a wheel in competition, but in 2022 Volkswagen took it on a promotional tour of America, and selected press were allowed to drive it. A second part-completed A59 with GTI engine and adjustable rear spoiler is reported to exist at Schmidt Motorsport.

OPPOSITE: Seen here in the Volkswagen museum, the outlandish A59 had two bulges molded into its Kevlar hood to clear taller suspension turrets and three cutouts to help engine breathing and cooling. (*Volkswagen Classic*)

BELOW: The A59's 2.0-liter engine was built to be capable of taking up to 400 bhp and made entirely out of aluminum. It remains the only engine of the program that was ever completed. (*Volkswagen AG*)

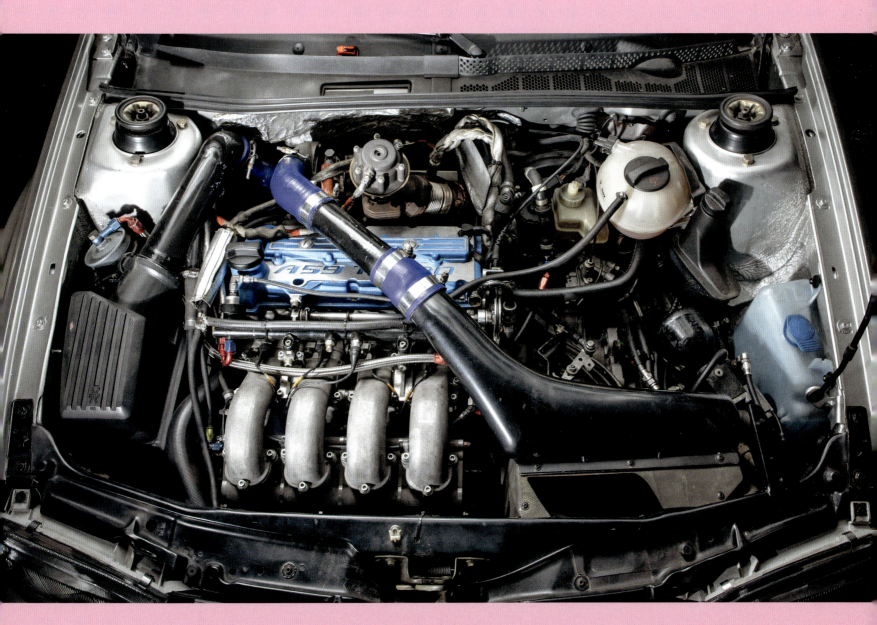

A GTI Six for the USA

The Mk3 Golf and Jetta were late coming to America, not arriving in the showrooms until late 1993, nearly two years after their European debuts. The Volkswagen faithful had been making do with warmed-over versions of the Mk2 models, and sales had slumped to 4,693. Unfortunately, the new '93 models were soon obsolete as they had passive seatbelts that were then replaced by twin airbags for 1994.

However, the larger Jetta Mk3 was a shot in the arm for sales, and for 1994 came as a GL or GLS with the 2.0-liter eight-valve 115 bhp engine (made in Mexico along with the car) but the main attraction was the 2.8-liter 172 bhp Jetta VR6 GLX.

Volkswagen Australia opted not to bring the Mk3 GTI in at all, just the VR6. Meanwhile, a four-cylinder GTI was no longer going to cut it with North American buyers. While the 115 bhp engine earned the Golf a GTI badge in Europe, in America it was demoted to GL status and described as "feisty" by its maker. The Mk2 GTI had been rapidly outgunned in the performance stakes, and now the Volkswagen hatchback faced rivals that unlike in Europe, were largely coupés such as the Eagle Talon, Mazda MX-6, and Ford Probe—the latter of which offered six-cylinder engines—and the Mitsubishi Eclipse.

When VWoA chose to launch the new Volkswagen GTI VR6 in autumn 1994 ('95 model year), it was an easy decision to also drop in the 2.8-liter VR6 and ask $6,000 less than the soon-to-be-obsolete Corrado at $19,190. In terms of size and space the closest rivals were the Acura Integra GS-R and a Nissan Sentra SE-R.

The GTI VR6 came with a five-speed manual gearbox only, its close ratios worked by the slightly rubbery long-throw shifting that

---

BELOW: The North American Jetta GLX VR6 (here a Canadian brochure) was launched ahead of the GTI as the top sporty model, sharing the trunk lid spoiler of the German Vento GT. *(Author)*

OPPOSITE: Launching the Volkswagen GTI only as a six-cylinder transformed a tarnished image. It was sold only as a three-door and was slightly longer than a European GTI thanks to 5 mph impact bumpers. *(Author)*

came from the cable operation. With a fraction less bhp (172 to Europe's 173) the GTI VR6 was easily the fastest ever tested by the magazines. *MotorTrend* managed 0–60 mph in 6.7 seconds. Its 129 mph top speed was curtailed against the European Golf VR6's 140 mph because the 15-inch alloy wheels were fitted with Goodyear (205/50HR15) Eagles GAs that were not speed-rated to match. They were also not very forgiving. "This car's ride leans toward harsh," wrote John Phillips in *Car and Driver* (September 1994), but he and the team found the GTI VR6 a "light-footed delight . . . which squirts and screams through traffic like some kind of motorcycle cop on a juiced-up Harley."

Anti-lock brakes and traction control were to be expected (in 1994 anti-lock brakes became standard on European Golf GTIs), and the 1995 model year GTI VR6 had a larger front anti-roll bar and firmer shock absorbers than a Golf GL. However, these seemingly had the same European settings that leaned toward luxury, so the expected GTI-like sharpness was found lacking around a test track. The GTI VR6 would gently lift its inside rear wheel as usual, but cornering was accompanied by a surprising amount of body roll.

Available as a three-door only, the GTI VR6 was Puebla-built with German engines and, for a market of cutthroat pricing, every possible goodie was thrown at it. The list included an electric sunroof, heated front seats, an alarm, and an eight-speaker AM/FM cassette. There were only two options: a six-CD player and clearcoat paint protection. This US Golf also had a lockable central storage box that held a remote release for the rear hatch and, of course, two cupholders up front and a pop-out at the rear. The black cloth seat fabric was more lively than in European GTIs, with splotches of red and blue triangles.

Clearly a suspension rethink had taken place for 1996, when the GTI VR6 was given firmer suspension all around and new gas rear shock absorbers, land lowered by 10 mm. It was "definitely more responsive than last year," said *MotorTrend*, but not at the expense of good rough highway composure.

Having been the Golf Sport in 1995, the 115 bhp four-cylinder was now available in GTI form, meeting the need for a slower yet still sporty GTI that was easier to insure. The 1996 American GTI range started at $16,000 and the VR6 GTI $19,685. The base GTI was distinguished from lesser Golfs by a two-bar grille, projector lens headlights, fog lamps, a roof-mounted "bee sting" antenna, 14-inch five-spoke alloy wheels, and air-conditioning but lacked electric windows. It rode on the standard suspension but with the rear stiffened by a 21 mm anti-roll bar.

VR6 GTI sales went from a planned 2,576 in 1995 to 7,406 in 1996 alongside 16,802 regular Golf Mk3s, but compared with this, 85,022 Jettas of all kinds sold in 1996, showing just how big a deal the Golf with a trunk was to the US market.

OPPOSITE: The 115 bhp Volkswagen GTI shared the two-bar grille of the VR6 but had its own five-spoke wheels and a red GTI grille badge. *(Revs Institute)*

RIGHT: Unlike European GTIs, there was body-colored rather than black side trim. It shared the same smoked rear lamp lenses of the GTI VR6 and the "bee sting" rear roof aerial. *(Revs Institute)*

BELOW: The VR6 was not a natural racer but had its time on American tracks—here at the 1995 Sports Car Club of America end of season mid-Ohio Runoff. *(Revs Institute)*

BELOW: Seen in a 1995 Canadian-market brochure, the GTI VR6 lacked a deep front spoiler because of the possibility of grounding on high parking curbs. Instead of BBS wheels, it had Canadian-made nine-spoke alloys. *(Author collection)*

A Splash of Color—1995–1997 GTI Color Concept

The inside of any European Golf Mk3 was a rather gray place to be, with a gray or black dashboard and gray seats only enlivened with subtle patterns. Introduced in Germany and Europe in 1994, then the UK in 1995, the GTI Color Concept was an additional model for those years based on the eight-valve 115 bhp GTI that came in five exclusive colors: Salsa Green, Yellow, Flash Red, Jazz Blue, or Diamond Black Pearl effect. Each came with leather Recaro sports seats where the center panels matched the exterior color, as did the stitching on the leather steering wheel, gear lever, side door trims, and floor mats. The instruments were silver faced. The 15-inch "Solitude" alloy wheels were unique to the GTI Color Concept. The £1,700 UK price premium for the Color Concept took it within £350 of the £15,345 16-valve.

If all this seems a little too extroverted for a GTI, consider the 1996 US-market Golf Harlequin (non GTI) special, a run-out model that followed a similar Polo in having its panels painted with four different colors. Cars were built in batches of those colors on the line in Puebla and then had their panels taken off and swapped around. Around 250 are believed to have been made.

The Diesel GTI Emerges

Back in Europe, the Volkswagen Group's diesel revolution was going at top speed, with the 1993 TDI engine range (also spelled TDi in Volkswagen advertising). The "T" was for Turbo and the "I" stood for direct injection of the fuel straight into the cylinder at much higher pressure rather than via a pre-combustion chamber. It addressed the public perception that diesel-engined cars, even with turbochargers, simply could not match their gas counterparts on performance. Coupled to the 1.9-liter diesel engine, the small turbocharger was fed with air from an intercooler, and had good low-speed torque, cleaner emissions (as measured at the time), and 15 to 20 percent better fuel economy than a gas engine.

Offered in addition to regular diesel engines, the TDI was soon used right across the Volkswagen brands and across the Golf (and Vento/Jetta) range. In 1995 it became available in the Cabriolet, the world's first diesel soft top. There was also a non-turbocharged direct injection diesel engine.

In 1996 the 110 bhp TDI from the Audi A4 was slotted into the Golf GTI, badged as the GT TDi (although not for the UK). On claimed figures it accelerated from 0–60 mph in 9.3 seconds, three-tenths of a second quicker than the eight-valve GTI, and its acceleration in fifth gear from 50 to 75 mph was even better at 11.1 seconds compared with 14.2. The torque was not far off that of the VR6, developed from only 1,900 rpm. The turbocharger had variable rate vanes that allowed exhaust gases to pass continuously through, even at low revs for better and quieter response.

GTI Anniversary

In summer 1996, to mark 20 years of the GTI, a limited run of 1,000 GTI Anniversary models was offered with both GTI engines and the 110 bhp TDI (again not the diesel for the UK). Bringing back what enthusiasts had been missing since launch, the Anniversary had special checkered Recaro front sport seats and matching rear seats bearing the GTI logo, red seatbelts front and rear, a half chrome and leather golf ball gear knob, and a red stitched leather steering wheel and handbrake gaiter. The red theme was continued externally with a red striping on the bumpers and red brake calipers. BBS cross-spoke alloy wheels replaced the normal items with larger 215/40 tires. In the UK, 700 cars were allocated in Anniversary trim, based on the eight-valve GTI.

OPPOSITE: The Europe-only GTI Color Concept series was a way to pep up interest in the 115 bhp car—at a premium. This one is finished in Jazz Blue Pearl effect. The center seat panels were matched in the same shade. *(Phil Talbot/Alamy Stock Photo)*

RIGHT: In 1997, those who missed the twin-lamp GTI could buy headlamp covers to create the illusion. The Votex shades here were offered by Volkswagen UK. *(Volkswagen UK)*

BELOW: While there were no factory Mk3 GTI rally campaigns, each country's importers were happy to support the car. This is Martin Rowe entertaining at the September 1996 Manx Rally round of the Mobil 1 Top Gear British Rally Championship. *(PA Images/Alamy Stock Photo)*

A Trailer for the Golf 4

By the late 1990s the GTI name was being spread around the Volkswagen Group. If you wanted something nearer to the size of the Mk2 Golf GTI there was now Polo-based Seat1 Ibiza GTI, with the 1.8-liter 130 bhp 16-valve engine or the bigger Seat Toledo GTI (which was based on the Mk2 Golf floorpan) with the 2.0-liter 16-valve engine.

When the third-generation Golf launched in 1991, Volkswagen claimed this would be a line that would run for ten years, but by 1996 it was clear this was not the case when the Audi A3 hatchback arrived. Launched in June 1996, underneath the A3 was the platform of the next Golf, with exactly the same dimensions in wheelbase, track, and width. This platform, called the A4 platform (PQ 34 internally), was also destined to be the basis of the Skoda Octavia, the new Seat Toledo and Leon, and there was speculation of an aluminum-bodied Audi sedan that turned out to be the Audi TT coupé, and finally the "new" Beetle.

The A3 was chasing after the BMW 3-Series Compact, but its launch engine choice included an impressive 20-valve 1.8-liter gas engine five valves per cylinder with 125 bhp or 150 when turbocharged both of which were an alternative to the Mk3 Golf GTIs, if not the VR6 (purposely not offered in the A3). The Golf Mk4 was launched in Europe in 1997 (chapter 4). The Audi A3 was more expensive and perceived as more prestigious, but if you wanted a full four-seater and five doors, the Golf was the only choice as the A3 was intentionally limited to three doors until 1999.

Meanwhile, the North American Mk3 GTIs served for another two years. For 1997 the GTI VR6 got its suspension lowered by 10 mm, then later in the year a limited-run GTI VR6 Driver's Edition, with unique seven-spoke alloys and even lower, stiffer suspension with progressive anti-roll bars; red brake calipers; chrome-tipped exhaust pipes; and lots of GTI interior badging. Many of these details made it onto the series production VR6 for 1998, and the four-cylinder GTI was dropped for the 1999 model year.

ABOVE: Inside the 1996 GTI Anniversary. Many fans welcomed the return of a tartan seats pattern in a GTI, and especially the golf ball gear lever. *(Volkswagen UK)*

Golf GTI Mk3 (Europe)

Model	GTI 1.8 8-valve	GTI 1.8 16-valve	Volkswagen GTI VR6 (US)
Engine type/capacity	4-cyls inline, single overhead cam 2.0-liter Digifant fuel injection	4-cyls inline double overhead cam 2.0-liter Digifant fuel injection	6-cyls narrow angle vee, single overhead cam, 12-valves, 2.8-liter Bosch Motronic fuel injection
Gearbox	5-speed manual	5-speed manual	5-speed manual
Maximum power/at rpm	115 bhp@5,400 rpm	150 bhp@6,000pm	172 bhp@5,400 rpm
Maximum torque/at rpm	122 lb ft@3,200 rpm	133 lb ft@4,800 rpm	173 lb ft@4,200 rpm
Acceleration 0–60 mph	9.9 seconds	8.1 seconds	7.2 seconds
Maximum speed	121 mph (*Autocar & Motor* 18 March 1992)	134 mph (*Autocar & Motor* 13 October 1993)	129mph (*Car and Driver* September 1994). 141mph Europe.
Suspension front/rear	Strut and coil springs, wishbone, anti-roll bar/trailing arms, coil springs, torsion beam axle, anti-roll bar	Strut and coil springs, wishbone, anti-roll bar/trailing arms, coil springs, torsion beam axle, anti-roll bar	Strut and coil springs, wishbone, anti-roll bar/trailing arms, coil springs, torsion beam axle, anti-roll bar
Wheels/tires	6 x 15-in alloy Pirelli P600 195/50 VR15	6 x 15-in alloy Uniroyal 205/50 R15	6.5 x 15-in alloy Goodyear Eagle GA M+S 205/50 HR15
Brakes front/rear	Ventilated disc/disc Anti-lock brakes optional	Ventilated disc/disc Anti-lock brakes standard	Ventilated disc/disc Anti-lock brakes standard
Length	4,020 mm	4,020 mm	4,075 mm
Wheelbase	2,475 mm	2,475 mm	2,475 mm
Width	1,710 mm	1,710 mm	1,695 mm
Height	1,405 mm	1,405 mm	1,423 mm
Unladen weight (kg)	1,035/1,060 (3/5-door)	1,090/1,115 (3/5-door)	1,285/1,315 (3/5 door)
Years produced	1991-1997	1993-1997	1994-1999

4.
GOLF GTI MK4 1997–2003

A Very Subtle GTI

Best-looking Golf? To many Golf fans the fourth generation remains a classic design that has aged rather well and as it turned out was built remarkably well—many were still on the road over 25 years later (it had a 12-year corrosion warranty).

The usual styling competition had taken place in 1994, with six full-sized designs ranging from the adventurous to the conservative, among them a Giugiaro design, yet this was judged too conservative. The winning shape was once more in-house, from chief designer Hartmut Warkuß. An ex-Audi stylist, he was among those who had backed the new Beetle through its bumpy journey into reality and had styled the distinctive 1996 Passat. Golf Mk4 took 31 months from the styling freeze to the start of production.

RIGHT: The Mk4 Golf aspired to a more premium feel; every version had bumpers painted in the body-color and the GTI lost the black wheel arch trims. This is a 2001 Golf GTI Anniversary model. *(Volkswagen UK)*

There was a family resemblance to the new Beetle and Passat in-as-much as the front door pillars had a gentle curve to them and the wheel arches were more pronounced to echo the new Beetle. For the first time, the tops of the Golf's doors folded over and blended into the roof panel.

From the side, the classic "C" pillar and the shut line of the rear bumper sloped neatly parallel to the line of the lower half of the rear door on the five-door car. The almost-oval headlamps of the Golf Mk3 continued with single or twin headlamps inside but now incorporated the front turn indicators and front fog lights, giving the front end of the car a smooth look.

All the versions of the fourth-generation Golf were presented to the European press in August 1997, then to the public at September's Frankfurt Motor Show, including a GTI—but which one was it? This was the first and only GTI not to feature the red stripe on the radiator grille. Nor was there any sign of the signature black side strips and wheel arch trim.

Instead, the GTI (or GTD) markers were side-rubbing strips in the body color rather than black, plus darkened tail lamp lenses. During the 1990s "hot hatchbacks" needed to become a lot more discreet after an explosion in European car theft, but perhaps this GTI blended in a little too well?

The 1997 Golf was 131 mm longer than the third generation, 30 mm wider, and the wheelbase was 39 mm longer to the benefit of trunk capacity and rear legroom. At 1,439 mm it was only a couple of millimeters taller. The standard wheel size had gone up, too, from 13 to 14 inches on regular cars to 15 or 16 inches on the GTI and GTI 1.8T. With the listed 1,109 kg unladen weight of an Mk3 16-valve three-door, it was notably heavier. This weight gain was later lamented by motor magazines.

The drag, or Cd factor, was still a respectable 0.31, around the same as the best models of the previous car, and two underbody trim panels smoothed airflow over the front and rear axles. The bodywork's torsional (twisting) rigidity, seen as a measure of how well the car would cope with poor surfaces, was now twice that of the 1974

BELOW: What's this? The fourth-gen Golf GTI didn't even have a GTI badge on the front grille. Front foglamps were integrated within the headlamps. *(Volkswagen UK)*

OPPOSITE TOP: On the tailgate, the GTI badge moved from the left to the right, making way for a Golf badge. This GTI is finished in Jazz Blue Pearl effect paint. *(Author)*

OPPOSITE BOTTOM: The European Golf GTI 1.8T was set out by its 16-inch Montreal alloy wheels. All Euro GTIs could be ordered with three or five doors. *(Revs Institute)*

Designed and engineered without compromise.

When Volkswagen's engineers first draughted the plans for the new Golf, safety was a primary objective. The result is clearly evident in its exceptional protection levels: Driver and front passenger airbags, ABS brakes and all-round disc brakes are standard across the range. To support Volkswagen's legendary build quality, you'll find the galvanised chassis is backed by a 12 year warranty against corrosion.

CHAPTER 4. GTI MK4 1997–2003   93

Golf, which Volkswagen attributed mainly to laser welding and advanced bonding techniques to mount the windshield and rear window. These also sped up manufacturing times, with the roof being welded as a single seam in 10 seconds.

Front suspension of MacPherson struts and wishbones was now the industry norm, but the additional "Plus" steering and suspension setting for the Mk3 Golf performance models were dropped, with one setting for all engines. Front and rear anti-roll bars were standard.

The trademark torsion beam rear axle reappeared (same as the Audi A3's apart from tuning) but instead of being one inside the other vertically, the coil springs and dampers were located separately, with the springs positioned under the side members. It meant a wider loading width in the trunk for the hatchback and the forthcoming estate.

However, pinning a torsion beam rear axle on the class-leading Golf was soon to seem last year's fashion. In 1998 Ford of Europe was to astonish the critics by replacing the dull Escort with the radical Focus, a real driver's car. One of the major investments Ford had made was in a multi-link fully independent rear suspension. More complex and hence costly, multi-link rear suspension is considered to give the best combination of handling, comfort, and space efficiency. Volkswagen was to be outfoxed by Ford.

On safety, VW chairman Ferdinand Piëch was so determined that the new Golf have the maximum five-star rating under the new European New Car Assessment Program (Euro NCAP) that he delayed production from September 1997 to November while the "b" pillar was redesigned. Side impact intrusion was claimed to have been reduced by 25 percent over the last Golf by the use of slanting side impact bars in the doors, roof cross bracing, and interlocking segments between the doors and sills. The engine and running gear were mounted on a subframe for both insulating road noise from the bodyshell and better crashworthiness. In the event of a collision, it was designed to direct the engine underneath the car.

Twin front airbags were now standard for all markets, and for some, a pair of side airbags were built into the sides of the front seats. Anti-lock brakes were also fitted to every Golf with Electronic Brakeforce Distribution (EBD) to correctly proportion the assistance given to each wheel, and this demanded the fitment of disc brakes all around. In the event of a crash, locked doors would automatically unlock.

Also standard, Electronic Differential Lock (EDL) was a development of traction control, monitoring the speed of the driving wheels and then braking the faster-moving wheel if the difference exceeded a pre-determined value, transferring more drive to the gripping wheel.

There was a new upscale feel inside, with options such as automatic air-conditioning, satellite navigation, and electric leather seats. No more slabs of boring gray and black plastic; depending on the color of the seat trim (there was a very smart beige), the new Golf's dashboard could be specified in a contrasting lower color (no more black-only GTI dashboards), in beige or gray, with the theme taken around to the lower halves of the door panels.

A technique called "slush molding" gave a soft, grained feel to the top section of the dashboard while the lower sections that you didn't

RIGHT: The standard 1997–1998 GTI interior had a black or beige dashboard top and front sports seats or Recaros on the 1.8T. Leather-wrapped steering wheel and gear lever were standard. *(Author)*

usually touch were made from a harder-surfaced plastic. It really did give the new Golf a "mini Mercedes" ambience.

Small details added to this premium feel. One often-noticed part was a little damper in the grab handles above the doors so that if you released them, they didn't thud back into place but returned silently—this had trickled down from the Passat, and generally Golfs started to gain the luxury features of their bigger brothers.

Five gas engines and three diesels were on offer for the 1997 Golf range, and with a cupboard full of nice new Audi A3 motors to use, there was none of the delay that the Golf Mk3 had suffered. Bosch multipoint fuel injection was now on all Golf gas engines, and all versions had a five-speed gearbox at launch, with a four-speed auto later, and further into the future, the first twin-clutch semi-automatic (DSG) Golf and a six-speed manual.

A new 75 PS (horsepower) 1.4 16-valve engine was introduced in the 1994 Polo, an all-aluminum unit (the first in a Golf), but the mainstay of sales was expected to be a 100 PS 1.6-liter 16-valve unit. It was derived from the old EA111 group 1.6 engine but had been redesigned with an alloy cylinder block and twin camshafts for use in the A3. This 1.6-liter four-cylinder produced similar power to the old Golf 1.8 and featured variable intake manifold geometry that changed the path of the air coming into the engine according to the engine load.

Euro-GTI Slips Down the Power Ladder

The European GTI had to regain some credibility after the 115 PS Mk3 (which had also shared its engine with the Golf GL station wagon). The new car would need more power just to overcome its extra weight.

European Golf Mk4s came with two choices of four-cylinder 1.8-liter (1.8-liter) engines, the Audi-developed EA113 with 125 PS and 150 PS turbo (15 and 25 PS more than before). Both of these 1.8-liter engines had 20-valve cylinder heads for better breathing. This meant that there were triple inlet and twin exhaust valves. All had to be proportionally smaller than before, demanding a new level of manufacturing precision.

Thus, the very first gas-engined production Golf with a turbocharger was thanks to Audi. The 1.8T engine was judged by road testers to respond very well with a relatively small turbocharger that gave no sensation of turbo lag and produced a wide spread of torque between 1,750 and 4,600 rpm. The performance figures were respectable, with a claimed top speed of 139 mph and 0–60 mph in around eight seconds. Although it was more tautly sprung than lesser Golfs, tes-

ABOVE: The first factory turbocharged GTI came with Audi's 20v 1.8T engine, which proved to be highly tunable, reaching up to 240 PS in the Audi TT Quattro Sport. *(Volkswagen UK)*
OPPOSITE TOP: The Golf V6 with standard 4Motion all-wheel-drive was the new range-topper, with a claimed 147 mph top speed. Its main distinguishing features were seven-spoke alloys and twin exhausts. *(Volkswagen UK)*
OPPOSITE BOTTOM: Compact as ever, the "R" had been dropped from VR6 across the Volkswagen range. The redeveloped 24-valve 2.8-liter was only offered in Europe in both Golf and Bora/Jetta. *(Volkswagen UK)*

ters felt this was a rapid GTI rather than a raucous one with slightly remote-feeling steering isolating the driver from the action. It continued the trend that Volkswagen had identified with the last model. Customers wanted refinement above all, and as the GTI also came in five-door form (unlike many competitors) some chose it for practical reasons. The GTI badge was a secondary pull.

In the British market, Volkswagen UK had chosen to replicate the former two-tier GTi (it used a lowercase "i") structure, but the 125 PS 1.8 was unique to the UK with a GTI badge—in Germany and other regions it was only offered in Highline trim. This backfired a little. "It's debatable whether VW should have christened this car GTi," sniffed *Autocar* in its December 1998 road test yearbook. "After all, it was the Golf that defined the hot hatch genre, and with just 125 PS to play with this GTi is anything but hot. . . . A top speed of just over 120 mph is hardly the stuff to burn up the overtaking lane on an autobahn. But VW has the 150 PS 1.8T GTi to cover those bases. As a mildly up-tempo Golf, this one doesn't disgrace itself."

The Golf GTI 1.8T was set apart from the lower-powered version by 16-inch alloy wheels, and the "i" part of the rear badge was red. Recaro seats and a glass sunroof were also unique to this model.

From VR6 Comes VR5

Not for GTIs, there was another new 150 PS engine in the European Golf range, the all-new 2.3-liter V5 engine, essentially a VR6 with one less cylinder and the same single overhead-camshaft operation of the valves (two per cylinder). Physically a little bigger than a four-cylinder but a little smaller than the VR6, the V5 (without the "R") could potentially be used in a wide variety of vehicles. A five-cylinder was unusual but not unique in the Golf class. Fiat had introduced a transverse five-cylinder in its Golf-sized Bravo and Marea ranges from 1995.

The alloy head/iron block 2.3-liter V5 was launched somewhat prematurely in the Passat in early summer 1997 when it was reported that development had fallen behind because of the rush to get the car to market, and that it had been held back in the Golf because of refinement problems.

When released into the Golf a year later, it was a smooth and flexible engine, which, when provoked, gave a satisfying growl. The Golf V5 was very much pitched as a small luxury car and offered in Highline or GTI trim in Germany, plain V5 in England, and could be had with a four-speed automatic with the Dynamic Shift Program (DSP) seen in the previous Golf, which was claimed to "learn" your driving pattern and adjust the gearchange points. In late 1998 it was the top-of-the-range Golf in the UK at £19,720 with very little on the options list.

Also launched in Europe in 1998, the Golf 4Motion V5 ushered in a replacement for the Syncro four-wheel-drive system used by the previous two Golfs. The viscous coupling was replaced by a multi-plate clutch developed by Swedish company Haldex with engine software by Steyr-Daimler-Puch and branded 4Motion by Volkswagen. It was the beginning of a long association between Haldex and Volkswagen.

A part-time four-wheel-drive system as before, the Haldex unit was mounted at the rear of the car, and once wheel slippage was detected, oil pressure to a piston was increased, which engaged the clutches and started to transfer drive to the rear wheels (in normal driving 90 percent of power went through the fronts) until the torque was split equally between front and rear axles—but it could, as with Syncro, send all the drive to the rear wheels in extreme conditions. The engine management system worked in tandem with the anti lock brake and traction control systems and was claimed to be extremely quick in reacting.

Adding a driven rear axle demanded new rear suspension, and this had been developed alongside the regular car. The V5 4Motion was the first Golf to feature multi-link rear suspension.

By 1999, the VR6 engine had now been in production for eight years, and European buyers got an updated version with a new cylinder head featuring four valves per cylinder for new range-toppers now badged Golf and Bora V6.

Compared with the Mk3 VR6, power increased from 174 to 201 bhp, making it the fastest Golf since the 210 bhp G60. The 24-valve Golf V6 was only offered allied to the 4Motion transmission with a six-speed gearbox, and while it had suspension lowered by 10 mm over a standard Golf and bigger brake discs, it didn't have sports suspension settings. This was a super-Golf for blasting down the autobahn at 140 mph, not the racetrack, but with hindsight it foreshadowed the later Golf R32 (see page 106).

Volkswagen Bora 1998—Or You Can Call Me Jetta

A year after the European Golf launch came the sedan version. Clearly the name Vento had not been a hit because now it was the Volkswagen Bora—another exotic wind name, no longer used by Maserati. The body—claimed to be 25 percent more rigid than the Golf—did finally break with the "Golf with a trunk" styling by being given its own rear doors and the distinctive curved roofline shared with the new Beetle and the Passat, emphasizing that the Bora was a smaller version of the former. The flagship Bora V5 could be had with leather-trimmed Recaro seats and wooden inlays to the center console.

A new Golf Cabriolet also appeared in 1998 but was not quite as it appeared; it was a skilfull reworking of the extensively (and expensively) developed Golf 3 Cabriolet introduced only five years previously. A fourth-generation Golf grille and smoothed front and rear bumpers helped give it a family likeness.

The next Golf estate followed in 1999, now a buyer favorite. The hatchback's new design of rear suspension improved access, and the load volume, at 1,470 liters with the seats down, was up by 45 liters. Trying to squeeze a new bunch of buyers out of the same design, a Bora was introduced in the German market in addition to the Golf estate, visually differing only in the front-end styling. The Golf wagon only had the smaller engines, the Bora the larger ones, with prices to match.

TOP: Volkswagen deftly remixed the Mk3 Cabriolet into Mk4 style with its front lights and grille and new front and rear bumpers (this is a US version). It stayed in production until 2002. *(VWoA)*

ABOVE LEFT: What appeared to be a smart Golf coupé appeared at the January '97 Detroit show, but the "Volkswagen CJ Coupe" just teased the front end of the new Bora/Jetta for '98. *(Volkswagen UK)*

ABOVE RIGHT: The production Bora/Jetta arrived with four doors as before—there would never be another two-door Jetta. Estate version for some markets (left) was identical to Golf apart from the front end. *(Volkswagen UK)*

THE OTHER GTIs

By 1999 and the fourth Golf, Volkswagen had added two Europe-only brands to its stable, Global web icon Škoda from the Czech Republic and Spain's Seat (also spelled SEAT). And thanks to the far-reaching platform strategy, buyers could choose all the mechanical parts of a Volkswagen GTI wrapped up in different shapes and brands.

Audis, Seats, Škodas, and Volkswagens based on the PQ34 platform had the same wheelbase, the same track between the wheels, and 20 "hard points" such as the center of the floorpan, wheel arch linings, suspension and engine mounts, and body side members. In addition to engines, gearboxes, and suspension, everything from sunroofs to fuel tanks was shared around the group at a cost savings of millions of euros.

The pressed-steel floorpans could have different front and rear sections added. At one end of the scale was the dinky Audi TT, the other the Škoda Octavia (wheelbase 4 cm longer than Golf). As well as in the A3, Audi's 20-valve, 125 PS 1.8-liter engine appeared first in the 1996 Octavia, which then jumped into the GTI hot hatch league in its 1999 RS version, with the same turbocharged 180 PS 1.8-liter engine that powered the Audi TT. If you wanted more space for the family but could give up the GTI badge, you made a neat saving: a UK Škoda Octavia was £15,100 in 2000 while a 150 PS Golf GTI was £16,245.

Also, in 1999 and perhaps somewhat forgotten now, the Golf-sized Seat Leon VT combined the 1.8T engine with Haldex 4Motion four-wheel-drive. The 1.8T got everywhere; from 2000 both American and European buyers could also have it in the new Beetle—another PQ34 car—giving it a GTI-like top speed of 132 mph and a claimed 0–60 mph time of 7.3 seconds.

TOP: European Volkswagen GTI fans had smaller GTIs; the city car Lupo GTI arrived in 2000, a 123 bhp pocket rocket smaller than the Polo GTI. *(Volkswagen UK)*

ABOVE: The Spanish Seat Leon VT was a left-field alternative to a GTI in 1999, and unlike the Volkswagen had four-wheel-drive plus the four-cylinder 1.8 turbo engine. *(Seat UK)*

TOP: Once a quirky low-price communist brand, the Czech Republic's Škoda had been transformed by VW. The Europe-only Octavia stretched the PQ34 to give a huge trunk, and the 1999 RS was a cut-price GTI 1.8T. *(Škoda UK)*

LEFT: The 1996 Audi A3 was the first offshoot of the PQ34 platform and underneath the base for the Mk4 Golf, launched a year earlier into a new market segment for Audi. *(Audi UK/Newspress)*

RIGHT: The most outrageous New Beetle was the 2001 RSI, which pre-dated the Golf R32. Based on the Beetle Cup race car, only 250 left-hand drive cars were ever built. *(Volkswagen AG)*

Diesel Does GTI Better?

While previous Golf GTDs had shared the sporty looks of their gas cousins but not the performance, Volkswagen brought forth a fourth generation that came the closest yet, while still just sipping fuel. Diesel was so "in" that Volkswagen UK finally decided to offer a sports diesel Golf for the first time.

In 1998 *Autocar* magazine preferred the 110 PS GT TDI to the 125 PS gas non-turbo GTI. "If 'diesel hot hatch' is a contradiction in terms, no one told VW. By finding a home for its 1.9-liter 110 PS turbo diesel in the nose of the MkIV Golf, VW has come up with a more effective GTi than the 20-valve 1.8 gas version. . . . This is because it has more torque—a walloping 173 lb ft at just 1900 rpm. So, while the TDi doesn't really make the GTi grade in the sprint to 60 mph, its 9.7 sec is still 0.3 sec better than the gas Golf GTi. And it's a different story when it comes to in-gear punch and flexibility."

In those days, Volkswagen's diesel technology continued to set the design benchmark. In 1999 the "PD" TDI diesels came in. PD stood for *Pumpe Düse*, which translated as "unit injector," a new injection system that operated at far higher pressures than the "common rail" diesels used lower down the Volkswagen range and by other manufacturers. Volkswagen claimed the higher injection pressures brought a better fuel and air mixture, resulting in higher torque but little or no change in fuel consumption. Introduced across the Volkswagen range, the first PD engines boosted the power of the 1.9-liter diesel to 115 PS.

North America Keeps Its Six-Cylinder GTI—1999

New for the North American market in early 1999, the German-built Volkswagen GTI (now named the GTI GLX) kept the 12-valve VR6 with a small increase in power to 174 hp (US horsepower, over 172) and 181 lb ft of torque (over 173). Three-door only, as before, a five-speed manual transmission was at first the only choice; goodies on

BELOW: It might have a Wolfsburg plate on it, but the side markers show this is a 1999 model year North American GTI, finished in the popular Cosmic Green Metallic paint. *(VWoA)*

the GTI GLX included 16-inch wheels, leather upholstery, dark wood trim, automatic climate control, trip computer, an automatic rain sensor, and heated windshield washer nozzles.

In early 1999 the 1.8-liter 125 PS European GTI engine was replaced by the 2.0-liter (2.0-liter) four-cylinder from the new Beetle, built in Puebla. Awkwardly, power actually fell to 115 PS so Volkswagen UK—continuing to call it a GTI—chose to just emphasize that it achieved the same maximum torque of 125 lb ft that was delivered earlier, at 2,400 rpm instead of 4,200 rpm. The company claimed a combined fuel consumption figure slightly improved from 34 mpg to 35.8 mpg (the new engine was aimed at improving emissions).

This 2.0-liter eight-valve was also the basis of the junior GTI in the American range as well as the Golf GLS, but as this engine was also the starter engine for the base Golf and Jetta of 1999, it was sporty in looks rather than action given the extra weight it had to haul.

The same engines could be had in the Jetta, the best-selling Volkswagen in the US, and the VR6 was very much appreciated under the hood of the Jetta GLS (the GLI name was dropped at the time, just GLS and GLX were used). "The 2 extra horsepower (to 174) gain over last year's 2.8-liter V-6 is negligible," said *MotorTrend*. "However, the 8 extra pound-feet of torque (now rated at 181) available at 3,200 rpm rather than 4,200 and more aggressive first and second gears make the Jetta VR6 a torquey and exhilarating car, rather than just another commuter sedan."

ABOVE: The European Golf VR6 didn't have sports suspension, so the body roll of the 1999 North America–only GTI VR6 drew attention. *(VWoA)*

RIGHT: The six-cylinder Golf GTI was a GTI GLX, but there was no exterior badging to show this, only the standout use of the VR6 engine. *(VWoA)*

Into the Next Century of GTI

In Europe, from the 2000 model year the V5 gained a multivalve cylinder head and twin overhead camshafts, releasing an extra 20 PS to bring its output up to 170 PS. Having already been dropped in the Beetle, Audi's 150 PS 1.8 turbo appeared in the 2000 GTI GLS for American buyers, a much-needed power boost, still with the same 15-inch wheels, but well equipped at a base price of $19,750.

Until now the North American market had never had a Golf estate/station wagon, but the German-made Bora estate crossed the Atlantic in 2001 re-christened the Jetta GLX wagon—a welcome addition to over 144,000 Jettas sold the previous year. For its first year it was either a 115 hp 2.0-liter GLS or 174 PS V6 GLX, with the 1.8T following on.

Meanwhile, Europe went all out on ever-faster diesel Golfs, helped by company car tax breaks and high gas prices. In 2001 the 130 PS GT TDi PD130 replaced the 115 PS car. It crushed its diesel rivals with a 127 mph top speed, a 0–60 mph time of 8.5 seconds, yet over 40 mpg, carefully kept apart from the GTI with comfortably soft suspension. It was followed by the rather more seriously sporty TDi PD 150, which liberated an extra 20 PS from a larger intercooler and turbo. The 150 shared the uprated suspension of the gas-powered GTI 1.8T and nearly matched its 0–60 mph time, if not top speed. The diesel clatter was the biggest clue from the outside.

OPPOSITE: With no rear spoiler, the Mk4 Jetta GLI really was a "sleeper" car, only marked at the rear by chrome-tipped exhaust pipes. *(VWoA)*

ABOVE: The North American Jetta GLI continued its role as a four-door GTI—17-inch wheels were standard. In 2002 it was offered with a 200 bhp V6 or 1.8T four-cylinder upped to 180 bhp. *(VWoA)*

THE FIRST GOLF R

At the start of the 2000s, European hot hatchbacks were more like mini rally cars, aiming at the all-wheel-drive Subaru Impreza WRX. As spy shots of the Ford Focus RS appeared in 2001, they were joined by pictures of what was then called a Golf RSI at Germany's famous Nürburgring racetrack; it was said to be running a 235 PS version of the 225 PS 2.3-liter V6 just seen in the Beetle RSI, coupled to the Haldex 4Motion four-wheel-drive system.

Volkswagen Motorsport had been renamed Volkswagen Racing (for now) and set itself up to produce small volumes of very high-performance versions of its road cars. This was initially set to be called the RSI line—the equivalent of the "M" badging used by BMW and Mercedes AMG.

At the Essen Motor Show in November 2001, Volkswagen exhibited what it termed a concept car, an aggressively styled three-door Golf with a deeper front bumper dominated by extra air intakes, a rear bumper with twin exhausts, and 18-inch OZ alloy wheels. Now simply called the R32, a new level of performance was provided by a 3.2-liter version of the 2.8-liter narrow-angle V6 A thanks to a bigger cylinder bore and longer stroke.

The concept was billed as delivering 240 bhp at 6,600 rpm, along with 228 lb ft of torque at 3,200 rpm; an increase of 36 bhp and 30 lb ft over the Golf 2.8 V6 4Motion. Drive was channeled to all four wheels via a six-speed manual gearbox and Haldex multi-plate clutch.

R32—THE FASTEST GOLF EVER

The Golf R32 was officially launched at the Madrid Motor Show in May 2002 as a flagship model sitting above the GTI range and went on sale in the UK in right-hand drive form six months later.

The details differed little from the concept of the previous November. The official power output was given as 241 PS, which was sometimes expressed as the same in bhp, when strictly speaking the PS conversion equated to 237.7 bhp. This maximum power arrived at 6,250 rpm assisted by continuously variable intake and exhaust camshaft timing. The new 3.2 V6 was not a peaky racing special but a full production engine also used by the luxury Phaeton and the Touareg off-roader. The exhaust system was specially tuned for a thrilling soundtrack.

The R32 had a claimed 0–60 mph time of 6.5 seconds and a top speed of 153 mph. Suspension was lowered by a further 10 mm compared with a standard Golf, with stiffer springs and anti-roll bars with the benefit of the 4Motion multi-link independent rear suspension. There was more responsive steering thanks to the quicker steering of the Audi TT (3.0 to 2.6). Over-enthusiastic R32 drivers were supported by standard and lock brakes and electronic stability control. The interior featured aluminum trim, Recaro Konig sports seats with integrated backrests and the "R" logo, and R32 markers on the door sills and floor mats.

THE FIRST DSG GEARBOX

While the standard gearbox for the first-generation Golf R32 was a six-speed manual, from 2003 German buyers could specify a new type of automatic gearbox,

also shared with the Audi TT. The Direct Shift Gearbox (DSG) was a new type of fully automatic gearbox, sometimes described as two gearboxes in one. It divided the odd and even number of gears (in this instance six) into two separate shafts each with their own clutch. As Volkswagen described it, when you turned the engine on and selected Drive mode, one shaft selected first gear while the second shaft put the next gear on "standby." As the gearbox changed to second, the second shaft was engaged and the original shaft reached third. As you shifted upward and then downward, the sequence continued. The next gear was always "ready."

The gear changes in a DSG gearbox were meant to be far quicker than those in a traditional automatic, with none of the power loss or increased fuel consumption (it was claimed the entire shift process was completed in less than four-hundredths of a second). You could drive a DSG car in fully automatic mode or change by tapping the gear lever forward and back. DSG went on to become widely applied across Volkswagen cars, eventually with seven speeds. Similar kinds of gearboxes were adopted by other manufacturers.

The Golf R32 was a rousing swan song for the Golf Mk4, just before the fifth generation appeared in 2003. Originally due to be a limited series of 5,000 (2,300 were eventually sold just in the UK), such was the European reception given to the Golf R32 that it was exported to America in 2004 after the regular Golf had been replaced. VWoA planned to sell 5,000 and did exactly that at 4,935 in just one year.

OPPOSITE: A unique front bumper molding helped the R32 gulp in extra air. It was offered in seven colors, including the unique Deep Blue Pearl Metallic here. *(Volkswagen UK)*
TOP LEFT: The Golf R's Recaro Konig seats (from the German *König* for king) became a classic design and were in gray or black leather or Alcantara. *(Volkswagen UK)*
TOP RIGHT: The DSG gearbox allowed the driver to do their own shifting (minus clutch pedal) by moving the lever to the right and going forward and back to go up and down the ratios. *(Volkswagen UK)*
RIGHT: Twin tailpipes from the specially designed exhaust system marked the rear of the R32. Initially only as a three-door in the UK, a five-door came later. *(Volkswagen UK)*

GTI 25th Anniversary 2001–02

As 2001 marked the 25th anniversary of the first Golf GTI, it was time for another special-edition GTI. Called the *GTI Jubiläum* (for jubilee) in Germany, this time it was more than a matter of cosmetics as it became the fastest Golf with a GTI badge, with the 1.8-liter 180 PS turbocharged gas engine from the Audi TT and Seat Leon VT. This also found its way into the Brazilian market Golf GTI Turbo.

Externally, this special GTI was distinguished by deeper front and rear bumpers, body-colored side skirts, a rear spoiler, chrome exhaust pipe, and 18-inch BBS alloy wheels. Inside were Recaro seats with red piping, various red interior trim items, and race-inspired aluminum pedals. Colors were Tornado Red, Reflex Silver Metallic, or Diamond Black. The PD150 diesel engine was also offered in Anniversary trim, and both units were coupled to a new six-speed gearbox with the first five ratios closely spaced and the sixth a higher cruising ratio.

In 2002 the German edition was followed by 2,000 examples of the GTI Anniversary for the UK, and—as the original GTI came much later to the American market—it was renamed the GTI 337 Edition for North America, picking up on the EA337 development code name, which lasted just one year. The GTI GLS and GLX tags were dropped.

The big performance Golf news of 2002 was the first Golf R32 (see page 106), and for a while Volkswagen was unsure whether the four-wheel-drive super-Golf would be sold in North America. Meanwhile—and crucial for sales numbers—for 2002 the Jetta GLI badge made a return with the 24-valve 2.8-liter VR6 and 200 hp plus a six-speed transmission and two-wheel-drive, a $22,950 competitor to a five-speed $27,745 BMW 325i, or for about the same dollars a Honda Accord or a Nissan Altima.

Toward the end of 2003 the European fourth-generation Golf began to be phased out after sales of more than 4.3 million units. The Bora/Jetta estate, which had been built in Brussels, Wolfsburg, and Mosel transferred to Karmann in 2003, where it outlasted the Mk4 Golf hatchback for a further three years.

US GTIs and Jetta GLIs had styling and equipment upgrades, such as new wheels, to see them through 2004 until the Mk5. For 2004 the GLI came with both the V6 and the 1.8 Turbo engines, the only time a Jetta GLI came with a choice of two engines.

TOP: The Anniversary was renamed the GTI 337 Edition for the US, just for the 2002 model year only sold in silver. A reported 1,500 units were allocated to the American market and 250 additional 337s to Canada. *(VWoA)*

ABOVE: The Anniversary interior featured perforated, red-stitched leather on the steering wheel, handbrake, and gear lever gaiter, a golf ball gear knob, and red-trimmed Recaro seats. *(Volkswagen UK)*

Golf GTI Mk4 (Europe)

Model	GTI 1.8 20-valve	GTI 1.8 20-valve Turbo	GTI 2.0 8-valve	Volkswagen GTI GLX (US)
Engine type/capacity	4-cylinder 1.8-liter Motronic ECU sequential injection	4-cylinder 1.8-liter Motronic ECU sequential injection, turbocharged	4-cylinder 1.8-liter Motronic ECU sequential injection	6-cyls narrow angle vee, single overhead cam, 12-valves, 2.8-liter Motronic fuel injection
Gearbox	5-speed manual	5-speed manual	5-speed manual	5-speed manual
Maximum power/at rpm	125 PS@6,000 rpm	150 PS@5,700 rpm (2001 Anniversary 180 PS)	115 PS@2,400 rpm	174 hp@5,800 rpm
Maximum torque/at rpm	125 lb ft@4,200 rpm	155 lb ft between 1,750 and 4,600 rpm (2001 Anniversary 173 lb ft@1,950 rpm)	125 lb ft@2,400 rpm	181 lb ft @3,200 rpm
Acceleration 0–60 mph	10.0 seconds	8.5 seconds	11.4 seconds (to 62mph)	6.8 seconds
Maximum speed	121 mph (*Autocar* 2 September 1998)	131 mph (*Autocar* 26 November 1997)	121 mph (Manufacturer claims)	140 mph (*Motor Week* and *Motor-Trend*)
Suspension front/rear	Strut and coil springs, wishbone, anti-roll bar/trailing arms, coil springs, torsion beam axle, anti-roll bar	Strut and coil springs, wishbone, anti-roll bar/trailing arms, coil springs, torsion beam axle, anti-roll bar	Strut and coil springs, wishbone, anti-roll bar/trailing arms, coil springs, torsion beam axle, anti-roll bar	Strut and coil springs, wishbone, anti-roll bar/trailing arms, coil springs, torsion beam axle, anti-roll bar
Wheels/tires	6J x 15-in 195/65 R15Y	6.5Jx 16-in 2015/55 R16 W	6J x 15-i 195/65 R15Y	6J x 15-in 195/65R H
Brakes front/rear	Ventilated disc/disc, anti-lock	Ventilated disc/disc, anti-lock	Disc/disc, anti-lock	Disc/disc, anti-lock
Length	4,149 mm	4,149 mm	4,149 mm	4,149 mm
Wheelbase	2,511 mm	2,511 mm	2,511 mm	2,511 mm
Width (without mirrors)	1,735 mm	1,735 mm	1,735 mm	1,735 mm
Height	1,439 mm	1,439 mm	1,439 mm	1,439 mm
Unladen weight (kg)	1,270/1,306 (with driver, 3/ 5-door)	1,270/1,306 (with driver, 3/5-door)	1,276kg (unladen)	1,311 (curb, 3-door)
Years produced	1997-1999	1997-2003	1999-2003	1999-2006

5.
GOLF GTI MK5 2003–2008

A Real GTI

The fifth Golf GTI needed to make an impact. No more parking lot confusion as to which Golf was the sporty one and a supersize serving of performance were needed.

Entering a tough European market and having lost the engineering advantage to the Ford Focus, Volkswagen spent all summer 2003 promoting the fifth-generation Golf until its autumn debut at the Frankfurt Motor Show. In August, anticipating high demand, production started simultaneously at the Wolfsburg, Brussels, and Zwickau plants.

For the first time, rather than launching the GTI alongside the regular range, at Frankfurt, Volkswagen held it back from sale but showed a "concept" GTI as a technique to build interest in the real thing.

RIGHT: In 2007, VWoA introduced the GTI and GLI Fahrenheit limited editions, each limited to 1,200 cars. The three-door only GTI came in Fahrenheit Orange with "European sport tuned suspension" and 18-inch "Charleston" alloy wheels. *(Andriy Baidak and Car Collection/Alamy Stock Photo)*

The concept GTI was, of course, red and had a black radiator grille in the new corporate V-shape shown on the Volkswagen Concept R, a two-seater sports car concept also shown at Frankfurt (that never made it to production). Beneath the new grille were three large air inlets in the bumper surrounded by a honeycomb structure.

The red stripe around the grille was back, and it had tartan seats! The three-spoke steering wheel also featured a GTI badge, and it had black trim along the sills and rear window frames. At the rear was a spoiler and twin exhaust pipes. Red brake calipers were visible through the newly designed 18-inch alloy wheels.

To have any credibility, a significant power boost was required for this new GTI. The Ford Focus RS, Honda Civic Type-R, and Renault Mégane Renaultsport were now beloved by the European car magazines and all were 200 PS-plus (197 bhp) cars. There was internal competition, too, from the Škoda Octavia RS and from Seat, cultivating a sporting personality with Leon Cupra models. To match the Cupra R alone (with the older 1.8-liter, 20-valve turbo engine), the fifth Golf GTI would have to have a power output of at least 200 PS, and indeed that's exactly what the 2003 "concept" had, via a turbocharged and intercooled EA113 2.0-liter FSI direct injection gas engine, termed the T-FSI.

Fuel Stratified Injection (FSI) gas engines had been rolled out across the brands. Fuel was injected directly into each combustion chamber at high pressures akin to a diesel common-rail fuel injection system. A flap in the intake manifold allowed an FSI engine to operate with a lean fuel/air mixture at low engine revs, and a conventional mixture when full power was required.

The diesel Golfs marched on, all *Pumpe Düse* "unit injector" engines. There was a new (2.0-liter) TDI with a 16-valve cylinder head offering 140 PS and meeting Euro 4 emissions standards. While it was 10 PS down on power from the Golf 4 GT TDI, it was praised for its refinement over the eight-valve 1.9, a broad spread of power from 1,500 to its 4,500 rpm limit, and claimed combined fuel economy of 52.3 mpg. It later became available in 170 PS guise. The Golf GTD had been absent from the European lineup since 1997 (although the Mk4 GT TDi was almost the same thing) and would not return until the sixth Golf.

ABOVE: Either non-turbo or turbo (seen here), the 2.0-liter direct FSI/TFSI engine included continuous inlet camshaft adjustment and a plastic variable intake manifold to boost efficiency. *(Volkswagen UK)*

OPPOSITE: A GTI is inspected for quality in Wolfsburg, March 2006. Gas-discharge (xenon) headlights provided a blue-white light more powerful than standard lights. The gloss black grille surround was unique to the GTI, the badge proudly back up front. *(Jochen Luebke/DDP/AFP via Getty Images)*

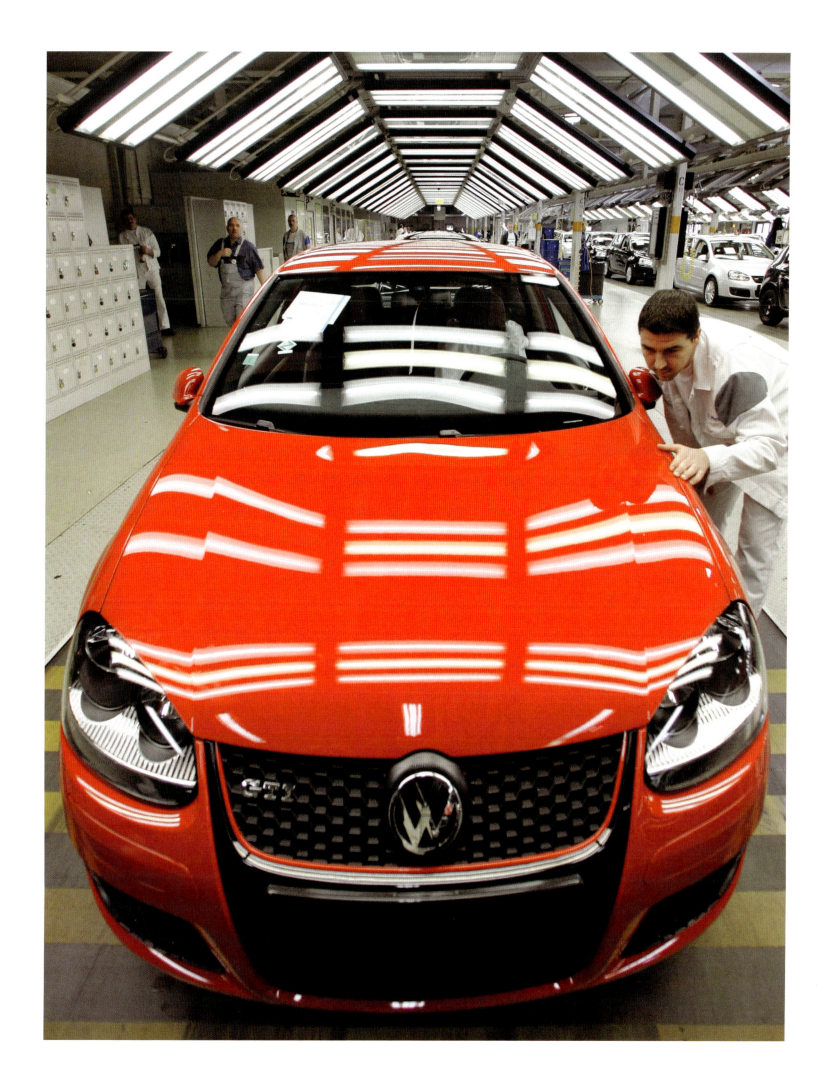

Returning to the latest GTI, it was a bigger car because it came from a bigger Golf. At 4,204 mm long, the Golf 5 was 57 mm up over the Golf 4 (4,216 mm for the GTI), and at 1,759 mm wide (without wing mirrors) up 24 mm. The wheelbase had grown by 67 mm to 2,578 mm for 52 mm extra rear legroom. The three-door GTI would have a curb weight of 1,336 kg, compared with 1,270 kg for a Mk4 GTI 1.8 three-door.

The Golf 5 was built on a new platform—internally known as PQ35—which provided not only the new generation of Audis, Seats, and Škodas, but extra-sized Euro-Golfs for extra-sized families. In the family car world, MPV fever—for multi-purpose vehicles, or minivans, or people carriers—had taken hold in Europe. Thanks to the 1996 Renault Scenic, everybody wanted a Golf-sized hatchback but with more seats, more space, and more pockets for the kids to cram things into.

Every European manufacturer in the lower medium (Golf) class scrambled to supply a mini multi-purpose vehicle (MPV). Ahead of the new Golf, the first Volkswagen MPV project was the 2002 Touran, more van than Golf-like ("Touran" from "tour" and "sharan," the ending "-an" was used to indicate Volkswagen's multi-purpose vehicles). It had a major connection to the van world as much of it formed the basis of the 2004 Caddy, but it could be had in five- or seven-seat versions.

How did this relate to the GTI? Well, what was under the rear floor of the Touran was very good news for the forthcoming Golf, especially the GTI—multi-link suspension. Road testers, who, of course, were naturally keen drivers and pushed a car to its limits, were besotted by most aspects of the multi-link-equipped Ford Focus but especially its ride and sharp responses. The Golf had always been regarded as a good car for enthusiastic driving, but now the Focus seemed a lot better. Worst of all, it was cheaper than a Golf. So, as the fifth Golf was in its early development stages, a considerable investment was made for a multi-link rear suspension, said to have been rapidly developed. It was a matter of prestige, no matter the cost—and that cost had to be spread across as many models as possible.

Considered to be best for both comfort and handling, multi-link is a more complex arrangement where the rear wheels can move fully independently of each other as they are carried in their own units, similar to the wishbone design of some front suspensions that allow up and downward movement and can be tuned to give a certain amount of rear wheel steering. Each wheel unit was in turn suspended on

forward facing trailing arms. Like other designs, the Volkswagen rear suspension unit was mounted on a subframe across the car that carried the spring for each wheel and a separate strut.

The second major mechanical change on the new Golf was electro-mechanical power steering. Instead of a pump with hydraulic fluid driven by a belt from the engine, the power steering was driven by an electric motor. Only in use when the vehicle was being steered, it varied the level of power assistance according to speed, thus maximum when parking, minimum when cruising. Perhaps most importantly, though, because the pump ran only when needed there was also a saving on the official fuel consumption figures, reckoned to be about 1.2 mpg on average over an engine-driven pump system. Electrically assisted steering was set to become widespread across the industry.

A five-star Euro NCAP safety rating was supported by a combination of electronic systems that intervened if the car appeared to be out of control, described by a string of acronyms. Anti-lock brakes (ABS) were standard, as was an Electronic Stabilisation Program (ESP). This sensed any tendency for the car to slide and could apply the brakes from one to four wheels. The car's systems could also sense if it was being emergency braked and increase pedal pressure while activating the ABS. If a crash happened, all Golfs had front airbags, side airbags for front and rear passengers, and anti-whiplash head restraints. An engine immobilizer, remote central locking, front electric windows, a CD player, height and reach adjustable steering column, and driver's seat height adjustment also featured as standard.

There would not be a new Golf convertible, but spring 2004 saw the launch of the Eos, a four-seater with a folding metal hardtop (see page 116). The December 2004 Bologna Motor Show would see the final Golf Mk5 European-market spin-off, the Golf Plus, which was another take on the compact MPV with the same wheelbase and width but 95 mm taller than a Golf for an extra 20 mm of headroom. The seating position was raised, and the rear bench, split 60/40, could be moved forward independently to extend the load space or fold flat. It was full of 34 various bins and storage slots.

OPPOSITE: The Golf 5's electro-mechanical steering system, like the suspension, was reprogrammed to suit the GTI and produced higher steering forces with more direct feel and feedback. The characteristic rear wheel lift remained.
(culture images GmbH/Alamy Stock Photo)
TOP: The new group-shared multi-link rear suspension was necessary to keep up with the competition and a world away in complexity from the 1974 simple twist beam axle.
(Volkswagen UK)
ABOVE: Tartan or plaid seat fabric returned for good with the Mk5 GTI, but in Volkswagen UK-speak it was Interlagos. The flat-bottomed steering wheel with GTI badge was new, and metal faced pedals an extra GTI touch. *(Magiccarpics)*

THE VOLKSWAGEN EOS 2004–2015

By the time the Mk3/Mk4 Golf Cabriolet retired in 2002, fabric-topped convertibles were out of fashion. Following the trend set by the 1996 Mercedes SLK, the latest breed of open-air cars (including spin-offs of family hatchbacks) had to have a folding metal hardtop that pivoted into the trunk via an electric and hydraulic system of cables, motors, and pumps. They provided better security, visibility, quietness, and a sidewalk sideshow when they folded down.

These hardtop coupés retained the front panels of the hatchbacks they were based on but had bespoke bodywork from the windshield backward and a large rear deck. Inevitably all were heavier, more complicated, and more expensive than traditional convertibles. Top up, there was a huge trunk—top down, luggage space took a big hit.

The European market had seen the small Peugeot 206 Coupé Cabriolet (CC) in 2000, then the Golf-sized 307 CC and Renault Mégane CC followed in 2003. With Ford and Opel planning similar cars, Volkswagen was bound to follow (Audi stayed with soft tops for its Cabrios) and had another base well covered with the soft-top Beetle Cabrio.

Volkswagen's new hardtop was a cocktail of Golf and Passat parts on a

ABOVE: Conceived under then Volkswagen chief designer Murat Günak, the 2006 Eos had a lot of Golf underneath but shared no exterior panels. The chrome grille surround was unique. *(Volkswagen UK)*

Golf platform, shown first as the Concept C at the spring 2004 Geneva show, then little different in production form at the following September's Frankfurt, with the name Eos for the Greek goddess of dawn. At 4,407 mm long, it was placed between Golf and Passat.

The Webasto-supplied folding hardtop was made up of five parts and was claimed to fold into a smaller space than other cars as a result. With the roof closed, trunk capacity was 380 liters and with the roof "off" 205 liters, and owners had to make sure a cover for the luggage section was fully in place before pulling the large, chromed lever between the front seats to start the show.

The Eos was built not by Karmann, which at the time built the Renault Mégane CC, but at Volkswagen's Autoeuropa factory in Portugal, which had been building the Ford Galaxy/Volkswagen Sharan minivan.

In Europe, the Eos engine range included the 200 PS 2.0-liter from the Golf GTI and the 3.2 V6, although the extra weight of the roof machinery blunted performance a little. However, it was still a far different driving experience compared with the old Golf Cabriolet and especially well received in the North American market in V6 form (from 2006).

A new Golf Cabriolet appeared in 2011 (see chapter 6), and a second-generation "new" Beetle convertible the following year. For 2012 the Eos received a facelift with the latest corporate front and rear styling, and the US engine choice was narrowed to the 2.0-liter GTI engine with six-speed DSG. It remained on US sale until 2015.

BELOW: The Eos's roof was made up of 470 components, including an eight-cylinder electro-hydraulic pump located under the luggage compartment cover behind the spare wheel. *(Volkswagen UK)*

A Stand-Out GTI

In October 2004 the fifth GTI was handed over to the European press at the Paul Ricard racing circuit in the south of France, with very little difference in looks or specification to the 2003 "concept." This time around there was only one Golf with a GTI badge, rather than a couple of versions with different power.

Now there was an official set of performance figures; a claimed 0 to 62 mph (100 kph) time of 7.2 seconds and a top speed of 146 mph. Whereas the rival Honda Civic Type-R gave its best performance at very high engine revs, the new GTI's power was delivered in the user-friendly fashion of its predecessors, pulling strongly and smoothly throughout with no hint of turbo lag. Its maximum torque of 207 lb ft was available from 1,800 to 5,100 rpm. The direct injection system was tuned to give a different blend of air and fuel entering the cylinders for performance over economy. The six-speed gearbox had more resilient synchromesh to handle the power of the new GTI.

"The 2-liter direct injection FSI is stimulating and effervescent," wrote John Barker for Britain's *Evo* magazine in November 2004. "A pleasant surprise given the turbo's delivery is capped to give linear torque between 1,800-5,000rpm. There's nothing linear about the delivery, though, and underpinning its strong, responsive performance is a genuinely engaging induction note. Somehow VW's engineers have given this turbo engine a normally aspirated voice—a guttural, appealing *bwarp* that swells with bass on large, low-rev throttle openings and then gradually thins out to a keen bark that reaches a natural peak and suggests an upshift."

Equipped with the new multi-link rear suspension, the GTI sat 15 mm lower than other Golfs with stiffer anti-roll bars, shorter, stiffer springs, and revised dampers. The "Monza" alloy wheel design was available in two sizes: 17-inch and optional 18-inch.

A larger brake servo was used, while the brake discs also increased in size to 312 mm at the front and 286 mm at the rear. All were ventilated, with red disc calipers. The power-assisted steering was recalibrated to give more "feel" and, as on lesser Golfs, the ESP could be switched off if you wanted to throw the car around and were confident you could handle extra understeer and a more abrupt turn into oversteer. The ESP system also provided an Electronic Differential Lock called EDL. If the anti-lock brake sensors detected front wheel slip, EDL braked the driveshaft of the slipping wheel, allowing torque transfer to the wheel with traction.

As it was then the top-of-the-range Golf, the European GTI was very well equipped, with convenience features such as rain-sensitive windshield wipers, automatic lights, and dual-zone climate control. The options list included heated front seats, gas-discharge (xenon) headlights, a parking distance control system, and a multi-function steering wheel with cruise control and paddle shift operation of the DSG shift.

ABOVE: Seen here on a 2004 test track drive, if the driver suddenly eased off in a bend, the ESP prevented the tail swinging out; all the driver felt was some mild oversteer, which slowed the car down. *(culture-images GmbH/Alamy Stock Photo)*
OPPOSITE: The second-generation R32's unique styling featured an aluminum-framed full-height grille and a new front spoiler. Suspension was lowered by approximately 20 mm over the GTI. *(Volkswagen UK)*

Comprehensive anti-theft measures included an alternating code alarm with interior movement protection, protection boxes surrounding the door lock mechanisms, and free-wheeling mechanisms for the locks, which meant that if an attempt was made to turn the lock cylinder with a screwdriver, the connection to the door opening mechanism was broken.

The First Automatic GTI

There was something new on the options list—an automatic gearbox—the six-speed dual-clutch Direct Shift Gearbox (DSG) first seen on the R32, creating the first self-shifting GTI. In the UK, this was offered at a not inconsiderable £1,325 extra (incidentally a 1:1 conversion from the German price in euros) against the £19,995 cost of the entire car.

By August 2004 almost 60,000 DSG systems (called S-Tronic by Audi) had been produced at the Kassel gearbox plant for the Golf, Touran, Audi TT, Audi A3, Seat Altea, and Škoda Oktavia. Volkswagen had applied for over 70 patents for the gearbox technology, and commentators were hailing it as the gearbox of the future.

Like the R32, a Golf GTI fitted with DSG could be left to run as an automatic or the driver could change up and down themselves by flicking the gear lever forward and back. At an extra cost, this could be done by a pair of paddle-like levers behind the steering wheel, and most GTIs fitted with DSG were specified with paddles.

According to Volkswagen's own performance figures, a DSG gearbox could change more quickly than a person using the manual gearbox, with 0–62 mph in 6.9 over 7.2 seconds. When tested by *Evo*, its figures revealed it was half a second slower but slightly more economical, with a combined mpg figure of 35.3—0.4 mpg better than the manual car.

The 2005 Golf R32

The second iteration of the V6-engined Golf R32 appeared at the 2005 Frankfurt Motor Show (full name Golf R32 V6 4MOTION), its six-cylinder 3.2 modestly uprated by 9 PS to 250 PS was not so much of a headline now that there was a 200 PS GTI (and tuners such as Oettinger could extract 280 PS), but the appeal was the same as that of its predecessor—discreet power in a compact and luxurious car. The same engine was offered in the Audi A3 3.2 S-Line.

The R32's only direct competitors were the Audi A3 3.2 Quattro and the Alfa Romeo 147 GTA, the latter with only front-wheel-drive. In Europe it was offered in three- and five-door forms with six-speed manual or six-speed DSG with standard paddle change.

The Haldex 4Motion four-wheel-drive system continued to direct most of the drive to the front wheels unless required at the rear. On official figures it was still just about the fastest Golf at 6.5 seconds to 100 kph (62 mph) compared with the GTI's 7.2 seconds (manual) and matched its 146 mph top speed.

The R32 reached the North American market for the 2008 model year as a 3.2, again in an allocation of 5,000 three-door only fully loaded (six-CD player, leather, and sunroof) DSG autos.

LEFT: The rear identity of the R32 once more included centrally positioned twin exhaust pipes and darkened rear lenses. The rear bumper was fully painted, without the black lower part of the GTI. *(Volkswagen UK)*

BELOW: In North America the Jetta GLI was clearly a four-door GTI. Here the optional 18-inch wheels were matched with low-profile 225/40R-18 Bridgestone RE050A tires. *(VWoA)*

The Twin-Charged Golf GT

In September 2005 European sub-GTI sporty Golfs saw the debut of new Volkswagen engine technology using both a turbocharger and a supercharger at the same time.

Reviving the ideas of the G-Lader of the 1980s, the new Golf GT's FSI 1.4-liter engine was dual-charged through a combination of an engine-driven supercharger plus an exhaust gas turbocharger arranged in series. The belt-driven supercharger operated at lower engine speeds, with the turbocharger coming in as the engine speed increased (the supercharger disengaged at a maximum 3,500 rpm in this case). Volkswagen claimed the result was excellent drivability and performance throughout the range with no turbo lag and high maximum torque.

The combination of these technologies enabled a small-capacity engine with a high compression ratio to cruise at part load on high gearing, combining improved performance with lower fuel consumption. It marked the start of a general automotive trend to reduce fuel consumption and emissions by downsizing engines, meaning reduced friction losses and engine weight but with performance and flexibility added by a turbocharger or supercharger.

The new 1.4-liter TSI engine could be set to produce either 140 or 170 PS (so no threat to the current GTI but nearly the power of the Mk4 GTI 1.8T). The 170 PS version was claimed to have the same peak power that the 2.3-liter V5 once had but with 20 percent lower fuel consumption, returning 38.2 mpg on the combined cycle. It also produced 177 lb ft of torque from 1,750 through to 4,500 rpm. Compared with the 1.4 FSI, it used a reinforced cast-iron cylinder block to withstand higher combustion pressures, plus modified six-hole injectors. This was still descended from the trusty EA111 series of engines that dated back to the 1974 Golf.

The use of TSI spread across the Volkswagen Group, with lower-powered cars using engines equipped just with intercooled turbochargers.

Jetta GLI and Volkswagen GTI 2005–2006

Introduced in Europe in summer 2005, the fifth-generation Jetta had already arrived in the North American market that March, well ahead of the next Golf as it was built in Puebla.

The new Jetta was around 300 mm longer than the Golf and only 200 mm shorter than the Passat, to which it looked very similar. The "vee" front grille of the GTI was used on all Jettas. The 200 PS gas four-cylinder seen in the GTI made it into the European Jetta range as the Jetta Sport.

Regular American Jetta Mk5s followed a different engine path. A new 148 horsepower 2.5-liter five-cylinder engine was the standard unit instead of the former 115 bhp 2.0-liter four-cylinder. The extra power was needed for this larger and heavier Jetta, and to keep up with similar-powered versions of the Honda Civic and Ford Focus. Developed "for the North American driver," it was about torque, 90 percent of which was claimed to be available between about 1,750 rpm and 5,125 rpm.

ABOVE: Inside, a 2006 Jetta GLI was exactly like a GTI, apart from the badge on the steering wheel. This car is a DSG automatic. *(Drive Images/Alamy Stock Photo)*

RIGHT: Now called Jetta for all markets, the fifth generation finally moved away from "Golf with a trunk," with no shared panels rearward of the central pillar and its own rear doors. *(Volkswagen UK)*

It bore no relation to the now-discarded European VR5 engine, but claims that it was half of the Lamborghini Gallardo's V10 were not quite true, although there was a connection in that it shared the same 82.5 mm bore and 92.8 mm stroke and used the aluminum-alloy 20-valve cylinder head found on one bank of the Lamborghini unit combined with variable intake-valve timing.

Introduced October 2005, the Jetta GLI was given the Golf GTI's 200 PS 2.0-liter turbo, which compared with the previous 180 hp 1.8 Turbo. There was less turbo lag, but to Tony Quiroga of *Car and Driver* (October 2005), it felt less frisky. That was put down to the extra weight, but the upside was Audi-like quality, even if once loaded with the DSG automatic it was an Audi-like $28,705.

This slightly too grown-up mainstream Jetta and other costly Volkswagens made sales droop to the extent (prices would be heavily cut) that when the Wolfsburg-built Volkswagen GTI hatchback arrived at the start of 2006, it had to re-inject some excitement. In an "edgy" press stunt, Golf GTIs were parked around the roads of Los Angeles surrounded by police cars ahead of the January 2006 LA Motor Show, suggesting they had been pulled over for speeding. This was followed by a quirky campaign that played on the brand's Germanness but that perhaps wouldn't have gone down well twenty years later—it introduced Helga, a blonde lady in white go-go boots who demonstrated the features of the new GTI alongside jokey catchphrases "Straight outta da Autobahn" or "Fast as schnell."

Such antics aside, the new GTI went down well with the enthusiast press that especially rejoiced in the return of the plaid (tartan) seats and concluded that it brought back the spirit of the Mk1 and the Mk2 GTIs. They were less convinced by the raised ride height—better to survive collisions with trucks and SUVs, which brought it back up 15 mm to regular Golf height but made for more body roll. It was lowered back down for 2007.

ABOVE: Some motoring magazines observed it looked a little high up on 18-inch wheels. The "Jetta" before GLI was dropped for 2008, to make it nearer the Volkswagen GTI. *(VWoA)*
BELOW: New for the 2006 model year, the North American GTI reverted to four cylinders but with the same output as European cars. Ride height needed to be dropped a little, though. *(VWoA)*

The Rabbit Hops Back

After the GTI, later in 2006 American buyers finally got their own Puebla-built Golf, a tardy three years after Europe, but quite unexpectedly bringing back the Rabbit name after 22 years. Perhaps it was because of the wave of Volkswagen nostalgia created by the new Beetle, perhaps because of retro American cars like Chrysler's PT Cruiser, but it caught the imagination. It was Rabbit-perky as well, with the 2.5-liter five-cylinder motor from the Jetta bumping up power from 115 to 148 hp. It was an easy driver rather than for fast thrills, but at $14,990 it was loaded with standard equipment such as air-conditioning and cruise control to out-spec the 2007 Honda Civic DX Coupe.

There was to be no return for the Rabbit GTI name, but for 2009 VWoA would offer the Thunderbunny Package, which included sportier front and rear bumpers, side skirts, and a bigger rear spoiler.

After the Touran and the Golf Plus, the Mk5 Golf estate or kombi was late on the scene, as the Golf 4 estate had remained quietly in production with a mild facelift and new engines at Karmann until May 2006. Then in spring 2007 a new Golf estate broke cover, now built at Puebla alongside the Jetta with which it shared frontal styling. In North America it was marketed as the Jetta SportWagen, with the 2.5-liter five-cylinder and diesel options, but no GLI version.

ABOVE: A five-door GTI (including the hatchback) was offered for the first time in North America for 2007, where it was referred to as a four-door. *(VWoA)*

GTI W12-650 —THE MONSTER GTI

Only eight weeks before the May 2007 Wörthersee festival, newly appointed Volkswagen AG chairman Martin Winterkorn tasked his engineers to come up with something special. The result was spectacular.

The GTI W12-650 design study was a highly modified Golf GTI three-door bodyshell (retaining the original production car's doors, hood, and lights) with a mid-mounted 6.0-liter bi-turbo W12 engine from a Bentley Continental GT (first seen on the Volkswagen Phaeton, the W12's roots were a pair of narrow-angle V6 engines set alongside each other).

The W12 was made from aluminum and had four valves per cylinder and two overhead camshafts per cylinder head. With two turbochargers, power came out at a mighty 650 PS at 6,000 rpm while peak torque was capped at 553 lb ft delivered at 4,500 rpm—overall, over three times more powerful than the conventional Golf GTI. A claimed 0–62 mph (100 kph) in 3.7 seconds and maximum speed of 202 mph were believable.

Volkswagen engineers created a unique aluminum subframe to house this beast of a powerplant. The W12-650 gained 160 mm extra width over the standard GTI to accommodate the mid-mounted engine, bespoke drivetrain, and side-mounted cooling systems.

The ride height was lowered by 70 mm, while the 19-inch wheels were styled to mimic the standard wheels fitted to the Golf GTI and wrapped in 295-profile tires to aid traction. This was no show pony—it worked, albeit with some limits on the speeds it could achieve in each gear to save the rear tires. The front brakes were from an Audi RS4.

The W12-650 was robust enough for a publicity tour around car magazines and TV shows like *Top Gear*. There was talk that if there was enough interest more would be built, but its destiny was to become a unique exhibit in the Volkswagen museum complex in Wolfsburg.

OPPOSITE: Its exterior designed by Marc Lichte, the GTI W12-650 had a carbon-fiber roof with an integrated cooling scoop to channel air into the rear-mounted radiators as well as two vents ahead of the rear wheels. *(VWoA)*
TOP: Extensive use was made of underfloor aerodynamic aids, including a diffuser, negating the need for a large rear wing. *(Volkswagen UK)*
MIDDLE: The cover above the engine compartment was carefully styled from carbon fiber, and a glass partition shielded the front seat occupants. *(VWoA)*
BOTTOM: The interior design for the concept car had racing touches, such as transparent switch guards for central functions, no door liners, and a fire extinguisher in the glove compartment. Note two turbo gauges. *(VWoA)*

Golf GTI Edition 30 and Pirelli Edition

As 2007 was the thirtieth anniversary of the on-sale date of the original GTI, Volkswagen opened the order books for a new 1,500-car special in late 2006. The Golf GTI Edition 30's engine was redeveloped to make it the fastest and most powerful production Golf GTI yet, at 230 PS (227 bhp)—although tuning companies could liberate more power by reprogramming the engine management system. Volkswagen added a larger turbocharger and intercooler, modified the fuel injection, and reinforced the engine block and pistons. The 230 PS took half a second off the 0–62 mph time at 6.8 seconds and pushed claimed top speed up to 152 mph over 146 mph.

New body-colored side skirts were paired with a new chin spoiler for the front bumper and a fully body-colored rear bumper. It sat 15 mm lower than the standard GTI (which *Autocar* judged made the ride too firm). Inside, there were new seats, Edition 30 sill plates, and a dimpled "golf ball" finish to the manual gear lever (DSG was also available).

TOP: The GTI Edition 30 was sold between 2007 and 2008 in unlimited numbers. It commanded a significant price premium of £2,000 in the UK. *(Volkswagen UK)*

RIGHT: The Edition 30 was further set apart from the regular GTI by unique 18-inch "Pescara" alloy wheels. There were six colors, from Candy White to Tornado Red. *(Volkswagen UK)*

The GTI W12-650 design study was the showstopper of May 2007's mass GTI pilgrimage to Wörthersee in Austria (see page 124), but for one you could buy there was the GTI Pirelli special edition, hearkening back to the first-generation Golf special of 1983 with its "P" pattern alloy wheels. Keeping the 230 PS engine and lowered suspension of the Edition 30, the GTI Pirelli was, of course, shod with the latest Pirelli P-Zero tires and had sports seats with a unique tire tread-style pattern.

There was further good news for German GTI fans when Volkswagen officially entered two factory-built racing GTIs to participate in the 24-hour race at the famous Nürburgring circuit from June 7–10, 2007 (see page 128).

TOP: A real rarity, the GTI Pirelli Edition evoked the prized Mk2 Pirelli. On German sale from October 2007, it came in blue, black, or a bright yellow "Sunflower" hue, but the best feature was "tire tread" seats. *(author's collection)*
ABOVE: For the 2008 model year North American GTI, VW offered an Autobahn Package that included a sunroof, premium audio system, leather upholstery, and heated front seats. *(VWoA)*
RIGHT: The Jetta GLI Fahrenheit was the sedan twin of the GTI Fahrenheit limited edition of 2007. The Jetta's shade was Fahrenheit Yellow, and each Farenheit car had its number on the orange-trimmed steering wheel.
(Andriy Baidak and Car Collection/Alamy Stock Photo)

2008—Time's Up

In June 2008, UK GTI Pirelli owners were getting their hands on their new cars, the end of the fifth-generation Golf was forecast as it approached just five years on sale, and the industry was already looking forward to seeing a sixth interpretation that autumn. The fifth Golf entered a difficult market and a period marked by Volkswagen battling to save costs caused by factory closures and restructuring.

The value of the dollar against the euro left the company debating whether to end imported Golf sales in America or start building it there once more. *The Wall Street Journal* reported that the company had struggled to make money with the Golf 5 and it had only been profitable from 2006. The next Golf was, according to the paper's sources, set to be €1,000 cheaper to build by carrying over the same platform.

And so, in September 2008 the sixth Golf was introduced to the European press (chapter 6), with a GTI on European sale in 2009. This time, North American buyers would only have to wait until 2010 for their new Volkswagen GTI.

A 24-HOUR TRIUMPH

Volkswagen officially returned to motorsport in 2007 with two GTIs for just one race—a very big race—the famous 24 Hours of Nürburgring, a car-chewing day and night through the Eiffel mountain circuit. Otherwise known as "the green hell," at the time one lap was just over 25 km/16 miles, made up of the combined length of the Nordschleife (North loop) and Nürburgring Grand Prix circuit.

The annual race drew in around 200,000 spectators, and it was now a matter of corporate pride just to be there because everybody else was. "We are not competing for overall victory," said Volkswagen Motorsport director Kris Nissen ahead of the race. "For us it is purely and simply a question of being a part of the action with two cars in this unique long-distance race. As the brand's best-selling model, the Golf, races in front of the largest conceivable motorsport crowd—a fitting backdrop."

It was the first trip for a factory team since 1996–97, which put the new TDI diesels to the test. Volkswagen Motorsport developed a pair of racing GTIs in four months, packing 300 PS and still attached to the six-speed DSG, gearbox, proving its strength. They were entered in the SP3T class for turbocharged cars up to 2.0-liters in a grid of 220 cars. They raced under Volkswagen's R-line brand, which had been launched in December 2003 and now covered models beyond the Golf and styling accessories.

Each car needed a crew of four drivers, and many companies would send their own management and invited journalists to take a turn (for example, Aston Martin). The number 101 GTI's drivers included Dr. Ulrich Hackenberg, board member of the Volkswagen brand, and Bernd Ostmann, editor-in-chief of *Auto Motor Und Sport*.

Much to Volkswagen's surprise the other GTI, number 111, finished first in class and eighth overall, ahead of racing versions of its showroom rivals the Opel Astra GTC, Ford Focus and Seat Leon, and many BMWs and Porsches. It was driven by a team of Volkswagen drivers who also raced Polos, Lupos, and Seats. Sadly, number 101 was one of the many retirements. The factory would return to the Nürburgring in 2011, with the purpose-built Golf 24 (chapter six).

ABOVE: On June 7, 2007, the racing GTI no. 101 crewed by Volkswagen top management takes a pit stop, having taken an inevitable knock during the close-packed race. *(imageBROKER.com GmbH & Co. KG/Alamy Stock Photo)*

Golf GTI Mk5

Model	**GTI 2.0 T-FSI**	**GTI 2.0 T-FSI Edition 30/Pirelli**
Engine type/capacity	2.0-liter 16-valve four-cylinder, turbocharged	2.0-liter 16-valve four-cylinder, turbocharged
Gearbox	6-speed manual or 6-speed DSG	6-speed manual or 6-speed DSG
Maximum power/at rpm	200 PS@5,100 rpm	230 PS@5,200 rpm
Maximum torque/at rpm	207 lb ft between 1,800–5,100 rpm	221 lb ft between 2,200–5,200 rpm
Acceleration 0–60 mph	6.7 seconds	6.8 seconds (0-62mph/100kph)
Maximum speed	136mph (*Autocar* 5 January 2005)	152mph (claimed)
Suspension front/rear	Strut and coil springs, wishbone, anti-roll bar/trailing arms, coil springs, multi-link axle, anti-roll bar	Strut and coil springs, wishbone, anti-roll bar/trailing arms, coil springs, multi-link axle, anti-roll bar
Wheels/tires	7.5J x 17 in Monza alloy wheels 225/45 R17 Bridgestone Potenza RE050	Edition 30: 7.5J x 18 in Pescara or Detroit alloy wheels Pirelli: 7.5J x 18 in 5-spoke Pirelli alloy wheels/Pirelli p-Zero tires
Brakes front/rear	Ventilated disc/ventilated disc with anti-lock and ESP	Ventilated disc/ventilated disc with anti-lock and ESP
Length	4,216 mm	4,216 mm
Wheelbase	2,578 mm	2,578 mm
Width (without mirrors)	1,759 mm	1,759 mm
Height	1,466 mm	1,466 mm
Weight (kg)	1,336 (curb)	n/a
Years produced	2004-2009	2006-2007

6.
GOLF GTI MK6 2008–2012

Marking Time

The volcanic rocks of Iceland made for a lunar landscape to launch the sixth Golf in September 2008, but it was already known that this was a bookmark Golf, a short-term improved version of the fifth generation until a ground-up new design was ready and equipped for stringent emission regulations—the 2012 Golf Mk7. Perhaps the 2008 version was more Golf 5:2, developed in a superfast four years. Buyers had to have a fresh reason not to choose an Opel Astra or a Ford Focus. The more expensive Audi A3—which shared its base with the Golf 5—was allowed an uninterrupted run from 2003 to 2012.

RIGHT: Look how big you've grown! The near-reality 2008 concept for the Mk6 GTI was in white, better to highlight the red grille stripe. Front style used horizontal lines to make the new car appear lower and wider than it really was. *(Volkswagen UK)*

LEFT: Visitors to the 2008 Paris show scrutinize the new Golf M6. Can you spot the difference over the Mk5? Takes a little work. The striking new 18-inch alloy wheels were called "Bilbao." *(Associated Press/Alamy Stock Photo)*

Volkswagen claimed that 60 percent of the components had changed, but the platform was essentially that of the previous car with its multi-link rear suspension. All the external panels were new apart from the roof, but the designers were constrained by using the same "hard points" of the Golf 5, so the wheelbase, door pillars, and seating positions couldn't budge. The sixth Golf carried over the 2,578 mm wheelbase of its predecessor and was about 17 mm shorter with its new bumper designs.

Although the development cost of the Golf Mk5's multi-link rear suspension had been spread across the Volkswagen Group, it had been too expensive to make, and this version was reported as being 5 percent cheaper to build. The front end was redesigned for faster assembly, and the doors were welded rather than clipped together, which was also faster on the line.

A major cost saving was to cut the number of European plants it was built in, dropping the Brussels assembly (the Audi A1 took its place) to leave the famous Wolfsburg and Zwickau plants. Until November 2008 Golf 5 and 6 were assembled alongside each other at Wolfsburg because the assembly tooling was so similar.

Inside the Mk6 Golf, the interior had been subtly refined. The overall shape of the dashboard was the same as the Golf 5 but it was positioned slightly higher and featured more soft touch grained plastics. The speedometer and rev counter were now in cowled binnacles with silver trim around them, like the Passat CC.

The interior door panels were redesigned so the armrests swept up to meet the base of the windshield, and the electric window switches were higher placed. The seats were slightly redesigned to offer more back and leg support and could be moved further back for taller drivers. The aim was a "premium" feel, and this was a genuinely quieter car, thanks to a new design of door and window seals, a new damping film sandwiched between two layers of windshield glass, and a new engine mounting system. There were 20 sections of noise insulation, including in the front pillars and the front bumper. The hood was double-skinned and insulated.

Standard safety was boosted by a knee airbag for the driver, bringing the total number of airbags to seven. A new head restraint system designed to reduce whiplash injuries and rear seat belt detection sensors were joined by new, more advanced Electronic Stabilisation Program (ESP) software.

There was nothing much to improve on the Golf's suspension, so the biggest change was optional Adaptive Chassis Control (ACC), again filtering down from the Passat CC and new Scirocco (see page 133). It allowed the driver to select from normal, comfort, or sport modes to change suspension, steering, and accelerator response settings for any particular journey. The damper units were pneumatically controlled.

The 2008–2009 engine choices for European Golfs were four gas and two diesel units, heralding a wholesale move to smaller-capacity turbocharged engines, which lowered emissions at the same time as balancing weight gain elsewhere in the car. In 2009 Volkswagen introduced a 1.2-liter 105 PS TSI unit for the Golf and Polo ranges, to replace the 1.6. Using gas direct injection and a turbocharger, it delivered the same performance but with greater engine flexibility with maximum torque developed at a notably low engine speed of 1,500 rpm.

A real novelty came with the super-economy gas-powered Golf BlueMotion model—stop start, when the engine cut out when idling in traffic only to restart when the car moved off. Volkswagen had been experimenting with such systems since the 1970s, and they were now being introduced by other carmakers.

For ultimate economy, Volkswagen diesels still ruled. The new-generation TDIs now had two balancer shafts to damp down vibrations. A particulate filter, which had been an option on the last Golf diesels, was now fitted as standard to meet emissions requirements.

A NEW SCIROCCO 2007–2017

By the time the Golf Mk6 was launched, the Scirocco coupé (last seen in 1995) had returned. Having teased and canceled several two-seater sports car concepts through the 1990s and early 2000s, in August 2006 Volkswagen surprised the press with a dramatic-looking concept car named Iroc (see what's happening here?) in Berlin and then publicly at September's Paris Motor Show. It was finished in Viper Green Metallic paint, one of the colors in the 1976 Scirocco range, and was clearly a prelude for a revival, as was a brief Scirocco history at the foot of the press release.

At 4,240 mm the Iroc was slightly longer (36 mm) than the Golf and its wheelbase over 10 cm longer at 2,680 mm. As concept cars often do, it sported large 19-inch wheels and an outlandish interior. It was touted as having a new Volkswagen "face," and the honeycomb pattern of the radiator grille was put forward as a link to the 1976 Golf GTI.

When the new Scirocco appeared in its definitive form in March 2008 (production started in autumn 2008), the gaping grille was gone. Styled by a team led by chief designer Klaus Bischoff, one of Walter de Silva's first edicts was to graft a new, more conservative, corporate grille onto the front, albeit with the VW roundel on the hood. The rear end styling stayed largely the same. The dashboard, while more conservative than the Iroc, was shared with the Eos and the two cars were built in the same factory in Portugal.

ABOVE: The 2006 Iroc concept—finished in 1970s Viper Green—built up a feverish appetite for a new Scirocco. The honeycomb structure of the radiator grille was meant to be a link to the Golf GTI. *(Volkswagen UK)*

Now firmly based on the PQ35 Golf platform, it had shrunk back to its standard 2,578 mm wheelbase, but this still allowed it to remain a full four-seater. Engines and transmissions were initially carried across from the faster Golfs, although not always with the same power outputs. It launched with a 200 PS EA888 TSI engine then the twin-charged and turbo-only versions down to the 122 PS 1.4 as an entry-level car. Once unheard of for a sporting car, diesels came later.

THE NEW MOTORSPORT SCIROCCOS

Rather than the soon-to-be-launched Mk6 GTI, the new Scirocco became the new (but modest) focus of Volkswagen Racing, and the Scirocco GT24 was on the tracks before the road-going car started production.

Initially, three GT24s were built for the May 2008 24 Hours of Nürburgring, the landmark event where two factory GTIs had a surprise success the previous year (chapter 5). Developed, built, and tested in only 75 days, the Scirocco GT24s were very close to the road car, stripped out and fitted with a roll cage but with the same 2.0-liter turbo engine from the GTI Mk5 with new injectors and the engine management remapped to produce 330 PS (315 bhp) and potentially 162 mph. This was coupled to the usual six-speed DSG gearbox, with its shift times remapped. To test the durability, an engine was put on a test rig for 72 hours, the only later modification a stronger flywheel (*Autocar* August 6, 2008). A limited-slip differential was added and AP racing brakes, but the suspension geometry was the same as the road car.

On Sunday, May 26, 2008, out of a field of 219 cars, the Scirocco of Austrian Hans-Joachim Stuck and his co-drivers Jimmy Johansson, Florian Gruber, and Thomas Mutsch won the 2.0-liter turbocharged class and finished 11th overall, four places ahead of the sister Scirocco piloted by double World Rally Champion Carlos Sainz and his Volkswagen rally teammates Giniel de Villiers and Dieter Depping; Stuck also took his turn at the wheel of this car. The works team's third Scirocco, whose drivers included Volkswagen board member Dr. Ulrich Hackenberg, also finished the event, taking fifth in class and 32nd overall.

As with the 2007 Nürburgring GTIs, there was some talk of building customer replicas of the Scirocco GT24, but at an estimated £95,000, the market proved not to be there. When three works Scirocco returned to the "ring" in 2009, their engines had been mildly adapted to run on compressed natural gas (CNG), the environmentally friendly fuel that was being rolled out as an option in production Volkswagens (which switched between gas and CNG).

The 300 PS GT24-CNG achieved victory in its class on its first appearance, yet emitted 80 percent less CO_2 than comparable competitors. For 2010, it became the basis of a one-make Bio-CNG-powered race series the Scirocco R Cup (replacing the Polo

TOP: The 2008 production Scirocco had the new VW corporate grille but the proportions were faithful to the Iroc. Its stance was retained by a track 29mm wider than the Golf at the front and 62mm at the rear. *(Volkswagen UK)*
LEFT: The new Scirocco gained its own dashboard, while the door pulls were more adventurously styled than the Golf GTI. Optional leather on this UK car. *(Magiccarpics)*
OPPOSITE: The Scirocco GT24's rear wing was tested for downforce using computational flow dynamics. It was good enough to worry Porsche 911 RSRs on the track. *(Volkswagen UK)*

Cup), supporting the German DTM Touring Car Championship.

Based on the Scirocco R, the CNG-fuelled cup cars developed less power at 223 PS but had a "push-to-pass" system that gave a short burst of 30 PS. The Scirocco Cup was replaced by the Audi Sport TT Cup in 2015.

SCIROCCO R

By 2009 the new Scirocco was a roaring success, cemented by rave reviews of its handling (*Autocar* said it handled better than a GTI), looks, and prices, which, in the UK, started at just under £20,000, which was level with a mid-spec Golf.

The fastest-ever production Scirocco, the Scirocco R, made its debut at the May 2009 24 Hours of Nürburgring ahead of the next-generation Golf R. Like the Golf R, it also used a highly developed four-cylinder EA113 engine (as opposed to the EA888 fitted to the conventional Scirocco and Mk6 GTI). The block was reinforced with an entirely new alloy head, uprated pistons, conrods, and high-pressure injectors. An uprated turbocharger generated 1.2 bar of boost supported by a new intercooler.

The resulting 265 PS and 258 lbs ft of torque were a rise of 65 PS and 51 lb ft over the Scirocco's current 2.0-liter TSI engine, but 5 PS less than the Golf R would offer. However, the Scirocco's low stance didn't allow it to be fitted with the Golf's 4Motion four-wheel-drive system, so having to channel its power through the front wheels only meant less power loss. Without the 4Motion system, the Scirocco R was claimed to be more than 200 pounds (91 kg) lighter than the all-wheel-drive Golf R.

With the same six-speed manual or DSG gearbox, the Scirocco R used the XDS electronic cross-axle traction control system first seen on the GTI. All Sciroccos were fitted with Adaptive Chassis Control (ACC), and the R's braking system was uprated with larger discs and calipers, the latter finished in gloss black. The headline figures were 0–62 mph in 6.4 seconds and a 155 mph top speed.

New front and rear bumpers marked out a Scirocco R as well as 18- or 19-inch five-spoke wheels. Like the Golf R, the "R" logo was across the car, including on new sports seats. There was a new three-spoke, flat-bottomed steering wheel finished in black leather with white stitching framing white backlit dials with blue needles unique to the "R" models.

The Scirocco R was priced at about 10 percent less than a Golf R and 10 percent more than a GTI. The US press was invited to drive the Scirocco R in the south of France in late 2009 but were told by Volkswagen that the US market couldn't support both the Scirocco R and the GTI without one cannibalizing the sales of

CHAPTER 6. GOLF GTI MK6 2008–2012   135

the other. "It's also the most brutal of the bunch, but it's sure to bring many smiles to its driver's face. It did to ours." Jens Meiners wrote for *Car and Driver* December 2009. "We'd now like to file another complaint with VW about the decision not to bring it here."

In August 2010, the 100,000th "new" Scirocco left the line. When the Mk7 Golf was launched in 2012 on the new MQB platform (chapter 7), there was speculation that a new Scirocco would follow, but the 2008 original just received a heavy facelift in 2014 (again Europe-only) with a new suite of more powerful engines: the 2.0-liter TSI 210 PS (since 2010) was replaced with a 220 PS (same power as the new Golf GTI) while the R rose to 280 PS. The last Scirocco was built in autumn 2017. A successor had been considered, but by now Volkswagen was reeling from the "dieselgate" scandal.

TOP: The two-tone Scirocco R seats matched the Golf R. All Sciroccos had two full-sized rear places, with folding seat backs. *(Volkswagen UK)*

ABOVE: With an extra 22-liter fuel tank, the Scirocco Cup cars used Bio-CNG, produced from renewable resources such as grass and refined biological waste. *Erdgas* means natural gas. *(Volkswagen UK)*

2009: GTI Concept Into Reality

Against the eager anticipation of Scirocco deliveries starting (see page 133), as was now the custom, the Mk6 GTI was launched as a "concept" at the October 2008 Paris Motor Show in pretty much the same specification as it would go on sale in 2009. Three VW designers were responsible for the GTI concept: Walter de Silva (director, group design), Klaus Bischoff (director, brand design), and Marc Lichte (director, exterior design).

The distinctive three-piece center grille had gone from sporting Golfs (and other Volkswagens), reverting to more conservative frontal styling, so once more there was less to mark out a GTI. But there was, of course, a red stripe around the top grille with a deep

TOP: Here in its production form, compared with a regular Golf the GTI was lower by 22 mm at the front and 15 mm at the back, and it had shorter front wishbones to narrow the track to improve turn-in. (*Volkswagen UK*)
RIGHT: For the Mk6 the GTI returned to fully body-colored bumpers (without the black lower half of the Mk5). A rear diffuser channeled air from beneath the car. (*Volkswagen UK*)
NEXT PAGES: By the time it was seen in the Mk6 GTI in 2009, the Volkswagen Group EA888 four-cylinder had been rapidly evolving. The 1.8-liter EA888 Gen 1 came in 2007 and the EA888 Gen 2 in 2008. (*Volkswagen UK*)

honeycomb air dam framed by vertical fog lights pushed out to the edges to emphasize width (the new GTI was 20 mm wider than the car it replaced).

At the rear, a diffuser sat between an all-new exhaust system with twin tailpipes with a subtle rear spoiler atop the tailgate and smoked rear light lenses. There were black extensions to the lower part of the sills, but that was the extent of the extra additions to the bodywork—an attempt to return to the simplicity of the original. Red brake calipers and the 17-inch Mk5 GTI Monza alloy wheels (some called the pattern "potato cutter") were carried over with 18-inch items optional.

Although it shared the same 2.0-liter capacity as the previous GTI, the engine for the Mk6 was part of a new range, the EA888 series, which had been developed by Audi as a family of larger engines for the North American market capable of high performance and better

ABOVE: The XDS limited-slip differential added another layer of electronics to the GTI's handling that would seamlessly allow you to accelerate hard out of a wet bend. *(Volkswagen UK)*

RIGHT: In the new dashboard, the instrument panel no longer glowed blue at night but white, and there was an optional touchscreen for the radio. Tartan seat fabric was called "Interlagos" in the UK and "Jacky" in Germany. *(Volkswagen UK)*

OPPOSITE: The GTD had silver grille trim instead of red. It featured all the chassis modifications of the GTI apart from the XDS electronic differential. *(Volkswagen UK)*

emissions, and which replaced the EA113 series in Europe. Already evolving, this was the EA888 Gen 2.

Once more turbocharged with direct gas injection, it had an iron block and alloy 16-valve cylinder head, modified pistons and piston rings, an improved oil pump, and a high-pressure fuel pump. The EA888 had a unique exhaust manifold design completely contained inside the cylinder head; so, the compact turbocharger mounted directly to the engine.

Both intake and exhaust camshafts featured continuously variable valve timing (newly developed by Audi), and the exhaust camshaft further added variable valve lift and duration through the use of two distinct camshaft lobe profiles. In combination, these systems were claimed to present a huge range of adjustability for a broad sphere of driving situations. The EA888 was designed to be very tractable at low rpm but to continue to make more horsepower as engine revs increased. Also fitted to the Scirocco, this was officially a TSI engine—not a TFSI.

In a bid to reduce servicing costs, the turbocharger and oil cooler were easier to access. It was also a selling point for some owners that the double overhead camshafts were run by a timing chain rather than a belt, considered to be much longer lasting. As before, the GTI could be specified with a six-speed manual gearbox or six-speed DSG automatic.

The new power figure was 210 PS (10 PS extra) delivered between 5,300 and 6,200 rpm for a claimed 0 to 62 mph (100 kph) in 6.9 seconds (the same claimed for the previous car), but emissions falling from 189 g/km to 170 g/km in the manual version (which meant that UK buyers paid less road tax) and economy improved from a combined 35.3 mpg to 38.7 mpg.

Bespoke springs and dampers were linked to a ride height lowered by 22 mm at the front and 15 mm at the rear compared with a regular Golf. The Adaptive Chassis Control (ACC) system was offered on the GTI.

Keeping the front wheels in the direction the driver intended was an electronically controlled limited-slip differential called XDS. Developed for the Mk6 GTI and later extended to other front-driven Volkswagen Group cars, it was an extension of the Electronic Differential Lock (EDL) integrated in the ESP system of the Mk5 GTI.

As soon as the electronics detected excessive unloading of the inside wheel of the driven front axle during fast cornering, the ESP hydraulic system built up braking system pressure in a targeted way on this wheel to restore optimum traction. XDS acted as a limited-slip differential to compensate for the understeer typical of front-wheel-drive cars during fast cornering.

This was a GTI for the head rather than the heart—capable, refined, a little cheaper to run overall, but not very exciting. The Seat Leon FR used the same engine and power output but was allowed to be a little more hard-edged. If you wanted rowdier thrills elsewhere, the 2009 Ford Focus RS (301 bhp) and Renaultsport Mégane 250 (247 bhp/250 PS) were on offer for not a great deal more money than a Mk6 GTI.

However, reprogramming easily released more power from the GTI's EA888. For example, in 2009, British firm APS offered a £599 remap of the engine ECU (electronic control unit) to increase power to 250 bhp at 5,800 rpm, while torque jumped to 292 lb ft at 2,650 rpm. The 0–60 mph time fell from 6.9 to 6.2 seconds, while top speed increased from 149 to approximately 155 mph.

For a more dramatic upgrade, in 2010 German tuner MTM's turbo kit plus new exhaust system would transform a Mk6 GTI into a 270 PS road burner with unique 18- or 19-inch alloy wheels and larger brake discs.

The GTD Returns

As the Golf GTI went on German sale, the GTD diesel made a return at the March 2009 Leipzig Motor Show after having skipped a generation in the UK. The 2.0-liter common rail TDI engine gave 170 PS, and while it wasn't as fast as the GTI, with 0 to 62 mph (100 kph) in 8.1 seconds and a top speed of 136 mph, the payoff was a claimed average fuel consumption of 53.3 mpg. There were few external differences to the gas GTI. It lost the red highlights around the grille for chrome and the alloy wheels were 17-inch "Seattle Black." Inside, the tartan seat pattern was gray, white, and black, rather than red, white, and black.

This time, the GTI's position at the top of the tree was safe, at least according to Germany's *Auto Motor Und Sport* in a 2010 back-to-back test of gas versus diesel. "The gasoline engine is much more alert to the accelerator. A VW Golf GTD driver will never experience this lustful marching across the rev range . . . but a look at the measured figures reveals a real surprise: In the flexibility rating, it gives the GTD a painful push and pulls through better than the diesel. Nobody would have expected that."

Farewell V6 —The Third Golf R

If the standard GTI's 210 PS was thought to lack sparkle, it was well known that the next R would take the battle to the Focus RS and Renaultsport Mégane 250, which unsurprisingly struggled to put all their power solely through the front wheels. It was also known that it would exchange six cylinders for four plus a turbocharger and just be called Golf R.

Given Volkswagen's policy of downsizing plus turbo and supercharging, there was, in Europe, no prospect of any more than four cylinders. Enthusiasts might have hoped that the Audi TT RS of 2009 would donate its turbo five-cylinder engine to the next-generation Golf R, but it was not to be.

Developed by Volkswagen's special projects wing, Volkswagen Individual, and launched alongside the Scirocco R at Frankfurt 2009, the new Golf R carried a 2.0-liter TSI four-cylinder engine, so it couldn't lay claim to being an R32 by virtue of capacity. However, it boasted 270 PS compared with the previous R32's 250.

This was not a hotter version of the EA888 Golf GTI engine but derived from the EA113 engine from the fifth-generation GTI,

essentially that of the Audi S3. *Evo* magazine reported that according to Volkswagen Individual this was because it lent itself more readily to tuning. The R engine had a reinforced block, new alloy cylinder head, uprated pistons and conrods, and high-pressure fuel injectors. The turbocharger ran at a boost pressure of 1.2 bar, claimed to be an unusually high figure. An uprated oil intercooler sat behind the front air dam to cope with the increased heat.

Like the Audi, power was channeled through a six-speed DSG gearbox to all four wheels via a Haldex system, now in its fourth generation. The system fitted to the R32 had relied on differing wheel speeds between the front and rear axles to engage the four-wheel-drive, but the system fitted to the Golf R was claimed to be quicker reacting thanks to faster coupling of the drive to the rear wheels by a hydraulic accumulator that was kept "pre-charged," so there was no drop in pressure. The improved system also limited torque when needed to maximize traction. It was possible for all of the drive to be transferred to the rear wheels in some situations. New front brake discs and calipers were joined by uprated suspension lowered by 25 mm with revised spring and damper rates and new anti-roll bars. The ESP was revised to offer two stages designed for track use (owners were increasingly using their cars on "track days"). The electro-mechanical power steering system was adjusted to sharpen responses.

Thanks to the physically smaller and lighter engine, there was more space in the engine bay. The Golf R was 35 kg lighter (albeit still much heavier than a GTI), so it had a better power to weight ratio than the R32. It was claimed to be the fastest accelerating Volkswagen ever produced, with a 0 to 62 mph (100 kph) time of 5.7 seconds. Although not top of most owners' lists, the claimed combined cycle of 33.2 mpg was around 4 mpg better than the R32 and CO_2 emissions of 199 g/km bettered 257 g/km.

OPPOSITE TOP: The 2009 Golf R had front bumpers with LED running lights and a trio of air dams, gloss black wing mirrors, sill extensions, and 18-inch five-spoke "Talladega" alloy wheels. (*Volkswagen UK*)

OPPOSITE BOTTOM: There was no longer a six-cylinder under the hood of the Golf R, and it would be gone for good. However, the 2.0-liter turbo four gave more power and better fuel consumption. (*Volkswagen UK*)

BELOW: The 2009 Golf R had new sports seats with "R" logos and piano black and silver highlights. Vienna leather sports seats or Recaro bucket seats were options. (*Volkswagen UK*)

Once road tested by the magazines, there was no complaint about any loss of flexibility minus two cylinders. The turbocharged Golf R came over as a much more eager car, starting to deliver its increased maximum torque of 258 lb ft (compared with 236 lb ft) at 2,500 continuing to 5,000 rpm where the V6 had tailed off at 3,000 rpm.

Volkswagen GTI 2010

In North America, the Rabbit revival had been very short-lived and when the Mk6 Golf arrived in August 2009, it was just plain Golf once more. Once more Puebla-built, the base five-cylinder's power was upped to 170 bhp and it was joined by a 2.0-liter turbo diesel. The Volkswagen GTI arrived as a 2010 model in October 2009 and continued the appeal of being German built. What wasn't new was the engine as North American GTIs carried over the previous EA113 turbo with the same 200 hp (PS) output. This is likely to have been down to the cost of emissions testing and re-engineering the EA888 for what looked to be a short time on sale.

Very on-trend, it was launched via a free iPhone app called Real Racing GTI (the Scirocco R had also been launched via an app), where virtual GTIs competed on a fictional racetrack. Registered players could win one of six limited-edition GTIs, fitted with most of the available options, including 18-inch wheels and simulated carbon fiber trim. In December, after some uncertainty VWoA announced it was bringing the R in for 2010, but it was not to arrive until autumn 2011.

It had plenty of more powerful rivals—the most frequent comparison was the 263 hp .3-liter four-cylinder Mazdaspeed3—but the GTI's agility, comfort, and, above all, quality soothed road testers such as Brian Vance of *MotorTrend* (October 2009). "It's a real eye-opener to be reintroduced to the incongruent notion that a fast car doesn't necessarily mean 0–60-quick. Really."

Golf GTI Adidas Edition 2010

If you wanted your GTI to match your favorite brand of sneakers, in 2010 Volkswagen Germany launched a limited edition of 4,410 Adidas GTIs just in time for Wörthersee, available as a three- or five-door model from the end of June. In addition to special wheels,

---

ABOVE: The super-exclusive Adidas GTI of 2010–2011 had 18-inch Serron wheels (optional 19-inch Glendale), could be painted in Candy White, Black A1, Tornado Red G2, and Metallic Oryx White 9099. Adidas logo on the "b" pillar. *(Author)*
OPPOSITE: The "White Stripes" sports seat design of the Golf GTI Adidas was joined by aluminum trim and a golf ball gear lever for the six-speed manual gearbox. *(Author)*

the sports seats were embroidered with the Adidas logo, its three famous stripes running down the middle.

There were unique door sill plates, interior accents in aluminum, fabric floor mats with decorative borders—and in versions equipped with the six-speed DSG, a gearshift grip with a golf ball texture. The Adidas ran (so to speak) in a small number of left-hand drive markets apart from a small amount for Japan.

Jetta GLI 2011

In the manner of the CJ concept of 1997 (chapter 4) the new Jetta was teased as a handsome coupé that failed to show up in the showrooms. Previewed as the New Compact Coupé at the January 2010 Detroit Motor Show, its hybrid drivetrain was of more significance than the styling, which morphed into an undramatic four-door sedan later in the year—but one of the new Jettas would be Volkswagen's first series production hybrid.

Although the dashboard was the same, this new Jetta shared no panels with the Golf and sat between the hatchback and the Passat in terms of size, its wheelbase extended by 70 mm to 2,648 mm over the Golf for better rear legroom. Trunk space was cavernous.

Even though they were built in the same factory in Puebla, Mexico, there were big differences between European and American Jettas, the latter determinedly built down to a price lower than the previous car to compete with the Toyota Corolla and Honda Civic. The European Jetta retained the Golf's multi-link rear axle, but regular US models had a specially developed torsion-beam rear axle, and the electric power steering was deleted in favor of cheaper hydraulic power steering. On some models, drum rear brakes replaced discs and even the gas struts holding the hood open were withheld. The

OPPOSITE TOP: Volkswagen CEO North America Jonathan Browning introduces the real, four-door 2012 Jetta GLI at the 2011 Chicago Auto Show. It's in Tornado Red with the Autobahn package's 18-inch wheels. *(UPI/Alamy Stock Photo)*
OPPOSITE BOTTOM: The 2011 GTI Edition 35 had new side skirts, revised front bumper, and bi-xenon headlights with LED daytime running lights. Its 18-inch "Watkins Glen" alloy wheels could be black or silver. *(Volkswagen UK)*
ABOVE: The 2010 Compact Coupé Concept was a handsome make-believe Jetta coupé that only previewed its front end and the idea of the later hybrid drivetrain. *(Volkswagen UK)*

gas engines of the US Jetta were unique to its market—the old 2005 Beetle's 115 bhp 2.0-liter four-cylinder and the North American Golf's 2.5-liter five-cylinder. The diesel was also popular.

However, the 2012 model year Jetta GLI (autumn 2011) came with all the right equipment: soft-touch dashboard and multi-link rear. At $24,515 it was some $4,000 less than the GTI. The 200 hp EA888 Gen 2 turbo engine supplied the power, which could be heard via the peculiar "Soundaktor," an audio file that played from a speaker under the hood to give a more rumbly engine note under acceleration. *Car and Driver* lived with a GLI for 40,000 miles and was not impressed: "Sometimes the car drones like a digital kazoo full of phlegm. Perhaps not surprisingly, YouTube has several videos explaining how to remove it."

THE 2011 GOLF24

In 2011, to mark the 35th anniversary of the GTI, Volkswagen Motorsport Golfs returned to the Nürburgring-Nordschleife for the first time since 2007 with three purpose-built Golf24s. The project had begun in August 2010 and was unveiled in February 2011.

Based on a three-door GTI bodyshell, the Golf24 had needed a major power boost to be competitive (the 2007 cars had 300 PS), so it used the five-cylinder of the Audi RS3, which in road trim made 340 PS with direct injection and a single turbo and was nearing the end of production. This was now tuned to give 440 PS, and like the RS4 it had permanent four-wheel-drive, which augured well for the sinewy curves of the forest track. The engineers developed two possible power splits 50:50 or 40:60 in favor of the rear wheels and chose the latter to save wear on the front tires. Rubber all around was supplied by Dunlop in wet or dry compounds. The gearbox was a six-speed sequential with paddle controls (the RS3 had a seven-speed DSG).

By the time of the June 25–26, 2011 24 Hours of Nürburgring, testing in Portugal and Italy had shown encouraging times for the Golf24s. They were piloted by three teams of drivers drawn from motorsport, management, and media, and joined by two Scirocco GT24-CNGs.

The 202 starters were formed of the usual very German mix of privateers, and independent, and factory teams, including two V12 Aston Martin Zagatos (at the time Aston's boss was German Dr. Ulrich Bez, who loved the race). On Saturday afternoon the cars were set off in three batches a few minutes apart, but sadly none of the Golf 24s finished; one had an accident and two retired with mechanical problems. The race was won by Manthey Racing's Porsche 997 GT3-RSR, then BMW Motorsport's BMW M3 GT and Audi Sport Team Phoenix took a class-winning 3-4-5 with its team of R8s.

OPPOSITE TOP: Built by Volkswagen Motorsport in Hannover, the monster Golf 24 was two meters wide, 22 cm more than a production GTI. The tires alone were 30 cm across. *(Volkswagen UK)*

OPPOSITE BOTTOM: Unlike the Scirocco GT24, the Golf24 was a complete racing machine with fuel tank in place of rear seats. The sequential six-speed gearbox with paddle shifters had a pneumatic system for rapid changes. *(Volkswagen UK)*

ABOVE: The Golf24 was powered by the 2.5-liter inline five-cylinder from the Audi RS3, related to the five-cylinder used in the US Golfs and Jettas but highly developed. *(Volkswagen UK)*

RIGHT: A front splitter, rear diffuser, rear wing, and smooth-surfaced underbody were designed for downforce—260 kg from the rear wing if the car reached 260 kph (161 mph). *(Volkswagen UK)*

2011: The Golf Cabriolet Returns

The only truly new derivative of the Mk6 Golf was the welcome return of the soft-top Golf Cabriolet. On European sale in summer 2011, it was for the first time ever a full convertible, without a rollover bar, forsaking the *Erdbeerkörbchen*, or strawberry basket, nickname of old. Body engineering having moved on from the 1990s, the rollover bar was no longer needed to keep the structure from flexing over poor surfaces, and the windshield could bear the weight of the car in a rollover accident. Extra safety systems were hidden until they were needed.

The Golf Cabriolet didn't supplant the Eos, but the complicated metal folding-roof cars were falling from fashion (they could leak, or worse, jam). Ford and Opel/Vauxhall had dropped their folding metal hardtops for their new Focus and Astra, leaving the Golf with few direct rivals apart from the BMW 1-Series Cabriolet and the 2008 soft-top Audi A3, built in Hungary, which provided much of the structural basis. Sharing the same wheelbase, the front panels were carried over from the Golf hatchback, but everything rearward was new, with a far more steeply angled windshield.

Reinforced window frames and structural modifications to the underbody, side panels, cross-members, and doors endowed the new car with a class-leading level of torsional rigidity, according to Volkswagen. To come close to the hatchback's level of hush, the fabric roof had an additional exterior skin as well as new window and door seals. As it had always been, the rear window was heated and made of glass.

The roof could be lowered electrically in a claimed 9.5 seconds, including on the move at speeds up to around 18 mph. A wind deflector could be fitted across the top of the back seat area when two were traveling to reduce buffeting at high speeds.

Cabriolet production returned to Karmann in Osnabrück or rather Volkswagen Osnabrück, as it was now wholly owned by the company as an assembly facility for smaller-volume cars.

2011 Golf GTI Edition 35 and New Racers

In June 2011 three purpose-built Golf24s competed at the 24 Hours of Nürburgring (see page 148) and the showroom special, the Golf GTI Edition 35, made its debut at Wörthersee. Its power output of 235 PS (up 25 PS) sat it between the regular GTI and the R, the most powerful production GTI to that point. It was distinguishable by a revised front bumper, distinctive lightweight 18-inch alloys, a "35" signature inside and out, and, yes, the golf ball gear knob.

OPPOSITE TOP: The Mk6 Golf Cabriolet dispensed with a rollover bar. In the event of a rollover, a pyrotechnic charge shot up two metal posts from behind the rear headrests. *(Volkswagen UK)*

OPPOSITE BOTTOM: The 2012 Golf GTI Cabriolet was unmistakable with the hatchback's grille plus side sill extensions and Monza alloys. Wind diffuser is in place behind the driver. *(Volkswagen UK)*

TOP: Unlike its predecessors, when it was folded, the hood sat flat on the rear deck as the final section that attached to the windshield was rigid, so it needed no separate cover. *(Volkswagen UK)*

RIGHT: Unlike the Eos, the volume of trunk space in a Golf Cabriolet didn't change whether the roof was up or down—250 liters over 205 for the Eos. *(Volkswagen UK)*

2012 and a New Golf GTI Cabriolet

Launched at Geneva in March 2012, the European finale to the Golf Mk6 range was the return of the GTI Cabriolet, last seen in the 1980s, but sadly not offered to North American buyers. The Puebla-built Beetle Cabriolet was the best seller.

Marked out with all the classic GTI design features, the radiator grille had a honeycomb structure with red edging and the GTI badge, while the front bumper incorporated a deep honeycomb air dam and the hatchback's vertical fog lights.

Using the same 210 PS engine as the hatchback, a weight penalty of 138 kg lowered the performance figures, but this was still a fast soft-top, with the claimed 0–62 mph (100 kph) covered in 7.3 seconds with either transmission (versus 6.9 seconds for the hatch), while top speed was 147 mph (146 mph for the DSG).

2013 Golf R Cabriolet

A year after the launch of the GTI Cabriolet an "R" version appeared, which met a somewhat mixed reception. Not four-wheel-drive like the hatchback R, it shared its EA113 2.0-liter engine set at 265 PS, connected to a standard six-speed DSG gearbox. It had an electronically limited top speed of 155 mph, with the benchmark 0–62 mph (100 kph) sprint taking just 6.4 seconds. This made it comfortably the fastest-ever factory-produced Golf Cabriolet, very much in need of the XDS differential to stop the front wheels from steering themselves sideways under hard acceleration.

It was lavishly equipped, but what everybody noticed was the initial price of £38,770, some £8,000 more than a GTI Cabriolet and more than a Porsche Boxster. Not long after delivery had started in June, Volkswagen UK dropped the price by £5,600. Most road testers preferred the more supple GTI Cabriolet, and it was short-lived, then dropped when all Golf Cabriolets bowed out in 2016, the last of the Golf Cabriolet line.

LEFT: Pictured in Shanghai in 2013, the Golf R Cabriolet was the fastest soft-top Golf but not a big seller. The following Volkswagen Cabriolet was the SUV-like T-Roc in 2019. *(Imaginechina Limite /Alamy Stock Photo)*

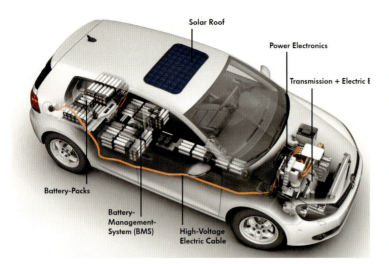

2013 Wolfsburg and Driver Editions

While European buyers began to take delivery of their Golf GTI Mk7s in 2013, North American buyers would have to wait another year, so interest was maintained in the usual way via special editions with added extra equipment for less than the total bill if ordered as options.

A GTI Autobahn package (there was also a Jetta Autobahn) had been running since 2011, which added LED daytime running lights and ten-spoke 18-inch Serron alloys, but the February 2013 Chicago Auto Show brought the limited-run Wolfsburg and Driver's Editions only available on the five-door GTI. The Wolfsburg Edition amounted to a set of nicer wheels, golf ball gear knob, and special floor mats, but was only $300 more than a base GTI (each alloy wheel cost that alone). The Driver's Edition also came with these extras but added partial-leather seats and the Sunroof and Navigation package. At $30,490, it was $900 more than a similarly optioned GTI, but that was the price of exclusivity—only 3,000 were expected to be sold.

TOP LEFT: Here's a Golf Mk6 nobody could buy. Between 2011 and 2013 a fleet of 500 prototype electric Golfs called the Golf Blue-e-motion began mass testing ahead of the production Golf Mk7 e-Golf. *(Volkswagen AG)*

TOP RIGHT: To prove their cars were genuine, each of the 3,000 Driver's Edition owners received a certificate of authenticity, a keychain, a parking sign, and a GTI hat. *(VWoA)*

ABOVE: The Volkswagen GTI Wolfsburg Edition and Driver's Edition were North American run-out specials for 2013 with 18-inch Laguna wheels and only came in black, gray, or white. *(VWoA)*

Golf GTI Mk6

Model	Volkswagen Golf GTI Mk6 hatchback (Europe)	Volkswagen GTI Mk6 hatchback (North America)	Volkswagen Golf GTI Mk6 Cabriolet (Europe)
Engine type/capacity	2.0-liter 16-valve 4-cylinder, turbocharged	2.0-liter 16-valve 4-cylinder, turbocharged	2.0-liter 16-valve 4-cylinder, turbocharged
Gearbox	6-speed manual or 6-speed DSG	6-speed manual or 6-speed DSG	6-speed manual or 6-speed DSG
Maximum power/at rpm	210 PS between 5,300–6,200 rpm	200 hp at 5,100 rpm	210 PS between 5,300–6,200 rpm
Maximum torque/at rpm	206 lb ft between 1,700–5,200 rpm	207 lb ft between 1,800–5,100 rpm	206 lb ft between 1,700–5,200 rpm
Acceleration 0–60 mph	6-7 seconds	6.1 seconds (DSG version, *Car and Driver*)	7.6 seconds (0–62 mph/100 kph)
Maximum speed	149 mph (manual version *Autocar* 3 June 2009)	124 mph (limited top speed)	146 mph (claimed)
Suspension front/rear	Strut and coil springs, wishbone, anti-roll bar/trailing arms, coil springs, multi-link axle, anti-roll bar, ACC Adaptive Chassis Control optional	Strut and coil springs, wishbone, anti-roll bar/trailing arms, coil springs, multi-link axle, anti-roll bar, ACC Adaptive Chassis Control optional	Strut and coil springs, wishbone, anti-roll bar/trailing arms, coil springs, multi-link axle, anti-roll bar, ACC Adaptive Chassis Control optional
Wheels/tires	17-in Monza alloys 225/45 R17 tires (18 in optional)	17-in Monza alloys 225/45 R17 tires (18-in optional). Detroit wheels from 2011	7.5J x 18-in Monza Shadow alloys 225/40 R18 tires
Brakes front/rear	Ventilated disc/ventilated disc with anti-lock and ESP/XDS	Ventilated disc/ventilated disc with anti-lock and ESP/XDS	Ventilated disc/ventilated disc with anti-lock and ESP/XDS
Length	4,199 mm	4,211 mm	4,258 mm
Wheelbase	2,578 mm	2,578 mm	2,578 mm
Width	1,779 mm	1,779 mm	1,782 mm
Height	1,479 mm	1,479 mm	1,898 mm
Weight (kg)	Dry weight 1,318/1,348 (3/5-door)	Curb weight 1,438 (DSG, 3-door)	1,555 (curb)
Years produced	2009-2012	2009-2013	2012-2016

7.
GOLF GTI MK7 2012–2019

Built to Impress

So much was new in the 2012 seventh-generation Golf: new body, new platform, new engines, and lots of new technology—and yet it was lighter. Was this peak Golf?

Kicking off with the platform, its versatility would underpin millions of Volkswagen Group cars of many shapes and sizes for over a decade. The Audi A3 had been the curtain raiser for the MQB system—*Modularer Querbaukasten*, translated as Modular Transverse Matrix. MQB was formally announced in February 2012 as the future basis for the Volkswagen Group A to B segment cars from Polo to the Volkswagen (Passat) CC. Volkswagen said that MQB would last for several product cycles and up to 40 models would be built using it.

Golf-sized cars from the 1990s had been obliged to share the same wheelbase, track between the wheels, and "hard points" such as the center of the floorpan, wheel arch linings, suspension and engine mounts, and body side members.

MQB went beyond this, expanding or contracting in nearly every dimension. While much of the frontal structure containing the engine mounts, suspension, and pedal positions were fixed, beyond these the length, width, height, and seating position of a car could all be changed—so, for example, the new Škoda Octavia's wheelbase was

RIGHT: Seen here at the 2012 Paris show, the Golf Mk7 was a clean-sheet design with an unprecedented range of powerplants for the European market. *(Abaca Press/Alamy Stock Photo)*

50 mm longer than that of the Golf. You could make different cars from different brands in different sizes on the same production line. The era of one factory being home to one model was ending. If demand for one car fell, another would take its place.

MQB provided the basis for cars powered by gas, diesel, hybrid, compressed natural gas, or electricity and significantly drove down weight. One of the key characteristics was the uniform mounting position of all engines—all transverse front-or four-wheel-drive. Gearboxes, steering systems, electronics, and infotainment systems could all be mixed and matched, as could exhaust gas treatment components (catalysts, particulate filters) to meet varying legislation.

There were other platforms designed on similar principles for others; the NSF (New Small Family) would be for small cars based on the Volkswagen Up. Audi used MLB for cars with longitudinal engines and front-, four-, or rear-wheel-drive—including Bentley—while Porsche had MSB, a sports car tool kit.

ABOVE: Paris 2012 and a new GTI concept enters a dance show, with costumes reflecting almost four decades of the Volkswagen Golf. It was faithful to the 2013 production GTI down to the wheels used. *(dpa picture alliance archive/Alami Stock Photo)*

By 2022 more than 32 million MQB-based vehicles had been produced across the group, more than 20 million of them under the Volkswagen brand from the Polo to SUVs such as the Atlas (USA) and the Teramont (China). With production of the Golf 8 in 2019 (chapter 8), it was still possible to use around 80 percent of the existing machinery in the body shop.

Back to 2012, the Volkswagen Group was immersed in "Strategy 2018" aimed at positioning the Volkswagen Group as a "global economic and environmental leader"—and that meant beating Toyota and General Motors, first and second at the time.

A Classic Look

Compared with the sixth generation, here was an apparently lower, sleeker Golf. The Golf Mk4 was referenced as a benchmark in styling, and looking at the sharp lines of the new car it was said that this was how that Golf might have evolved had it continued without diversion into the rounded forms of the 2003–2008 series.

At 4,255 mm the seventh Golf was 56 mm longer than its predecessor, with a 59 mm longer wheelbase at 2,637 mm. The MQB platform allowed the front wheels to be placed 43 mm further forward, which helped interior space and also gave the designers the chance to be relatively radical within Golf constraints. The passenger compartment was moved further toward the rear, to follow the proportions of premium-class vehicles, on which the hood is long and the passenger compartment a long way toward the back. It was also 13 mm wider, at 1,799 mm, and 28 mm lower, at 1,452 mm. There was a claimed 10 percent improvement in the drag coefficient at 0.27 Cd, the lowest ever for a Golf.

BELOW: The versatile MQB platform could be varied to underpin every size of Volkswagen Group car above city cars and was used for well over ten years. *(Volkswagen AG)*

BOTTOM: On the five-door Golf Mk7 the profile of the "c" pillar was likened to the string of a taut bow and arrow but was still an unmistakable Golf design. *(Volkswagen UK)*

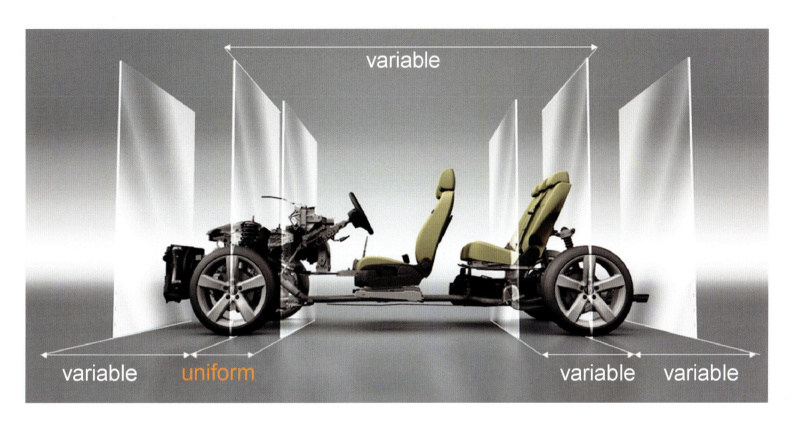

BELOW: In 2013 Wolfsburg built the 30 millionth Golf. The factory dated to the 1930s, but the production line used the latest techniques. *(Sean Gallup/Getty Images)*

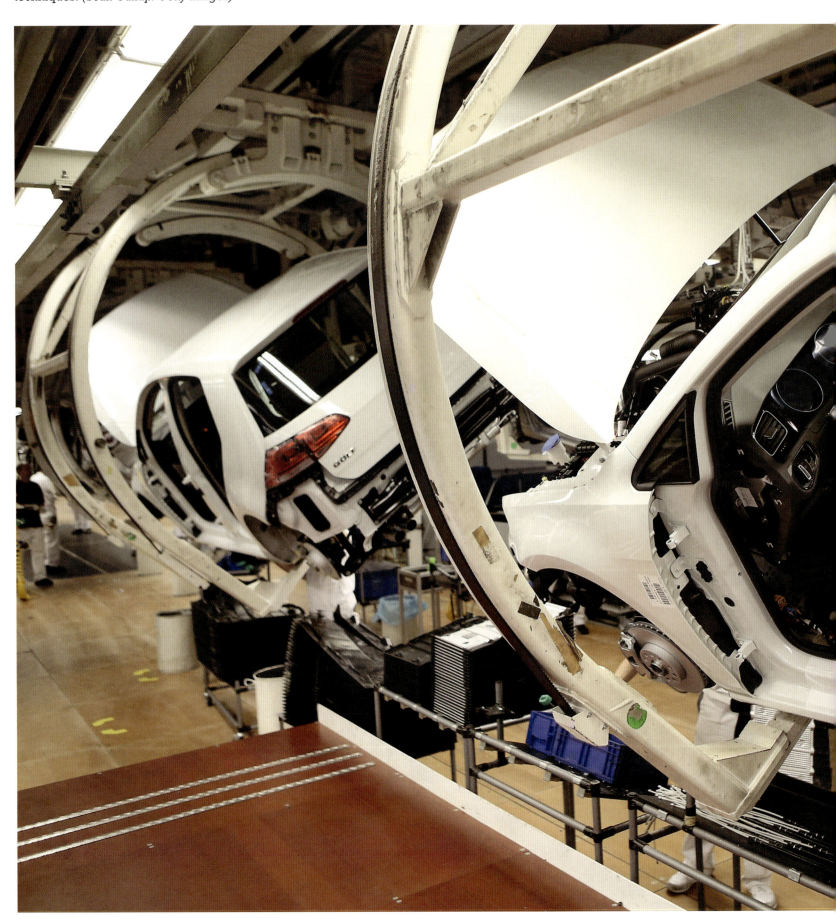

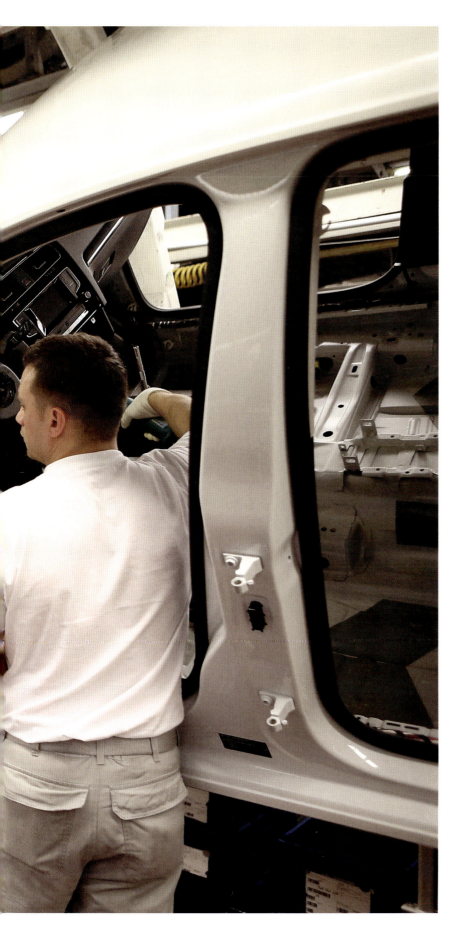

Bigger, but a Little Lighter

The billions invested in MQB were aimed at reducing weight across the range and improving emissions, both to meet legislative requirements and to cement Volkswagen's then image as an environmental leader. By 2015 the average CO_2 figure of all cars sold in Europe had to be 130 g/km and would be 95 g/km by 2020. Radical solutions had to be found, and high-volume Volkswagen models had to subsidize the thirst of Bugattis and Lamborghinis.

For a selection of examples where components had shed weight, the air-conditioning weighed 2.7 kg less through changes in the thickness of various system component walls, reduced diameter pressure lines, and a new heat exchanger. The new seats saved up to 7 kg depending on version, especially the rear backrests with lighter latch mechanisms. The bare bodyshell weighed 23 kg less.

The fuel tank had shrunk from 55 to 50 liters, which was fine as the fuel economy had improved once more, but this also helped to reduce some weight figures as it held less fuel for official measurements. Relative to the competition, *Autocar* listed the curb weight (with a full tank) of a new UK-market Golf 2.0 TDI SE at 1,354 kg compared with a similar Ford Focus at 1,421 kg. The comparison was not quite so marked against the 1,395 kg of a BMW 118d Sport.

All-Turbo Engines

The greatest overall weight loss was claimed to be the Golf's new range of gas and diesel engines, which could weigh up to 40 kg less mainly by all-aluminum cylinder blocks replacing cast iron. They were either major redesigns or all-new series. Only the six- and seven-speed DSG automatic gearboxes came across unchanged from the previous generation.

The new EA211 series replaced the EA111 engines, which had been vastly developed since their 1974 namesake had appeared. A modular series that could be three- or four-cylinder, in the Golf 7 the EA211 series was first presented in four-cylinder 1.2-liter or 1.4-liter displacements, all with turbochargers and intercoolers (developed with Bosch Mahle and Mitsubishi Heavy Industries).

The path to the EA211 started with the twin-charged 1.4 TSI engine of 2006. It was a complete redesign based on an aluminum cylinder block. The exhaust manifold was integrated into the cylinder head to speed up warming times and help exhaust gas flows, with a smaller diameter turbocharger reducing weight further.

EA211 rotated from the traditional position where the exhaust manifold had faced forward to be inclined rearward toward the bulkhead. It meant the driveshaft and gearbox mounting position could be standardized for all engines. Dozens of small design changes had been made so the engine took up as little space as possible, with items like the water pump bolted directly to the engine instead of a bracket.

The European Golf launch lineup was a 1.2-liter TSI 85 PS eight-valve unit from the Polo, later joined by a 105 PS version then a 16-valve 1.4-liter TSI with 122 or 140 PS. Combined fuel economy figures for these ranged from 54.3 to 57.6 mpg with CO_2 emissions from 113 to 120 g/km. Illustrating that power outputs for these engines were governed primarily by the engine management unit, German tuner ABT pretty soon offered a reconfiguration of the 85 to 105 PS and liberated 165 PS from the 140.

Engine downsizing was now common even among luxury brands, which increasingly had the facility to shut down banks of cylinders at lower and cruising speeds. Now there was a Golf with a 1.4-liter turbocharged EA211 engine of 140 PS featuring Active Cylinder Technology (ACT). From 2012 the system started to be used across the group from the Polo to the Lamborghini Aventador. However, Volkswagen UK opted to offer the ACT engine as the only gas unit for the high-spec Golf GT model (the equivalent was Highline in Germany, which also offered ACT in the next trim-down, Comfortline).

Working between an engine speed range of 1,400 and 4,000 rpm, the engine management system adjusted the ignition and throttle settings to smooth the transitions, and the road testers concurred that the change was indeed almost imperceptible with only a dashboard light showing when two-cylinder mode was operating.

The twin-charged 160 PS TSI engine was no longer fitted to the Golf, and the next highest gas-powered version in the new lineup was the third generation of the 2.0-liter EA888 unit, with a new cylinder head design destined for the GTI. All EA888 TSIs had variable valve timing with dual camshaft adjustment.

Although the difference in emissions and economy was becoming less marked between gas and diesel, many countries enjoyed a price advantage at the pumps. There was also a range of Volkswagen TDI engines that earned a new designation of EA288. The switch having been made to common rail fuel injection with the Golf 6, the induction system for the turbocharger benefited from some of the new design features of the gas engines and reached operating temperature more quickly.

The "BlueMotion Technology" badge was now liberally spread around the trunk lids of Golfs, and all Golfs were fitted with a stop/start system and battery regeneration plus a visual indicator of the best economy gear to be in displayed on the multi-function computer in front of the driver.

With Golf Mk6 having sold on its refinement, the seventh had to maintain this serenity while not resorting to heavy sound-deadening materials. However, as the car was virtually all new, many components such as the engine induction systems, suspension, and subframes benefited from acoustic tests as they were being designed. It was recognized that with less wind noise and outside noise kept out by the sealing of the bodyshell, the occupants of a new Golf might notice ancillary noises more, such as the heater blower or the turbochargers, so these were tackled directly. The sound-damping film between two layers of windshield glass was carried over.

Torsion Beam Suspension for Some

Following the example of the 2010 North American Jetta, for the first time ever, the Golf was offered with two types of rear suspension. The front suspension stayed true to McPherson strut and lower wish-

bones, while at the rear there was either a multi-link setup or a "modular lightweight suspension," which marked the return of the simple torsion beam, albeit engineered to the latest standards. Applied only to Golf models with power under 122 PS, of course there was a manufacturing saving, and the MQB system was flexible enough for both types of suspension to be fitted on the same production line. There was also a weight saving of 11 kg over the multi-link unit.

Indicating that the changeover point to multi-link rear suspension according to engine power was perhaps more down to price and marketing than the abilities of the torsion beam, the Seat Leon was fitted with it for versions of over 150 PS and the Škoda Octavia only received it for the 220 PS vRS, another Golf GTI in Škoda clothes.

OPPOSITE: Touchscreen operated with the same kinds of finger gestures people were using on their mobile phones, sensed the approach of a finger, and presented the choices available. *(Volkswagen UK)*
ABOVE: In 2013, lifting a small button and hearing a whir as the electric parking brake applied itself was a very new sensation. *(Volkswagen UK)*

Techno-Fest

The 2012 Golf came packed with the latest driver aids. All dashboards had touchscreen systems as standard to operate the DAB digital radio, CD and MP3 players, plus a mobile phone, starting in the UK with a 5.8-inch color display system and rising to satellite navigation with 8-inch color display. It responded to the same kinds of gestures people were using on their mobile phones, sensed the approach of a finger, and presented the choices available.

Where once there had been a large lever, only a small square button indicated the presence of a handbrake. Instead of being activated by a cable, the brakes to the rear wheels were activated by two electric motors once the button was pulled upward. To drive away you pressed the brake pedal and flipped the button again. An auto hold function applied the brake if the car rolled while stationary and would enable the driver to perform a hill start. This had trickled down from upper-range Audis, the Passat, and Tiguan. The latest Opel/Vauxhall Astra also featured an electronic handbrake, so there was keeping up to be done.

The benefits of a button handbrake were more space in the center console and a further contribution to vehicle weight loss. However, electronic handbrakes were not universally liked by car buyers, some of whom bemoaned their complexity and potential repair costs. The Audi A3 had the same parking button as the Golf but the Seat Leon and Škoda Octavia had a traditional lever. Mexican-built Golfs and

Golf GTIs for North America (see later in the text) would also have a manual parking brake, while the estate/Sportwagen had the electronic brake as it was exported to Europe.

Golf passive safety was achieved by seven airbags as before, with standard anti-lock brakes and ESC stability control extended to provide the same electronic differential lock (XDS, now called XDS+) previously fitted to the GTI and GTD, which was claimed to improve traction and handling through bends. XDS+ would be fitted to the new GTI and GTD.

MQB didn't just allow various types of body structures, it allowed a host of electronic systems to be shared around. To begin listing a few of the new technical names for gadgets on the Golf 7 (each given capital letters), Automatic Distance Control (or intelligent cruise control) was now a radar-based system available on UK market cars where the car would cruise at a set distance from the vehicle in front. It was combined with Front Assist, which on its own could warn the driver if they were getting too close, and at low speeds City Emergency Braking would halt the car. If a DSG gearbox was fitted, the car would restart itself and drive away when the traffic started to move.

A Driver Alert System, as on the Passat, could detect signs of tiredness in the driver, a camera-operated Lane Assist system kept the car in a specific lane, and the Dynamic Light Assist system dropped the headlamps onto dipped beam automatically when it detected another car approaching on full beam.

For the first time, Driver Profile Selection allowed the user to select Eco, Sport, Normal, and Individual modes by changing the throttle mapping and engine management to their chosen style. Bringing back the old concept of freewheeling, when a DSG gearbox was fitted on the Eco setting it dropped into coasting in neutral under certain conditions. The Park Assist option had evolved to offer parallel and reverse parking at right angles to the road.

TOP: The only way to distinguish a Performance Pack GTI was by "GTI" lettering on the red brake calipers, here behind the 18-inch Austin alloys standard in the UK. *(Volkswagen UK)*
ABOVE: The EA888 Gen 3 four-cylinder of the GTI was used across all the Volkswagen Group brands made across the world, including Mexico and China. *(Volkswagen UK)*
OPPOSITE: As the top-end Golf of 2013, the GTI Performance was a showcase for the latest Volkswagen technology. *(Volkswagen UK)*

The Seventh GTI—2013

The all-new Golf made its press debut at Berlin's national gallery in early September 2012 before a full public showing at the Paris Motor Show that October where a GTI Concept was the star car, very near to production form while waiting for the official fuel consumption figures to be homologated. By spring 2013 the European order books were open for GTI and GTD.

For the GTI, the 2.0-liter EA888 (Gen 3) continued with the same cylinder head and integrated exhaust manifold introduced with the Mk6. The water-cooled exhaust gas channels ran through the cylinder head to the turbocharger (to efficiently reduce full-load fuel consumption) combined with a dual injection system of direct injection and multi-port injection. The crankshaft bearings were reinforced, and the direct fuel injection modified. Torque was much improved rising from 206 lb ft to 248 lb ft at 1,500 rpm to 4,400 rpm.

For the first time Volkswagen offered the GTI with two power outputs: the standard 220 PS (up 10 PS on the Golf 6) and the GTI Performance with 230 PS, larger brake discs, and a mechanical front limited-slip differential called VAQ, which stands for *Vorderachsquersperre*, or transverse front axle lock. As before, the gearbox choices were six-speed manual or six-speed DSG.

The headline performance improvements were relatively small; the standard car claimed 62 mph in 6.5 seconds rather than 6.9 and a top speed of 152 mph, and the GTI Performance was 6.4 seconds and 155 mph. The torque on the Performance was the same.

The Golf GTD continued to offer the same combination of looks as the gas car and a performance jump from 170 to 184 PS, although it was the usual different kind of performance, with peak torque available between 1,750 and 3,250 rpm and maximum power at 3,500 and 4,000 rpm (gas 4,700 to 6,200 rpm) and 0–62 mph in 7.5 seconds. There was no GTD Performance Pack option, but then there was a potential 67.3 mpg. Both versions also had the stop/start system to meet 2014 EU-6 emissions standards.

Made by BorgWarner, unlike the purely electronic XDS+ system where individual wheels were braked, the additional VAQ limited-slip front differential (it would also be termed an e-diff) on the Performance Pack GTI consisted of a multi-plate clutch between the differential cage and right driveshaft, which controlled locking torque electro-hydraulically. Monitoring the data from each wheel sensor, including vehicle and wheel speed as well as yaw and lateral g-force,

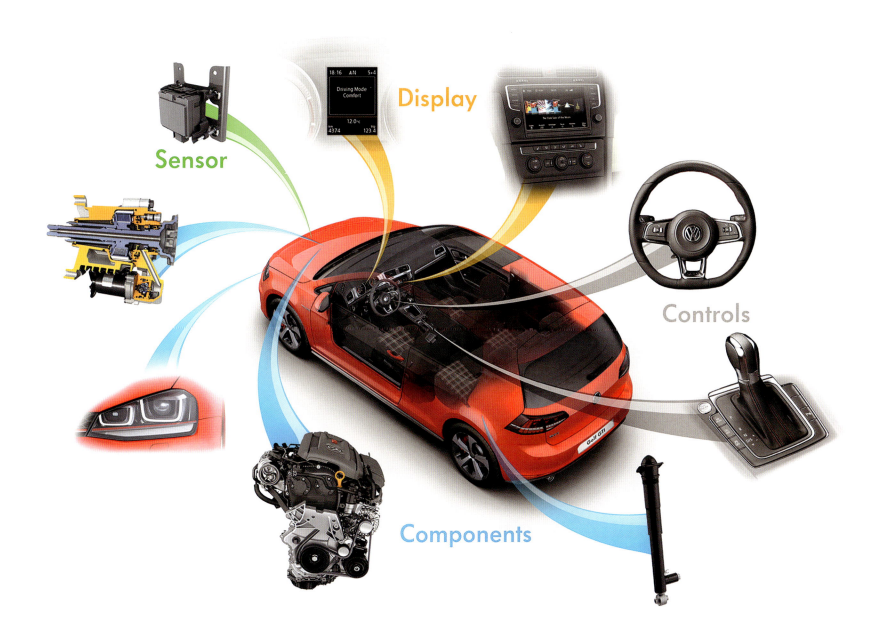

the system constantly made precise adjustments to help maintain an optimum torque balance between the left and right front wheels. This proactive system was claimed to eliminate the understeer and torque steer that could afflict powerful front-wheel-drive cars. It was very difficult to come unstuck in a GTI Performance.

Performance Pack buyers also received uprated brakes. The ventilated discs increased from 312 x 25 mm to 340 x 30 mm, while the rear discs, which were 300 x 12 mm solid discs on the "standard" GTI, were changed to 310 x 22 mm ventilated discs.

The GTI and GTD both had a "progressive" version of the electro-mechanical power steering that varied the steering ratio so it became faster-acting, winding on lock the quicker you went around a bend and then releasing it more quickly. On a standard Golf the wheel took 2.75 turns lock-to-lock and on the GTI Performance this was reduced to 2.1 turns.

All the safety and driver convenience features of other Golfs were standard on the new GTI, and in the UK optional equipment included 19-inch Santiago alloy wheels, Vienna leather upholstery, keyless entry, High Beam Assist, Lane Assist, Park Assist (parking sensors were standard), a rearview camera, ACC Adaptive Chassis Control, touchscreen satellite navigation, and a Dynaudio sound pack with 10-channel amplifier and eight speakers.

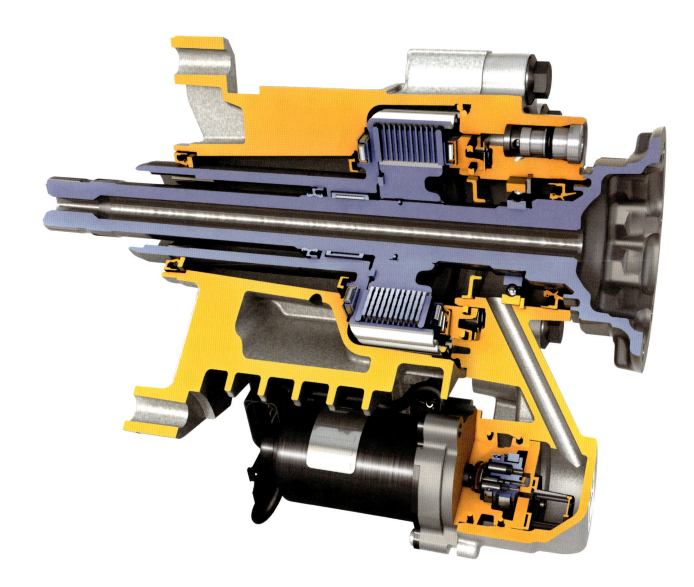

Britain's *Car* magazine scooped the first drive for the April 2013 issue and made it the cover star. Behind the wheel of a standard power pre-production model was European editor Georg Kacher. He concluded that once more Volkswagen had got it right and supplied a great drive and an emphatic all-rounder: "It is an everyday, any road, everyman car that makes its owner shine because it is so easy to drive, astonishingly quick, totally benign, and yet more rewarding than many extrovert crackerjacks."

In the UK, prices started at £25,845 on the road—£195 more than the previous model. The Performance Pack added £980, which was close to the price of the set of 19-inch alloys. The European order books opened in March 2013, and the GTI price premium was in play against the 250 PS Ford Focus ST (£21,995) but on a par with the 280 PS Opel/Vauxhall Astra GTC VXR (£27,010), Mercedes A250 AMG Sport (£27,105), BMW 125i M-Sport (£26,285), and Renault Mégane Renaultsport 265 Coupé (£26,455).

As for in-house rivals, that same year the Škoda Octavia vRS appeared with the 220 PS GTI engine, and in 2014, against the background of a growing motorsport presence for the brand, the Seat Leon Cupra 280 (the Leon another MQB car) was the fastest-ever Seat with 280 PS and more of a Golf R alternative.

The First Mexican-Built Golf GTI

In early 2013 VWoA announced that production of the new Golf would begin at Puebla the following year, and the model range was unveiled in late March at the New York Auto Show with basic detail. Hearkening back to the days of the Westmoreland-built Volkswagens, the need to localize content had become increasingly important to safeguard against currency fluctuations and to be closer to the market in which the manufacturer sold. Golf models, later to include an estate (Golf rather than Jetta Sportwagon) made at Volkswagen de México's plant, would be supplied to the North and South American markets.

Investments of more than $5 billion were planned in the US and Mexico over the following three years, key to these the opening of

---

OPPOSITE: The seat fabric was the same, but in UK the tartan center panels were Jakara and for the US Clark plaid. *(Volkswagen AG)*

ABOVE: The VAQ front limited-slip differential consisted of a hydraulic pump (below) that pumped fluid into the clutch pack (the fins in the center around the driveshaft). *(Volkswagen UK)*

new plants in Silao, Mexico, for the 1.8- and 2.0-liter turbocharged EA888 (Gen 3) TSI engines and a planned Audi production facility in San José Chiapa.

The Mk6 GTI Wolfsburg and Driver's Edition were offered to North American buyers during 2013 (chapter 6) while the new Golf would go on sale in 2014 as a 2015 model year range. The standard gas-engined North American Golfs would be powered by a 170 hp 1.8-liter direct injection turbocharged EA888 Gen 3, thus spelling the end of the 2.5-liter five-cylinder Golfs. Jettas and Beetle would also get the 1.8.

Compared with the Gen 2, engine weight had been reduced by eight pounds (3.6 kg), to 290 pounds (131 kg) overall thanks to a thin wall crankcase casting, exhaust headers integrated into the cylinder head, smaller-diameter main bearings, roller bearings for the twin balancer shafts, and a crankshaft with four counterweights instead of eight. The single-scroll turbocharger was jointly engineered by IHI and Volkswagen. The TDI Clean Diesel model used the new turbocharged, common-rail, direct-injection 150 hp four-cylinder EA288 engine.

The Puebla GTI would also use a locally built EA888 Gen 3. In February 2013 the Beetle Turbo and the Jetta GLI had already been announced as the first recipients of this Mexican-built engine.

For those cars peak power of 210 hp was generated 200 revs higher in the engine range than the Gen 2, at 5,300 rpm, and torque was unchanged at 207 lb ft. In contrast, the GTI was then billed to make "about" 210 hp and 258 lb ft of torque. Unlike European Golfs, all the North American cars had the XDS+ electronic differential lock and the new GTI's progressive steering. The TSI models had multi-link rear suspension and the TDI Clean Diesels torsion beam.

Back in Europe, the 2013 Geneva show had seen the first all-new Golf estate in six years. With the hatchback already boasting an increased trunk capacity and longer wheelbase, the estate's trunk volume expanded from 505 to 605 liters and loaded up to the front seat backrests 1,620 liters (versus the 1,495 liters of the Golf 6). It looked better, too, with the distinctive C-pillar close to the design of the hatchback model and similar rear light clusters.

The Fourth Golf R

At the October 2013 Frankfurt Motor Show the new Golf R was the new stablemate for the front-drive-only Mk6-based R Cabriolet (chapter 6). Mechanically, it was now much closer aligned to the Mk7 GTI, replacing the EA113-based four-cylinder with a development of the EA888 with 300 PS (more than some Porsches of the time) thanks to a modified cylinder head, exhaust valves, valve seats and springs, pistons, injection valves, and turbocharger.

Maximum power was produced between 5,500 and 6,200 rpm and peak torque of 280 lb ft from 1,800 to 5,500 rpm. Zero to 62 mph (100 kph) took a claimed 5.3 seconds (versus 5.7 seconds for the previous Golf R), or 4.9 seconds with the DSG gearbox. The top speed was electronically limited to 155 mph. And yet with lower emissions and fuel consumption, the new R was claimed to be 18 percent more efficient than its predecessor.

The new R's ride height was lowered by 20 mm compared with a regular Golf and 5 mm lower than the GTI, with reworked front and rear suspension. The four-wheel-drive was the fifth-generation Haldex system (in 2011, the Haldex Traction division was acquired by US powertrain specialist BorgWarner). Under low loads or when coasting, the rear axle was decoupled, helping to reduce fuel consumption. An electro-hydraulic pump was claimed to improve its engagement

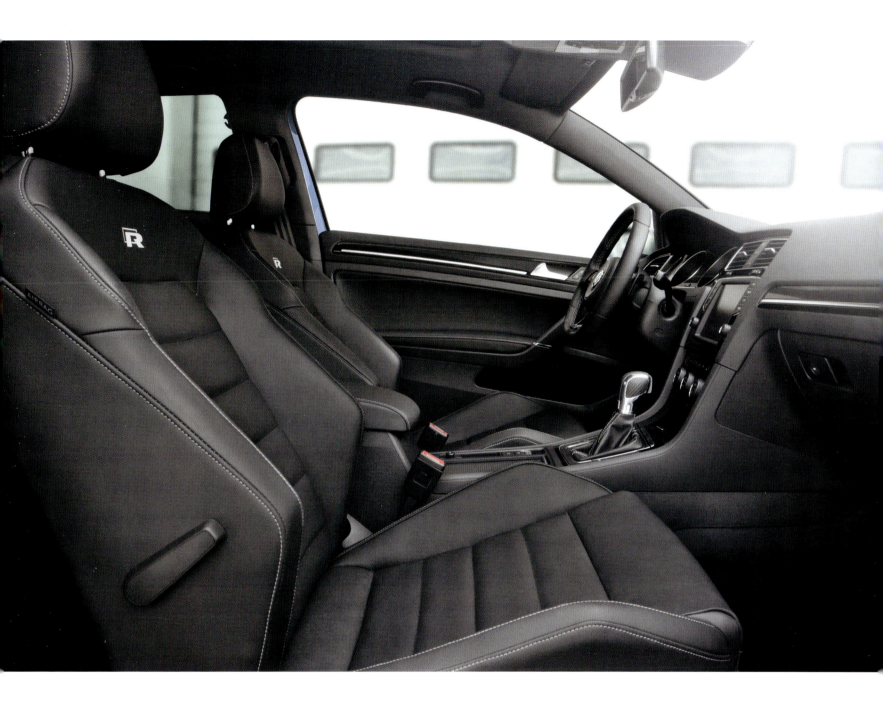

time. It also offered the Driver Profile Selection of other Golfs but with an extra setting, "Race," which attenuated throttle response and altered the shift pattern of the DSG gearbox and fully disengaged the electronic stability control. The engine sound was tuned to appeal to the driver and for the first time for Europeans enhanced by a sound synthesizer under the hood (the Soundaktor, which had appeared on the Jetta GLI and was little appreciated by the critics).

OPPOSITE: Lapiz Blue was the signature Golf R color, not available on the GTI, as well as the Cadiz alloy wheels. Compared with the GTI, there was a unique front bumper design with daytime running lights integrated into bi-xenon headlights. *(Volkswagen AG)*
ABOVE: The Golf R interior was as discreet as ever. In the center, the electronic parking brake button common to all European Mk7 Golfs increased console storage space. *(Volkswagen UK)*

The R was naturally top of the Golf range, from £29,900 for the three-door model with six-speed manual gearbox in the UK in 2014, and £31,315 for the three-door with six-speed DSG gearbox. The five-door versions added around £500. North American buyers would need to wait a further year for their Rs in four-door form only (five-door hatchback).

Jetta GLI Edition 30

In December 2013 a special edition of the Jetta GLI was announced for 2014 to celebrate the 30th anniversary of the first GLI. Through 2014 the Jetta would be sold only as the Edition 30, in two trim levels: the Edition 30 and the Edition 30 with Navigation. All 2014 Jettas had the multi-link rear suspension.

Compared with the regular 2014 (model year) Jetta, the GLI Edition 30 was distinguished externally by 18-inch Laguna alloy wheels, red trim on the front grille, a trunk lid-mounted spoiler, and Edition 30 badging inside and out.

THE WILD ONE-OFF GTIs

Since the spectacular mid-engined GTI W12-650 was the star of the 2007 Wörthersee GTI-fest, there was a little grumbling in the press that annual offerings of a bodykitted GTI concept were getting a bit dull. The 2013 Design Vision GTI was a return to the showstopping GTI.

It was a one-off no-holds-barred styling exercise by Golf designers Marc Lichte, Andreas Mindt, and Philipp Römers, reported to have cost €4 million (£3.4m) to build. There was a likeness to the seventh-generation GTI, but every styling element of its carbon-fiber body was pulled out and stretched to comic book proportions, notably the C-pillar, which appeared to be detached.

Highlighting how the MQB platform could be adjusted, it sat on the same wheelbase as the production GTI but was 15 mm shorter, 57 mm lower, and 71 mm wider with specially designed 20-inch wheels and suitably large 15-inch ceramic-disc brakes.

A 3.0-liter front-mounted V6 TSI with twin turbos sent drive to all four wheels via a 4Motion system, and the unit was reported to be destined for the next-generation Passat. Although its headline power output of 503 PS was less than the 2007 W12, a claimed 300 kph (186 mph) top speed with 0–62 mph (100 kph) in 3.9 seconds was quite respectable.

Like the W-16 650, the Design Vision GTI could be driven by selected press to an accompaniment of glorious noise—there was no need for any soundproofing as it was never let loose on a public road or even a racetrack. "The engine whoomps and bangs like a World Rally Car," wrote *Autocar*'s Matt Burt after a drive in Los Angeles (November 27, 2013). "Lifting off the accelerator prompts an equally pleasing array of chirrups from the turbos. It is impossible to drive without a broad grin across your face."

The interior was finished with Alcantara-trimmed plastic panels and the number of switches in front of driver and passenger reduced to an artistic minimum, while a large display to the right of the driver was said to be able to show the circuit the car was racing on and information about the times driven.

OPPOSITE: The only component that the 2013 Design Vision GTI shared with the real GTI was the windshield. It could only be driven around gentle curves because the wheels could not go onto full lock. *(Volkswagen UK)*

ABOVE: Reflecting the millions of euros spent on creating it, the Design Vision GTI's engine bay was fully finished. The new three-liter V6 was also featured in the CrossBlue Coupé SUV concept. *(Volkswagen UK)*

GTI ROADSTER CONCEPT 2014

Back in Austria again, May 2014 saw the GTI Roadster Concept leap from the virtual world of the Sony PlayStation 3 game, *Gran Turismo 6* (GT6). To celebrate the 15th anniversary of *Gran Turismo*, designers Malte Hammerbeck, Domen Rucigaj, and Guillermo Mignot came up with a winning design that was selected by Volkswagen design chief Klaus Bischoff and Kazunori Yamauchi of Sony Computer Entertainment.

Even more extreme than the Design Vision GTI, its 2,494 mm wheelbase was 137 mm shorter. A height of barely over a meter and almost double that in width (1,894 mm) helped create video game proportions. With the same 503 PS twin-turbo V6 but a relatively modest weight of 1,420 kg, it was claimed to be even faster than the Design Vision with 0–62 mph in 3.6 seconds, a top speed of 190 mph.

TOP: The 2014 GTI Roadster Concept was finished in a new color called Gran Turismo Red. Doors swiveled upward to open. If they wanted one, GT6 players could download their own. *(VWoA)*

ABOVE: The GTI Roadster Concept had its cockpit display mounted directly to the exposed steering column. It was four-wheel-drive like the 2013 car. *(Volkswagen AG)*

LEFT: The 2015 Golf GTE Sport was more of an electric/gas ideas lab than before. Painted in Pearlescent White Club, its two gullwing doors swung forward like the super-frugal XL1 hybrid. *(VWoA)*
BELOW: The Golf GTE Sport was said to preview the next-generation Volkswagen Golf hatchback. With hindsight it did show the shapes of the front and rear lights. *(VWoA)*

GOLF GTE SPORT 2015

Owing a lot in looks to the previous two concepts, the 2015 Wörthersee wild card was a GTE rather than a GTI and packed with motive complexity. However, it shared stand space with one you could buy, the GTI Clubsport (see page 180).

Once more largely made of carbon fiber, it was powered by a total of three motors for a plug-in hybrid drive with system power of 400 PS. A 299 PS 1.6-liter TSI adapted from the Polo R World Rally Car was fitted up front, assisted by two electric motors. The first 115 PS electric motor was within the housing of the six-speed DSG (like the production Golf GTE) and the second was at the rear with the same power but slightly lower torque. Whenever possible, the concept car was powered solely by electricity with an electric-only range of 50 km (31 miles). The total power output came to 400 PS.

The GTE Sport was capable of switching to four-wheel-drive with both electric motors in play, and since the energy for driving the rear axle flowed by wire not a spinning tube here, Volkswagen referred to it as an "electric propshaft" and, hinting at future use, pointed out that it had protected the German equivalent of the phrase under copyright law.

Able to move (silently) under its own power, the Golf GTE Sport appeared at the 2015 Frankfurt show and then November's LA Auto Show, but by that point Volkswagen was engulfed in the "dieselgate" scandal and the days of expensive concepts were over.

ABOVE: The 2015 model year Mk7 Golf range for North America was placed as a premium product at a value price, with initially no engine smaller than 1.8 liters. *(VWoA)*
OPPOSITE: The E-Golf was Volkswagen's first mass-produced EV, designed to ease buyers into the new fuel by looking very much like any other Golf aside from its c-shaped LED daytime running lights. *(Volkswagen AG)*

The Electric Golfs Begin

On January 14, 2014, the first Mexican-built Golf 7 came off the line at Puebla, a red GTI, at a ceremony marking the 50th anniversary of Volkswagen de México attended by industry and political leaders.

Next, the path to a future filled with electric Volkswagens began in February 2014 with the debut of first series production electric Golf, the e-Golf. The world had known it was coming for several years thanks to the 2011 public trials using modified Mk6 Golfs. But Volkswagen had first built experimental electric Golfs back in 1976.

The MQB structure of the Golf 7 allowed the e-Golf to have batteries under the rear seat where the fuel tank once was, running up the center of the floorpan to the electric motor and controls under the hood. The 85 kW/115 PS electric motor reached 100 kph (62 mph) in 10.4 seconds and the 24.2 kWh battery was claimed to give a potential range of 190 km (118 miles). Mass-market electric cars were only just getting going; in Europe the 2010 Nissan Leaf came first, then the Renault Zoe in 2012, and BMW i3 in 2013. The e-Golf was to be the first electric Volkswagen sold in North America, from late 2014.

Like all electric cars the e-Golf could sprint away from a standing start (as electric motors can instantly deliver all their torque), but sustained speed killed the range and the e-Golf had no sporting pretensions. However, when Volkswagen launched its first Golf plug-in hybrid at Geneva in March 2014, that car most definitely had a sporty flavor: the Golf GTE (see page 182).

The One-Off Golf R400

Was a 400 PS Golf R in prospect? The April 2014 Auto China show in Beijing brought the wild Golf R400 Concept, the 400 for 400 PS (or 395 bhp).

Developed by Volkswagen R GmbH, the arm responsible for high-power and customization projects, the Golf R400 used a modified version of the Golf R's engine with a newly developed turbocharger with a higher maximum charge pressure and reinforced crankcase. The mighty performance claims were 0–62 mph (100 kph) in just 3.9 seconds, a second faster than the 300 PS R, and a top speed governed at 174 mph.

At 1,420 kg, the Golf R400 weighed the same as the standard Golf R but had flared wheel arches reminiscent of those on the 1988 Rallye Golf G60. Filling those arches were 19-inch alloy wheels on an increased offset. The wheels were a development of the Golf R's standard "Cadiz" wheels, with high-gloss back inserts acting as air vanes helping to cool the reinforced braking system. At the front, the bumper was redesigned to take into account the greater cooling requirements of the R400. A carbon-fiber splitter and aerodynamic "wing element" helped to push air toward the honeycomb mesh of the grille.

The redesigned rear bumper included vents on each side, and the Golf R's four tailpipes were replaced with two centrally mounted

items. Showgoers peering inside would see motorsport shell seats with integrated head restraints and belt openings. These were upholstered in cross-quilted panels covered in Alcantara, and "carbon leather," as were the two individual rear seats.

The R400 was said to only be a concept to showcase Volkswagen R's talents rather than a production car, but based on past Golf concepts it was logical for *Autocar* to speculate that such a beast would cost £38,000 and rival the Mercedes A45 AMG. In July the magazine reported that VW had confirmed it had gone into initial development and an appearance at the November 2014 LA show only reinforced the sense that it was a runner.

OPPOSITE: Shown at Auto China 2014 in Beijing (the Chinese market was then booming for VW), the R400 was the hottest Mk7 Golf never built. The body was 20 mm wider on each side. The "R" badge on the gloss black radiator grille sat on a Lemon Yellow background. *(Imaginechina Limited/Alamy Stock Photo)*

ABOVE: New sill extensions on the R400 Concept bridged the gap between the widened arches. Unlike the regular Golf R, there were two instead of four exhaust pipes, centrally mounted. It was a runner, shown worldwide. *(Imaginechina Limited/Alamy Stock Photo)*

Three-Tier GTIs— The 2014 North American Launch

The ready-to-order 2015 model year GTI was announced in all its detail in May 2014. And in a small but significant move it was a Volkswagen Golf GTI, no longer a Volkswagen GTI, part of the Golf family as it was in Europe. It was part of a move to make the North American Golf family a distinct offering in addition to the Jetta, which positioned the cars as more of a premium model. The first customer received his car at the end of the month—one of the reasons behind Puebla production was so North American GTI buyers wouldn't wait long.

The US Golf GTI's competitors were the Ford Focus ST, Honda Civic Si, and Subaru WRX. There was a three-tier model lineup of Golf GTI S, SE, and Autobahn. The S began at $24,395 for the manual three-door hatch with the usual option to add doors and a DSG gearbox. The SE's main extra goodies were a power tilt and slide sunroof, keyless access with push-button start, a rearview camera, automatic headlights, rain-sensing windshield wipers, a Fender Premium Audio System, and leather seats. The five-door-only Autobahn started at $29,595 and added a navigation system, 12-way power driver's seat, and Climatronic automatic air-conditioning. Compared with the European GTI, some standard features such as the Forward Collision Warning system and front and rear Park Distance Control were optional according to trim ($695 Driver Assistance Package).

The engine specification was as previously billed: the 2.0-liter EA888 Gen 3 did develop 210 hp and a healthy 258 lb ft of torque. The optional $1,495 Performance Package, due later in the model year, would bring 220 hp, plus, as Europe, the VAQ limited-slip differential and larger brakes.

The US motoring press reaction was an emphatic thumbs-up for this first MQB GTI. "From the moment you open the door of the new, seventh-generation Volkswagen GTI, there's an overwhelming sense of quality and precision," wrote Jared Gill of *Car and Driver*. The test car was fitted with the Performance Package: "A 0-to-60-mph time of 5.8 seconds won't shock your passengers in the way that makes for good YouTube videos, but that just means you get to wring out the turbo four longer before drawing undue attention."

Finding it hard to pick any faults apart from the pedals being spaced too far apart, he concluded that even the much-liked Ford Focus lacked the "space and liveable civility of the GTI." Optioned up, the tested five-door manual Golf GTI was $28,305. "That's getting pricey, but this rare level of excellence is worth it. The GTI doesn't just feel better than its predecessor; it feels better than almost any other car on the road today."

OPPOSITE: Orange side reflectors within the headlight unit featured on the North American Golfs and the GTI, which were all a little longer thanks to their bumper design. *(VWoA)*

BELOW: A chrome-finished manual handbrake lever further distinguished a North American Mk7 GTI from its European relations. It still had space for two large cupholders next to it. *(VWoA)*

BOTTOM: The first-ever Golf R estate was an appealing package. Its closest rival was the Seat Leon ST Cupra 300 estate. *(Volkswagen AG)*

The First Golf R Wagon

If you wanted to move a bookcase/surfboard/lawnmower superfast, then the November 2014 Los Angeles Auto Show brought the debut of the first-ever Golf R Variant (or estate/station wagon). It had the same 300 PS engine and four-wheel-drive as the hatchback, a DSG-only transmission, a lot of extra cargo space yet only a little more weight (79 kg). Claimed performance was little different to the DSG hatchback R at 5.1 seconds to 62 mph compared with 4.9. Why not a GTI estate, one might ask? Those in Wolfsburg were reported to favor the R brand because it had more flexibility. With it on sale in Europe in 2015, US buyers missed out, despite the LA launch. It seems this was one wagon too many against the relentless rise of the SUV. However, North America did get its own version of the regular Golf estate, as the Golf Sportwagen, when Puebla production began in early 2015, joined a year later by the Golf Alltrack, a 1.8-liter four-wheel-drive Sportwagen with 20 mm higher ground clearance, pronounced wheel arch moldings, and flared side sills.

Summer 2015 saw engine downsizing as the 1.4-liter EA211 four-cylinder turbocharged and direct-injection TSI was introduced into the Jetta range, replacing the previous naturally aspirated 2.0-liter in the S model and the 1.8T TSI engine in the SE. The 150 hp 1.4 was claimed to bring a respective 13 percent and 7 percent economy improvement over the former engines. The Jetta GLI, of course, kept its 210 hp EA888. For the 2016 model year it had a front and rear bumper redesign.

The Golf GTI Clubsport/ Clubsport Edition 40

As the Golf GTI headed toward its 40th anniversary in 2016, European hot hatch buyers had an increasing choice of track day versions—cars you might take to the supermarket then on the weekend to a track day, where, for a fee, a twisty circuit could be anybody's playground for an hour or two (or until you needed new tires). These versions were a little faster, a lot stiffer, and had sometimes shed some weight by losing the rear seats.

The GTI and Golf R's direct track day competition were cars like the latest Honda Civic Type R GT (310 PS/306 bhp) and the Renault Mégane RS 275 Trophy (275 PS/271 bhp), both still front-wheel-drive yet commanding Golf R money. Furthermore, there was some competition from within the Volkswagen family—as was often pointed out by the journalists—in the shape of the entry-level Seat Leon Cupra 265 (for 265 PS), for around €2,500 less. *Auto Motor und Sport* reckoned that if you looked through the group brands from Audi to VW, there were then eight sports models with a 2.0-liter turbo and Golf architecture in the range offering between 200 and 300 PS.

Unveiled as a concept at Wörthersee 2015, then in production form at September's Frankfurt show, the Golf GTI Clubsport was both the most powerful factory-built GTI to date and a special edition ahead of the anniversary, with a promise of an even faster S version to come (although neither was bound for North America).

It was easy to tell a Clubsport from a regular GTI, with its new front bumper, two-piece rear spoiler design for extra downforce, rear diffuser, and new side sills. A black side stripe reading "Clubsport" paid homage to the 1976 Golf GTI's stripes.

For the GTI Clubsport the output was set at 265 PS like the Seat, which positioned it between the standard GTI (230 PS with the Performance Pack) and the 300 PS Golf R. However, it had a party trick in the shape of an overboost function, achieved by raising the turbocharger boost pressure 10 percent to a maximum 1.2 bar, whereby mashing the accelerator to the floor in squirts of about ten seconds the driver could boost engine power to "over 290 PS" (equaling the Seat Leon Cupra 290).

It was offered with either a six-speed manual gearbox or a six-speed DSG. The performance claims were 0 to 100 kph (62 mph) in 6.0 seconds with a six-speed manual gearbox, 5.9 seconds with the DSG. The latter was also equipped with launch control as standard to get away in a controlled manner from standstill using its maximum overboost power.

It had a unique suspension setup, with stiffer springs, dampers, and bump stops than the GTI, and on the first press drives on the Portimao race circuit in Portugal late in 2015, more agile handling was noted, also thanks to the newly available option of Michelin Pilot S Sport Cup 2 tires.

When the GTI Clubsport order book opened in spring 2016, it had been re-christened the Clubsport Edition 40, complete with the usual Edition badges. It only went on UK sale during the latter half of 2016 after the Clubsport S allocation had sold out (see further on) limited to 1,000 cars. At £32,350, the DSG-equipped three-door added just under £3,500 to the price of an equivalent "standard" GTI. UK reviews of the temporary overboost were mixed, but *Auto Express* thought it fun, adding, "Although VW won't tell you this, concealing that 25 bhp in a quick spurt overboost mode is a deliberate ploy to ensure that the Clubsport doesn't quite tread on the toes of the 296 bhp, but heavier, Golf R."

The D-Word

As is well documented elsewhere, in September 2015 Volkswagen's relentless progress toward being the world's number one carmaker was brought to a shuddering halt by what may prove to be the worst crisis in its history. Most call it the diesel emissions scandal, or, invoking US President Nixon's fall following the Watergate tape scandal, "dieselgate."

Volkswagen was found by US regulators to have been cheating tests to certify the emissions and fuel consumption of diesel-engined cars in the early 2000s. To make them pass laboratory tests, the TDI Clean Diesels were found to have been fitted with a software change known as a "defeat device" that installed software in the model years 2009 to 2015 2.0-liter diesel cars to circumvent EPA emissions standards.

Eight Volkswagen and Audi models with the affected EA189 diesel engines, including the Golf, Jetta, Beetle, and Audi A3, were recalled, then other models with the 3.0-liter TDI. The European 2012 Golf 7 had been launched with new EA288 diesel engines, meeting the Euro 5 standard and fitted with an NOx storage catalytic converter and diesel particulate filter. In the run-up to the crisis, North American Golfs, Beetles, Passats, and Jettas had been offered with the 2.0-liter EA288 diesel for the 2015 model year.

In the fallout, there were major changes in Volkswagen senior management, massive criminal and civil penalties, and long-running lawsuits. North American Volkswagen diesel sales were halted in 2016, never to restart. It changed the way that consumers thought about all diesel cars and changed the direction of the mighty carmaker.

Electric cars would be the new trademark of Volkswagen. North American sales would get another push: first, stepping up introductions of large SUVs and cars, then a new range of electric vehicles. September 2016's Paris Motor Show saw the debut of the Volkswagen ID electric concept car, to be launched in 2019 as the ID.3 and the first of an extensive line.

Volkswagen AG embarked on a massive cost-cutting program and began to axe low-volume models. A new Scirocco was dropped, as was the Golf Cabriolet and the three-door Audi A3—reflecting a trend to axe three-door cars. A four-door Golf with a sloping roofline like the Passat CC never appeared, and the Golf R400 remained a one-off show car.

OPPOSITE: The 2016 GTI Clubsport Edition 40 was marked out by front strakes and extra air ducts to cool the brakes and reduce drag around the front wheels. The redesigned roof spoiler was much larger than the regular GTI. *(Volkswagen UK)*
LEFT: GTI Clubsport Edition 40 seats were folding racing bucket instead of sport seats partially covered with Alcantara. Edition 40 badging was also on the door sills. *(Volkswagen UK)*

THE GOLF GTE

In 2012, decades after its first experiments with VW Transporters and diesel Golfs, Volkswagen's first series production hybrid car became the North America–only gas/electric Jetta hybrid, a range-topper above the Jetta GLI to compete with the likes of the Toyota Prius, Honda Civic hybrid, and range-extending electric Chevrolet Volt.

A full hybrid has an internal combustion engine and an electric motor powered by a small battery. The power sources can move the vehicle independently or both can work together, but the small battery means that the car can only cover short distances (about one to ten miles) on pure electric and will usually be seamlessly swapping between gas and electric for low overall fuel consumption.

The Jetta had a 1.4-liter 150 PS TSI gas engine and seven-speed DSG automatic coupled to a 20 kW electric motor. Under pure electric power it could be over a typically modest distance of 2 km (1.3 miles), depending on conditions.

Two years later, the first Europe-only hybrid Golf was a plug-in hybrid version, to complement the all-electric e-Golf. A plug-in hybrid vehicle (PHEV) has a bigger battery than a hybrid's (not as big as full electric). If the driver switches to electric-only mode, range is normally around 25 to 50 miles. They can choose to plug in at home or at a public charger or let the engine do the charging. Plug-ins were seen as a halfway house to full electric without the worry of a fully discharged battery.

The Golf GTE 1.4 TSI had a 150 PS 1.4-liter TSI gas engine coupled to an electric motor within the gearbox rated at 75 kW/102 PS. Drive was channeled to the front wheels through a six-speed DSG gearbox designed for hybrid drive. When energy ran low, the engine management system engaged the engine and used the electric motor as an alternator to generate some energy for the battery.

Compared with a gas Golf, the GTE's fuel tank was relocated beneath the trunk floor to make way for the lithium-ion battery. There was, however, a weight penalty. The battery weighed 120 kg, giving the GTE an unladen weight of 1,599 kg—300 kg heavier than a GTI.

When used together, a combined maximum power of 204 PS was quoted, a near-GTI figure, with a claimed 0–100 kph (62 mph) figure of 7.6 seconds. To go fully electric, you pressed an "e-mode" button. Unlike the Jetta hybrid, the GTE was claimed to be good for 31 miles depending on conditions. If you wanted all of the performance, you pressed the "GTE" button. Based on the then current European test procedure, a provisional combined fuel consumption figure of 188 mpg (using a great deal of electric power) was quoted, but press tests of pre-production cars in December 2013 saw 70 mpg displayed.

On sale in the UK from early 2015, the Golf GTE was dressed up like an eco-GTI (blue was Volkswagen's highlight color for super-economy models). Inside and out, the GTE featured blue highlights where the GTI had red, including stitching on the steering wheel, gear lever gaiter, and seats, and a blue stripe in the tartan pattern on the sports seats. As on the GTI, there was no Golf badging.

This, and the potential total power, set up a sporty expectation that was partially satisfied, mused Michael von Maydell in Germany's *Auto Motor und Sport* (October 2014). "With the VW Golf GTE, Volkswagen is indeed managing the balancing act between a practical electric car and a sporty compact car. Nevertheless, it is likely to remain a rare show object. All those who want to have driving fun above all else continue to reach for the more agile and cheaper GTI." The price was the biggest snag—€39,600 compared with €31,500 for a five-door DSG GTI.

By 2017 and the introduction of the facelifted Golf "7.5" range (see page 187) there were more hybrids and plug-in hybrids on the European market. Still five-door only, the 2017 Golf GTE also received all the cosmetic exterior and interior upgrades of the rest of the 7.5 range. The complex powertrain was left alone, but Volkswagen UK reduced the price by £3,420 compared with the previous model. The starting price was now £28,135 after the Government Plug-in Car Grant.

The appeal of the upgrades, new price, and a concerted advertising push was reflected in perkier sales, and in October 2017 Volkswagen UK reported that GTE orders were up by more than 300 percent compared with September 2016, and 2017 sales had already beaten 3,000. At the start of 2018 Volkswagen UK paused new orders to deal with a reported production backlog due to unprecedented demand. By November 2019, the Golf 8 having been announced the previous month with a GTE version set for 2020, total Golf 7 GTE production had reached 51,000. In Germany there was a 200-unit Golf GTE Edition loaded with extras.

OPPOSITE: An e-Golf was only charged behind the rear filler flap while the GTE (here) added a front charging port. Five-door only, it had the daytime running lights of the e-Golf and aerodynamic horizontal fins like those on the GTI. *(Volkswagen UK)*

BELOW: As the GTE's battery sat beneath the rear seats, the fuel tank moved to below the trunk floor and was smaller as a result—but needing less fossil fuel was the whole point of the GTE. *(Volkswagen AG)*

Golf GTI Clubsport S 2016

The Golf GTI Clubsport S was eagerly awaited, very rare, and also a timely reminder of the power of the GTI badge when Volkswagen's reputation was being battered by the diesel emissions scandal. May 2016's Wörthersee GTI gathering saw the premiere, limited to only 400 examples worldwide (including 100 for Germany but 150 for the UK, the GTI's second-biggest market). Tuned for 310 PS, it outpowered the Golf R.

With the Clubsport S developed over a year, the team headed by chassis development chief Karsten Schebdstat drew on their experience with the 330 PS racing Golf GTI TCR (see page 196). The power boost came by a modified engine management unit and a new exhaust system, with a diameter ahead of the exhaust tailpipes of 65 instead of 55 mm, reducing the exhaust back pressure and producing a deliberate "backfire" when braking. It also had a new fuel pump with increased throughput. Performance was quoted as 0–100 kph (62 mph) in 5.8 seconds and an unlimited top speed of 265 kph (165 mph).

There was a weight-reduction program similar to that of the contemporary and similarly exclusive Renault Mégane RS 275 Trophy-R, a car, like the Clubsport S, designed to lap the Nürburgring Nordschleife circuit in record time (7 minutes 54.36 seconds in 2014). In the 2010s, how fast a car would go around the tortuous twisty German forest track was a marketing prize every hot hatchback wanted to grab. The record was always swapping hands—only one month before the Renault, the Seat Leon Cupra 280 had claimed the 2014 record for a front-drive hatch, and the pre-production Honda Civic Type R took the record in 2015.

The Clubsport S was a three-door two-seat only—gone were the rear seats, insulating material, luggage compartment floor, parcel shelf, and floor mats. There was a smaller battery and manual transmission only. There was also an aluminum subframe for the front axle and aluminum brake covers. Total weight reduction was stated at 30 kg for a fully unladen weight of 1,285 kg. There was no air-conditioning, but it was a no-cost option. Unlike the Renault Mégane RS 275, there was no option to have a roll cage or racing harnesses fitted.

ABOVE: Benjamin Leuchter laps at Nürburgring in spring 2016 in a GTI Clubsport S. He said the key to a good lap time was to use the curbs as much as possible. *(Volkswagen UK)*

OPPOSITE TOP: "Benny" Leuchter, then 29, leans on the production Clubsport S launched at Wörthersee in May 2016. His Nürburgring lap record adorns the side of the car. *(Volkswagen UK)*

OPPOSITE BOTTOM: Doing away with the rear seats, including the central armrest, gave the most noticeable weight savings in a Clubsport S, but the rear cupholders remained. *(Volkswagen UK)*

CHAPTER 7. GOLF GTI MK7 2012–2019 185

Externally, the aero package was unchanged, but markers were the larger twin exhaust, S badging, and larger 19-inch wheels with the semi-slick Michelin Pilot Sport Cup 2 tires as standard. Front and rear axles were re-tuned compared with the Clubsport, with changes to the geometry. Paint colors reflected those of the original GTI: Tornado Red, Pure White, and Deep Black Pearl Effect, and the roof of the red or white cars was painted black.

The Clubsport S arrived at Wörthersee 2016 with a record in its pocket. On the evening of April 20, Volkswagen Golf TCR racing driver and instructor Benjamin Leuchter and the Clubsport S had broken the lap record for front-wheel-drive production cars on the 13-mile Nürburgring Nordschleife, with a time of 07:49:21 and at times topping 157 mph. For comparison, a Golf GTI Performance Pack had lapped the Nürburgring at 8 minutes and 26 seconds.

Even if they would never visit the track, each driver of a Clubsport S could select a Nürburgring driving profile setting that tuned the adaptive chassis control (DCC), engine, steering, and sound to suit the circuit. Even at £33,995, by the start of August all 150 examples of Golf GTI Clubsport S allocated to the UK had been sold on release.

"The Clubsport S makes for a fitting 40th birthday present to GTI aficionados," wrote *Autocar* in its test conclusion (August 24, 2016).

"It does this by not only being plainly faster and fitter than the basic Clubsport but also by exalting the badge's traditional virtues even as it gently revises them."

Clubsport Not Fast Enough?

Power boosts for GTIs and Golf Rs were well established, but the Clubsport and Clubsport S triggered more German tuning conversions that sometimes went well over 450 PS.

In 2016, ABT, which had tuned seven generations of GTIs, added a second engine management unit to the Clubsport that would wind it up to 340 PS—even higher than the S. A 0–62 mph (100 kph) time of 5.6 seconds was claimed. To control this power, ABT added re-developed sports suspension and six-piston front brake calipers for the 370 mm diameter brake discs. The €2,500 upgrade also added a new front spoiler and grille, rear spoiler and side skirts, with a choice of 18- to 20-inch wheels.

OPPOSITE: Still based on the Mk6 GTI, for 2016 the Jetta 2016 GLI had bumpers designed to incorporate the fins of the Mk7 GTI. *(VWoA)*
LEFT: The 2017 GTI Mk7.5 facelift was subtle, only bringing a red surround to each of the headlights.
(Volkswagen UK)

BELOW: The GTI 7.5's instrument panel was fully digital and could be configured as the driver wished. The infotainment display almost filled the width of the console. *(Volkswagen UK)*

For a more modest €549, Speedbuster would add an extra tuning chip that boosted the power of a Clubsport by 61 PS, retained the temporary overboost, and was claimed to improve fuel consumption.

In 2017, O.C.T. Tuning offered to delve into the engine control software to increase the output of the Clubsport S from 310 to 370 PS and also reprogram the DSG for faster shift times. It offered an additional oil cooler that lowered the oil temperature by up to 20°C.

Also in 2017, for €12,950 B&B would boost a Clubsport or Clubsport S up to 480 PS with a larger turbocharger, high-pressure gas pump, high-performance intercooler, racing exhaust system with sports catalytic converter, and reworked air induction paths. Boost pressure was increased and the injection and DSG transmission remapped. An additional oil cooler was also installed.

Golf GTI Mk7.5 2017

The Golf Mk7 was designed for a long career, and at the midway mark it was time for an upgrade. The mechanical parts were still top-notch, but it needed an interior technology refresh.

Car center consoles were increasingly resembling multimedia tablets. While the Golf 7 had been groundbreaking with its touch-sensitive dashboard media system and adaptive cruise control, all the new rivals were crammed with similar technology. When full details of the updated Golf 7 (soon called the 7.5) were presented in November 2016, the major change was inside. On the higher-level trims the screen for the Discover Navigation Pro system grew from 8 inches to 9.2 inches and filled the space in the center console with a flat glass screen. All other Golfs had either a 6.5- (formerly 5) or 8-inch screen.

The Discover Pro screen could be operated via gesture control where the motion of your hand would be enough to swipe between menus without touching the screen. This was a first for the Golf class. There was voice activation, and keeping up with its rivals, your mobile phone screen could be mirrored on the car's center screen by an app such as Apple CarPlay. Wireless charging of your mobile was also an option by placing it on a pad in the center console. A digital display could replace the analogue driver's instruments, where the speedometer and rev counter could be altered to show different information within the dials and in between them, such as a navigation view.

The safety and assistance systems were a little smarter (adaptive cruise control went between standstill and 125 mph). Emergency As-

ABOVE: The 2018 GTI TCR borrowed elements of the Clubsport and Clubsport S. In addition to red and white, black and pure gray were new. The honeycomb decal could be deleted at no cost. *(Volkswagen UK)*

6.2 seconds (6.4 previously) in the six-speed manual as well as the newly developed seven-speed DSG automatic. The DQ381 had a pair of "wet" clutches that ran in oil, so it was considered more durable than the "dry" six-speed.

The Golf R was also facelifted and upgraded in 2017. It gained an extra 10 PS to arrive at 310 PS, keeping it at the top of the Golf performance league, above the GTI Performance and the Clubsport S. However, from mid-2017 the Volkswagen Group rolled out particulate filters to the exhaust systems of all its gas engine models. Similar to those already fitted to diesels, the company claimed emissions of fine soot particles would be reduced by up to 90 percent. Sometimes there was a slight power trade-off, so the R returned to 300 PS for 2018. The North American 2017 model year R stayed with 292 hp.

Later in 2017 both the European hatchback and estate Golf Rs became available with a factory fitted Performance Pack option consisting of an "R-Performance" brake system, a de-restricted top speed, and 19-inch Spielberg alloy wheels (over the standard 18-inch Cadiz). The hatchback version also received a rear roof spoiler claimed to add 20 kg of downforce.

The brakes had silver-painted calipers, and having aluminum brake pots (which house the pistons) saved 2 kg and the material was more durable for track use. And if you did run your de-restricted R on a track, the claimed maximum speeds were 166 mph for the hatch and 168 mph for the estate.

Instead of (or on top of) the Performance Pack, buyers could choose to spend a heady £2,975 just on a titanium exhaust system—a metal of low density and high strength—made by Slovenian exhaust specialist Akrapovič. The tailpipes were round, rather than oval, and Volkswagen said it produced an "incomparable" sound at high revs and when shifting gear.

2017—The Short-Lived GTI Sport

While North American Golfs waited for their Mk 7.5 facelift, VWoA popped in a new trim level to go between the Golf GTI S and the GTI Autobahn called the Sport. It had the Performance Package as standard (no longer an option on the S) consisting of brakes from the Golf R, the limited-slip VAQ differential, and a ten-horsepower increase to 220 (which demanded premium fuel) as well as 18-inch Nogaro alloy wheels and bi-xenon headlamps with LED daytime running lights. The Sport also had unique floor mats, KESSY keyless access with push-button start, and black mirror caps. Joey Capparella of *Car and Driver* (March 2017) reckoned that the GTI Sport, "Just may be the ideal version of this ideal car. It bundles the GTI's most desirable optional content into one handy trim level that starts at $28,815."

The facelifted North American Golfs, with the standard LED daytime running lights, LED taillights, and new bumpers, were announced in April 2017 as 2018 model year cars on sale that fall. The GTI range was pared back to S, SE, and Autobahn, all with the 220 hp engine with six-speed DSG or manual gearboxes. SE buyers got the essential GTI goodies, such as a red stripe outlining new LED running lights and Clark Plaid cloth seat surfaces. The range-topping Autobahn included the new eight-inch touchscreen for the Discover Media navigation system and DCC suspension control. As before it came with a power tilt and slide sunroof, leather seating surfaces, and Fender premium audio system.

sist was capable of noticing if the driver was incapacitated, initiating various measures to rouse them or getting to the point where the car carried out its own emergency stop.

There were no sheet metal changes for Golf 7.5, but it had new front and rear bumper designs (the latter with fake exhaust outlets). The tailgate featured LED (light-emitting diode) lights, and the new headlight design contained LED daytime running lights and a chrome-effect strip that extended across the grille.

The European Golf GTI had a small power hike from 220 to 230 PS, and so there was an extra 15 PS for the Performance Pack GTI to 245 PS. This resulted in a torque increase to 273 lb ft (over 148) from a broad band from 1,600 to 4,300 rpm. Zero to sixty was a claimed

2018—The MQB Jetta

In Europe, sales of the 2010-era (PQ54) Jetta had completely fizzled out. *Autocar* reported in November 2017 that after sales of just 379 between January and October, Volkswagen UK and Germany no longer listed it for sale. Over 52,0000 Golf hatchbacks had reached UK buyers in the meantime, and the Passat made decent numbers. This lack of Jetta enthusiasm (and the rise of the SUV) was also felt to a less dramatic effect in North America, so an all-new MQB-derived Jetta was big news at the January 2018 Detroit show—billed as a global debut even though there were no plans for a European version.

A 2019 model year car arriving in dealers mid-2018, the new MQB Jetta expanded in all directions, including the wheelbase, up from 105.7 inches (2,685 mm) compared with 104.4 inches (2,651 mm) and the Golf's 2,637 mm. The dashboard owed nothing to the Golf and on most versions had a digital cockpit.

The GLI was a year way, so the 147 hp 1.4-liter turbo was carried over with a new optional eight-speed automatic (not offered on the Golf) in S, SE, a new R-Line, SEL, and SEL Premium trims. As a lower-powered MQB car it ran on the torsion beam rear suspension.

Generally cheaper, bigger, and better equipped, to finally persuade buyers the new Jetta had a warranty European owners could only dream of called the "Every People First Warranty," claimed to be America's best with coverage for six years or 72,000 miles.

The GTI TCR Road Car—2018–19

With the Clubsport GTIs long sold out, in May 2018 a Golf GTI TCR Concept was unveiled at Wörthersee and production started in Wolfsburg at the end of 2018.

This was a hard-core run-out special edition for the seventh Golf GTI. The headline figures were a full-time (rather than on-demand) 290 PS and—optionally—a claimed unrestricted 164 mph (264 kph) top speed thanks to uprated engine management. As with the Golf R there were two extra radiators to ensure sufficient cooling for the engine. A gas particulate filter was fitted.

Unlike the Clubsport Edition 40, the GTI TCR came only as an automatic, this time with the seven-speed DSG introduced on the Golf 7.5 with paddle shifts plus the electronically controlled front-axle locking differential—as fitted to the GTI Performance. Also like that car, it sat 20 mm lower than a standard Golf. The standard 18-inch Belvedere/Quaranta wheels concealed an uprated braking system with the composite brake discs and 17-inch calipers of the Clubsport S.

Two option packs removed the top speed restriction. The first pack brought 19-inch Reifnitz wheels, revised springs, and dampers sitting 5 mm lower, and Dynamic Chassis Control with electrically adjustable shock absorbers in Comfort, Normal, and Sport modes. The second included Pretoria 19-inch rims with the racetrack-ready Michelin Pilot Sport Cup 2 tires of the Clubsport S.

LEFT: The TCR's front sport seats had a new microfiber/fabric design, seatbelts with red edging, plus an exclusive sports steering wheel. *(Volkswagen UK)*

The TCR's distinctive looks came from a newly designed front bumper with a splitter (front spoiler) and black lower sill panels coupled to a new rear diffuser. The doors carried TCR lettering and could be customized with an additional decoration in GTI honeycomb style.

The GTI TCR was available to order in the UK in early 2019, where prices started at £34,135—into four-wheel-drive Golf R territory. The regular GTI was discontinued in favor of the 245 PS GTI Performance. British car magazines found the TCR likable but wondered if it was that much of a step up over a GTI Performance, and the Honda Civic Type R was a favorite and cheaper rival.

Rabbit Returns

The autumn 2018 changes for the 2019 model year North American GTI gave all models 228 horsepower standard (achieved with premium fuel), an 8 hp increase from previous years, plus Golf R brakes and the VAQ differential. These would soon be seen on the new Jetta GLI.

The Rabbit Edition briefly revived an old name for a limited production run of Golf GTIs. Fitting in between the base GTI S and mid-level SXE, the Rabbit had 18-inch gloss black alloys, a black rear spoiler, LED headlights with the Adaptive Front-lighting System (AFS), black mirror caps, Rabbit-badged seat tags, red-stitched floor mats, keyless access with push-button start, Front Assist, Blind Spot Monitor, and Rear Traffic Alert.

The 2019 Volkswagen Jetta GLI

On sale in February 2019, the all-new Jetta GLI was hailed as the return of a long-lost friend by enthusiasts, a reasonably priced performance sedan where reasonably priced performance sedans were becoming hard to find with a manual transmission. For the price, the closet rivals were the Honda Civic Si, Subaru Impreza WRX, and Hyundai Elantra Sport.

The new GLI could be recognized by LED projector headlights with LED daytime running lights aside a black honeycomb grille with a red accent line and Golf R brakes (13.4-inch vented front discs). Riding with the multi-link rear suspension of the GTI, it sat just over half an inch lower than a regular Jetta. A 35th anniversary model out at the same time had unique black wheels with a red stripe, a black roof, black mirror caps, black tail spoiler, and 35th anniversary badging inside and out.

Starting at $26,890, or $1,600 less than the Golf GTI, it majored on value and space (largely in the trunk), even if the testers thought the interior plastics not as good as the Golf's and disliked the standard instrument panel. But it had exactly the same 228 hp engine as the GTI (81 more horses than the standard Jetta) and in sport mode a sporty sound was once more piped in.

A six-speed manual transmission was standard, with the seven-speed DSG optional. Like the GTI, the GLI was fitted with the VAQ

LEFT: The 2018 GTI Rabbit Edition was for North America only and came in Cornflower Blue, Urano Gray, Pure White, or Deep Black Pearl. *(VWoA)*
ABOVE: The all-new 2019 Jetta GLI had unique front and rear bumpers compared with other Jettas, 18-inch alloy wheels, and a black honeycomb grille. *(VWoA)*

LEFT: The Jetta had evolved far from being a "Golf with a trunk" to have a fastback rear window style more akin to the Passat CC. Rear spoiler and dual chrome exhausts were GLI markers. *(VWoA)*

OPPOSITE TOP: There were no Clark plaid seat inlays on any of the 2019 Jetta GLI variants. Unlike the North American Golfs, it had an electronic parking brake. *(VWoA)*

OPPOSITE BOTTOM: The 2019 ID.3 was the first mass-produced Volkswagen designed as a pure electric car. The company said the 3 was for the start of a third era after the Beetle and the Golf. *(Volkswagen UK)*

limited-slip differential. The 35th anniversary model added the DCC adaptive damping system. "There's more car to love here than in the GTI," said *Car and Driver* editor Tony Quiroga. "And for those who buy by the inch, the Jetta GLI will be an easy choice."

As an aside, in 2019 Volkswagen launched a range of cars in China under a new JETTA brand name rather than Volkswagen, aimed at budget drivers. There was a restyled Volkswagen Jetta sedan and a couple of Seat-based SUVs. These sold alongside a long-wheelbase version of the Volkswagen Jetta, the latest Sagitar (by 2024, Volkswagen had 39 plants in China).

Sights on the Golf 8

During 2019 stories and spy shots of the Golf 8 circulated in the automotive press for months. There were so many that Volkswagen decided to spoil their sport in August by releasing its own picture of a camouflaged Golf 8.

It began to look as if the regular Golf might end its long career on the North American market with the next generation. In May 2019 Chris Perkins of *Road & Track* reported, "A VW spokesperson confirmed to *Road & Track* the Mk8, Golf R, and GTI are confirmed, but other Golf models are still under consideration for the North American Region."

There was a logic to this, in 2018 alone, the GTI had outsold the base Golf by 10,000 units in the US. The Golf R wasn't as popular as the GTI, but with a base price almost twice as high it was figured to be "nicely profitable." Puebla was preparing for new model lines, and 2019 saw the last Beetle leave the line and the end of the Golf Sportwagen and Alltrack.

The 2020 model year North American GTI saw a minor equipment boost with previously optional driver-assistance technologies (such as frontal-collision warning or blind-spot monitoring) now standard.

And seven years after it had gone on sale, the Mk7 GTI still commanded respect. In November 2019 *Car and Driver* announced that the 2020 Volkswagen Golf GTI and Jetta GLI had made its "10 Best" list for 2020, the 14th consecutive year that a Volkswagen Golf had appeared. "These VWs check every box and do everything well. They are affordable; they are efficient; they are spacious, fast, and fun," said the editors.

The same month Volkswagen celebrated production of the 100,000 e-Golf, at the Transparent Factory—*Gläserne Manufaktur*—in Dresden. Series production of the ID.3 began in Zwickau the same month, but the e-Golf lived on into 2020, 74 a day still rolling off the Dresden line that summer. It had done its job and would not be replaced.

In Europe, the Volkswagen Golf managed to hold on to its spot as the number one best seller for 2019, with 410,330 units registered, and the tenth year in that top spot. In October 2019 the eighth-generation Golf made its debut in a star-studded show at Wolfsburg (see chapter 8). The GTI was scheduled to appear at the 2020 Geneva Motor Show, but the show was canceled due to the COVID-19 pandemic.

With stalled production of the Golf 8 during 2020, a full range of Golf 7.5s were available from stock. In Puebla, the "short roof" (non-estate) Golfs were made until January 2021 while the Jetta continued, and in February Volkswagen de México began production of the Taos compact SUV for export markets beyond its homeland. In July Volkswagen of America introduced the 2022 (model year) Mk8 Golf GTI and new Golf R at the Chicago Auto Show.

THE GOLF GTI TCR RACERS

In early 2015 VW Motorsport announced that it would develop a track-focused Golf for customer racing based on the seventh-generation car. It would run in the new Touring Car Racer International Series (TCR) for "c-class" or Golf-sized hatchbacks, in which most of VW's rivals were fielding cars. In 2015 the series consisted of 11 events as far apart as Singapore (supporting Formula 1) and Spain.

The class rules specified four or five-door vehicles with engines of no more than 2 liters and 350 PS, powering the front wheels through six-speed sequential transmissions.

In 2015 the TCR Golf was shown as a concept "for evaluation." Volkswagen Motorsport worked in conjunction with the sport department of Seat, drawing on its experience with the Leon Cup Racer.

The 2.0-liter EA888 turbo engine was derived from the Golf R, tuned for 330 PS with a six-speed sequential racing gearbox but only driving the front wheels as per the rules. Thanks to an MQB chassis about 15 cm wider than that of the production Golf, it was roughly 40 cm wider overall. It also featured a front splitter and carbon fiber rear wing for improved aerodynamics. Inside was a racing seat with head protectors, a racing safety cell, and a safety fuel tank in accordance with FIA regulations.

During the final stages of the 2015 TCR series, Liqui Moly Team Engstler ran two development cars, and at its first race weekend, the Golf won the second race at the Red Bull Ring in Austria.

There was immediate customer interest in the new Golf racer, and all 20 cars planned had been sold by January 2016. Deliveries of the now-named Golf GTI TCR were timed for March and the start of the season. Each car cost €95,000 before tax, capped by the TCR regulations under

OPPOSITE: May 2018 and SLR's Mehdi Bennani (25) is head of the pack at the Nürburgring, the TCR chased by an Audi RS3 LMS and Peugeot 308 TCR. *(DPPI Media/Alamy Stock Photo)*

BELOW: This Golf TCR at Daytona in January 2018 shows the second design of squared-off wheel arch extensions and an adjustable aluminum-alloy rear wing. *(VWoA)*

€100,000 to keep the series as close as possible to production cars. The Volkswagen Group fielded the Golf, the Seat, and the Audi RS3 LMS for the series.

Compared with the 2015 development cars, the GTI TCR's front spoiler was reworked and the side air intakes with horizontal slats were more similar to the GTI Clubsport S. The GTI was a successful racer from its first season, with Swiss driver Stefano Comini coming straight from the Seat Leon Cup Racer to the TCR with Team Leopard, the top driver in the 2016 TCR International Series. Overall, the Golf TCR won 17 races and two championships.

Thirty new GTI TCRs were built for 2017, and power was increased to 350 PS with an improved gearchange and steering. The wheel arches were just as wide and more angular, with open vents at the rear to dissipate exhaust heat. A GTI won the TCR class in the VLN Endurance Championship on the Nürburgring Nordschleife and went on to win the TCR International Series in 2017.

The TCR International Series only ran between 2015 and 2017, then merged with the new FIA World Touring Car Cup (WTCR). For the 2018 season the next batch of TCRs received a front end that more closely resembled the current road-going GTI. Volkswagen was always keen to stress how closely related the racer and road car were. "For example, the engine comes directly from series production," said Volkswagen Motorsport Director Sven Smeets. "And only requires minimal adjustment for competitive racing. This is proof that the Golf GTI provides the perfect foundation for our customer racing cars."

Further linking the TCR to the production Golf, Volkswagen offered the Golf GTI TCR both with DSG for €95,000 before tax and with a sequential six-speed gearbox for €115,000. Proving how tough the DSG gearbox was, the engineers just lengthened the first gear ratio and shortened the sixth.

Before the season started, in January 2018 the Volkswagen GTI TCR made a guest US appearance at the Daytona Motor

198 THE COMPLETE BOOK OF VOLKSWAGEN GTI

Speedway. The #31 GTI TCR of Rumcastle Racing took part in the BMW Endurance Challenge at Daytona, part of the IMSA Continental Tire Sports Car Challenge series and the first of the 10-race IMSA Continental Sports Car Challenge.

Also in the US, FCP Euro entered a pair of GTI TCR race cars (with DSG gearboxes) in the Pirelli World Challenge's TCR class, with drivers Nate Vincent and Michael Hurczyn, and finished third overall.

WTCR did not allow factory teams, so Volkswagen was pleased to announce that a new private team buyer for the 2018 season was Sébastien Loeb Racing (SLR), co-owned by the world rally champion himself. SLR ran two GTI TCRs driven by Englishman Rob Huff, the 2012 world touring car champion, and Morocco's Mehdi Bennani, 2016 WTCC Trophy champion. The 100th Golf GTI TCR track car was delivered in March 2018, to Team Engstler, while SLR finished fourth of twelve teams in the end of the 2018 WTCR season standings.

FCP Euro re-entered their pair of GTI TCR race cars (with sequential gearboxes) for the eight-fixture 2019 TC America championship. Hurczyn became the 2019 champion driver with Vincent in second place.

In European showrooms, 2018–2019 buyers could now go for a TCR edition of the roadgoing GTI—more of a Clubsport replacement than a true racer (see page 184). On the tracks for 2019, SLR ran four Golf TCRs supported by Volkswagen, driven by Mehdi Bennani, Rob Huff, Johan Kristoffersson, and Benjamin Leuchter, and once more ended in fourth place.

This would be the Golf GTI's last year in factory-supported racing and the end of the Golf TCR race cars. In November 2019, Volkswagen announced that it would end all motorsport programs that did not involve electric vehicles. Production of the Golf GTI TCR track cars stopped at the end of that year, but they would continue to race in the year ahead. Volkswagen Motorsport closed at the end of 2020 as the company focused on its electric strategy. A TCR based on the Golf 8 was abandoned and consigned to the company museum in 2021 but would resurface in 2024 (chapter 8).

OPPOSITE TOP: Ready to race with a quick release hood and roll cage, the 2015 Golf TCR Concept was badged as neither a GTI nor an R (although it was based on the latter). *(Volkswagen UK)*

OPPOSITE BOTTOM: VW stressed it retained 60 percent of the regular Golf. A massive rear wing for increased downforce was allowed on all TCR cars and made in carbon fiber. *(Volkswagen UK)*

ABOVE: Only the front door trim remained from the original Golf. Changing for the sequential gearbox was by column shift paddles. Note the washer bottle is relocated inside the car. *(Volkswagen UK)*

Golf GTI Mk7/7.5

Model	European Golf GTI/Performance	North American Golf GTI/Performance
Engine type/capacity	2.0-liter 16-valve 4-cylinder, turbocharged	2.0-liter 16-valve 4-cylinder, turbocharged
Gearbox	6-speed manual or 6-speed DSG (from 2017 GTI Performance 7-speed DSG)	6-speed manual or 6-speed DSG
Maximum power/at rpm	220 PS from 4,500–6,300 rpm/GTI Performance 230 PS 4,700–6,200 rpm (from 2017 GTI Performance 245PS)	210 hp at 4,500 rpm/GTI Performance 220 hp at 4,700 rpm (from 2018 228 hp all models)
Maximum torque/at rpm	350 Nm (258 lb ft) from 1,500–4,400 rpm/GTI Performance 1,500–4,600 rpm	350 Nm (258 lb ft) at 1,500 rpm (both models)
Acceleration 0–62 mph Maximum speed	Claimed (manual): 0–62 mph in 6.5 sec; top speed 152 mph/GTI Performance 0–62 mph in 6.4 sec; top speed 155 mph (from 2017 GTI Performance 0–62mph 6.2 sec manual or DSG, 155 mph)	(manual GTI Performance, *Car and Driver* 2014): 0–60 mph in 5.8 sec; top speed 124 mph (limited)
Suspension front/rear	Strut and coil springs, wishbone, anti-roll bar/trailing arms, coil springs, multi-link axle, anti-roll bar, optional adaptive dampers (DCC)	Strut and coil springs, wishbone, anti-roll bar/trailing arms, coil springs, multi-link axle, anti-roll bar, optional adaptive dampers (DCC)
Wheels/tires	18-in Austin alloy wheels 225/45 tires, optional 19 in Santiago wheels	18-in alloy wheels P225/40HR18 tires
Brakes front/rear	Ventilated disc/ventilated disc with anti-lock and ESP/XDS+ (plus VAQ differential Performance)	Ventilated disc/ventilated disc with anti-lock and ESP/XDS+ (VAQ differential on Performance and all models from late 2018)
Length	4,255 mm	4,268 mm
Wheelbase	2,637 mm	2,631mm (differs from Europe)
Width (without mirrors)	1,799 mm	1,799 mm
Height	1,452 mm	1,442 mm
Weight (kg)	From 1,351 (unladen)	From 1,348 (curb weight, manual 3-door)
Years produced	2013-2020	2014-2021

Golf GTI Clubsport Edition 40/Clubsport S	Golf GTI TCR
2.0-liter 16-valve 4-cylinder, turbocharged	2.0-liter 16-valve 4-cylinder, turbocharged
6-speed manual or 6-speed DSG (Clubsport) Clubsport 6-speed manual only	7-speed DSG
265 PS at 5,350 rpm, overboost to 290 PS/310 PS at 5,800–6,500 rpm	290 PS at 5,400–6,400 rpm
280 lb ft at 1,700 rpm/280 lb ft at 1,850–5,700 rpm	280 lb ft at 1,950–5,300 rpm
Clubsport DSG 0–62mph 6.3 secs (*Autocar* 2016) 155 mph limited Clubsport S manual 0–60 mph 6.1 sec (*Autocar* 2016) 165 mph (claimed)	5.6 secs (claimed) 155 mph limited or 164 mph unlimited (claimed)
Strut and coil springs, wishbone, anti-roll bar/trailing arms, coil springs, multi-link axle, anti-roll bar, adaptive dampers (DCC)	Strut and coil springs, wishbone, anti-roll bar/trailing arms, coil springs, multi-link axle, anti-roll bar, optional adaptive dampers (DCC)
18-in alloy wheels 225/45 tires optional 19-in Brecia wheels/19-in Brescia alloy wheels 235/35 ZR19 Michelin Pilot Cup 2 tires	18-in Quaranta alloy wheels 225/40 R18 tires optional 19-in Reifnitz wheels 235/35 ZR19 Michelin Pilot Cup 2 tires
Ventilated disc/ventilated disc with anti-lock and ESP/XDS+ VAQ differential	Ventilated disc/ventilated disc with anti-lock and ESP/XDS+ VAQ differential
4,255 mm	4,255 mm
2,637 mm	2,637 mm
1,799 mm	1,799 mm
1,452 mm	1,452 mm
1,375 (curb)/1,285 (unladen) 1,360 (curb)	1,410 (curb)
2015-2017	2019-2020

8.
GOLF GTI MK8 2019 TO DATE

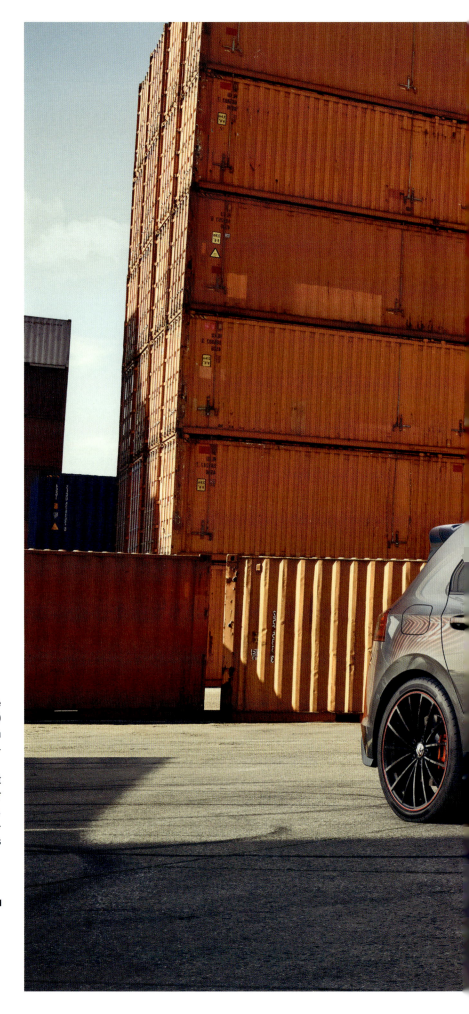

After the 2019 Frankfurt Motor Show had been given over to the groundbreaking electric ID.3, the eighth Golf was launched to 600 guests on October 24, 2019, at the Wolfsburg Autostadt museum in the 45th year after the first Golf started production in the neighboring factory.

Once more the Golf 8 looked reassuringly Golf, with the greatest change reserved for the front end, with a lower hood line, slimmer upper radiator grille, and LED lights for all versions. The optional IQ. Light LED matrix headlights had 22 separate LED lights for the indicator function. Information from the front camera adapted the beams for corners, city, and motorway lighting.

RIGHT: The Clubsport Edition 45 marked the next European GTI anniversary. In addition to decals, an Akrapovič exhaust system was standard, as were 19-inch Scottsdale alloy wheels. (*Volkswagen UK*)

Structurally, it was a very thorough remix of the previous car, and as it was still based on the MQB platform of the Golf 7 (and able to use existing production tools) the dimensional changes were marginal. At 4,284 mm long, 1,789 mm wide (excluding door mirrors), and 1,491 mm high (non GTI), a Golf 8 compared with a Golf 7 five-door's 4,255 mm length, 1,799 mm width (also excluding door mirrors), and 1,452 mm height. The Golf 8's wheelbase was 2,627 mm, whereas the Golf 7 posted 2,637 mm. Seats up, the trunk volume was an identical 380 liters.

Other group models got an MQB stretch. The new 2020 Seat Leon had a 2,686 mm wheelbase for improved rear passenger space. The 2020 Škoda Octavia shared the same wheelbase as the Leon but retained its trademark generous trunk, 600 liters with the seats up. The MQB platform had also provided Škoda with a further Europe-only Golf-sized hatchback for sub-Golf money, the 2019 Scala.

Reflecting cost-cutting and changes in automotive trends, for the first time in its history, there would be no three-door (hatchback) Golf, only five-door cars. The Polo three-door had already been axed, nor would there be three-door Audi A3s or Seat Leons.

The Golf Sportsvan MPV would also not be replaced, the MPV/Minivan trend having completely given way to SUVs. For a while, the prospect of a Golf estate (Sportwagen) wasn't confirmed, but it arrived in 2020. As mentioned in earlier chapters, there would still be no return for the Golf Cabriolet or Scirocco.

With the same running gear as before, there were no major changes to the already wel-respected ride and handling for the non-performance Golfs. The standard electro-mechanical steering rack's response was quickened compared with the outgoing 7.5's, and the Progressive Steering option (non-GTI cars) brought variable tooth spacing on the steering rack-and-pinion system and a more powerful electric motor for greater assistance at lower speeds and a more direct response in corners. As before, Golfs with less than 150 PS and front-wheel-drive had torsion-beam rear suspension, those with 150 PS and above or with all-wheel-drive, a multi-link setup.

ABOVE: Volkswagen started issuing a "generations" lineup image from the Golf Mk7 on. Aerodynamic improvements of the Mk8's shape and a lower front cut the drag coefficient (Cd value) to 0.27 from 0.29. *(Volkswagen AG)*

Mild Hybrids for Most Golfs

All the gas and diesel engines were turbocharged direct-injection units, and many of the gas units were available as mild hybrids—a new concept then but soon to be used by most carmakers.

A mild hybrid system is essentially a small electric motor and lithium-ion battery coupled to the conventional gas engine. The motor only acts in short bursts and the battery recovers energy lost through braking. It's good for a small boost of acceleration from standstill but mostly good for lowering emissions and fuel consumption.

Applied to the smaller EA211 engines, a conventional 12-volt electrical system was joined by a 48-volt belt-integrated starter generator and a 48-volt battery. Volkswagen explained that the 48-volt system enabled a higher amount of energy to be saved for coasting support and for instant restarting. Energy would be recouped from regenerative braking, where in the process of deceleration and braking, the alternator's voltage was boosted and used for bulk recharging of the battery.

Gas Golf 8 outputs would range from 90 to over 300 PS, capacities from one liter to two. It was complicated: engine prefixes would be TSI (gas), TDI (diesel), TGI (gas), eTSI (mild hybrid gas), and eHybrid (plug-in hybrids).

Gearboxes were five- and six-speed manual, six- and seven-speed DSG. In 2014 Volkswagen declared that the 2019 Golf GTI, R, and GTD would have a ten-speed DSG automatic gearbox (eight was a big deal at the time) also due to be fitted to the R and GTD for improved fuel consumption and gear shifting. After dieselgate, by 2016 the ten-speed DSG was mothballed, leaving developed versions of the six- and seven-speed DSGs to continue.

The EA888 Evo4

Volkswagen considered a mild hybrid powertrain for the Golf 8 GTI, but as the boosting benefits were more apparent on smaller-capacity engines at lower speeds, it opted not to. There were ample reserves of torque from the 2.0-liter EA888 and no need to add the extra weight of a mild hybrid electric motor.

Instead, the EA888 evolved into its fourth generation, called Evo4. Built in a state-of-the-art facility in Gyor, Hungary (the Puebla Jetta GLI had the EA888 Gen3), the turbocharged and direct-injected units for the GTI and the next Golf R continued to use very high compression ratios for turbocharged engines, of 9.3 to 1 for the Golf R and 9.6 to 1 for the GTI. The new GTI Evo4 got a new high-pressure direct-fuel-injection system at 5,076 pounds per square inch, compared with 2,900 psi on the previous generation. Switchable piston oil jets activated under high load conditions.

With the promise of a new Golf R to come and then a GTI Clubsport, the 2020 GTI had one power output, its EA888 Evo4 set to deliver the same 245 PS at 4,700 to 6,200 rpm and 273 lb ft of torque between 1,600 and 4,300 rpm as the former 2017-on GTI Performance model.

OPPOSITE AND ABOVE: For Europe, the front-wheel-drive performance Golfs came even closer together for the Mk8. Wheels and signature colors were how to tell them apart. *(Volkswagen AG)*

Diesel Not Down Yet

Diesel car sales had peaked at 55 percent of the European market in 2011 but plummeted in the wake of the emissions scandal and never recovered, but there was still a demand from high-mileage drivers. Volkswagen rationalized the Golf 8 diesel offering. The 1.6-liter Golf diesel was no more, in its place the 2.0-liter EA288 Evo TDI in 115 or 150 PS versions. The GTD reappeared, tuned to provide 200 PS (previously 184). It now came only with the seven-speed dual-clutch DSG gearbox.

These diesels were as clean as they could be. In 2018 SCR (selective catalytic reduction) technology began to be used on Volkswagens to reduce nitrogen oxides in the exhaust gas. A close-coupled SCR catalyst was located between the turbocharger and the diesel oxidation catalytic converter. Then AdBlue (synthetic urea) was injected into the exhaust gas upstream of the SCR catalytic converter. From 2019 a twin AdBlue dosing process was introduced on the Passat 2.0 TDI Evo engines and then into the Golf 8, which had a second SCR catalytic converter fitted. This reduced NOx by around 80 percent compared with the previous generation, it was claimed.

GTE Gets More GTI

With the advent of the ID.3, there was no all-electric Golf 8, but strikingly, the new version of the Golf GTE plug-in hybrid was upgraded to equal the power of the new GTI with a higher combined gas-electric output of 245 PS. It was expected to account for 15 percent of Golf global sales (although again, not for North America).

Depending on the market there were two plug-in hybrid Golf 8s. The e-Hybrid, with a combined output of 204 PS and the new GTE with exactly the same power as the GTI at 245 PS, (but with its battery it did weigh some 176 kg more than the GTI). The claimed 0–62 mph (100 kph) figure of 6.3 seconds gave barely half a second away to the GTI.

The 245 PS GTE's plug-in hybrid drive was similar to the previous generation: a 1.4-liter TSI engine, electric drive motor (85 over 75 kW), six-speed DSG—modified for smoother low-speed changing—and a new lithium-ion battery with 50 percent more capacity (13 kWh over 9) so the all-electric range was now 38.5 miles (62 km) over the Golf 7.5 GTE's 31 (50 km).

LEFT: The new Golf was still a world car. Here, Guo Yongfeng, president of Faw-Volkswagen Sales, presents the new GTI during the April 2021 Shanghai International Automobile Industry Exhibition. The launch color was Kings Red Metallic. *(Hector Retamal/Getty Images)*

Both the Golf 8 GTE and GTD used the same chassis and suspension set-up as the GTI. Why had Volkswagen chosen to dial up the sportiness of the GTE? "It's important that the GTE feels more like a GTI," Matthias Rabe, Volkswagen's chief technology officer, told *Autocar* ahead of the performance Golf reveal in March 2020. "The GTE has a very smooth electric powertrain. For me, it's on the next level in terms of driving, handling, and agility. I'm a GTI fan and I really think for the first time this GTE is an option for the GTI driver. I think there will be some movement from the GTI to the GTE in future."

The All-Digital Golf 8

While the styling of the Golf 8 and its mechanical makeup were evolution rather than revolution, on the inside Volkswagen had made true years of promises to make the new Golf all-digital. Putting a touchscreen down in the center console was suddenly out of fashion after the 2018 Mercedes A-Class ditched traditional instruments and infotainment for what resembled a vertically mounted tablet that stretched from the driver's door to the middle of the dashboard. The 2019 BMW 1-Series offered twin 10.25-inch screens as an option, controlled by touch and the traditional dial by the gear lever. A tablet-like screen atop the center console became universal from city cars to SUVs.

In all Golf 8s, the driver now faced a digital instrument cluster with a 10-inch display. The optional Innovision Cockpit incorporated Digital Cockpit Pro with a 10.25-inch screen binnacle and the Discover Navigation touchscreen infotainment system, which could project speed and navigation information onto the windshield.

On the upper trim levels including the GTI, all the functions on either side of the steering wheel (such as the Digital Cockpit or adaptive cruise control) were controlled by what was a single molded pad that had different areas to push for each function. The surface was smooth but each area pushed gave a small vibration—for example, to increase the speed on the cruise control you gave a firmer push. Other controls such as audio volume worked by sliding your finger across the surface. To the side of the driver, a touch pad of grouped functions sat where the rotary auto/side/fog light switch had been before.

The nerve center of the car was the central screen, which was aligned with the instrument display at the top of the dashboard above the central air vents. The majority of the Golf's settings were controlled through menus in the 8.25-inch touchscreen (10-inch for some markets), including things like the heated front seats, temperature controls, and fan speeds. There were four shortcut keys for the menus.

The screen would mirror the display on your mobile phone (which on some versions could become your entry key). When the optional Dynamic Chassis Control (DCC) was fitted, on the central touchscreen the Eco, Driving, and Sport modes were joined by an Individual icon. This brought up a further menu of choices, including engine sound. In the DCC the driver was presented with a 15-stop slider with Comfort at one end and Sport at the other. You could play at being a chassis engineer all day.

It was either touch, swipe, or speak to access the infotainment system, but Volkswagen had controversially completely done away with rotary knobs for heating and ventilation. In addition to using the touchscreen, the temperature could be varied by sliding a finger along either side of a pad below it, and volume in the middle of the pad. Alas, this new buttonless Golf landed badly with some of the press because the temperature slider wasn't lit at night, but chiefly because in its launch state the infotainment system was judged slow to respond to swiping and the steps to go through the menus somewhat laborious. Worse, the haptic steering wheel buttons didn't always do as they were told.

However, you could ask your Golf 8 to perform certain functions by voice in a similar way to an Amazon Alexa, the Volkswagen Group having bought access to the Alexa software. It was activated by saying, "Hello Volkswagen," or by pressing the voice button on the steering wheel. Then, for example, you could ask the car to "Take me home" (navigation) or say, "I'm cold" (turn the heating up).

Every new Golf was fitted with assist systems, including the Lane Assist lane-keeping system, Front Assist Autonomous Emergency Braking with Pedestrian Monitoring, the XDS electronic differential lock, and Car2X (local communication with other vehicles and the traffic infrastructure). As before, driver and passenger airbags were complemented by side seat impact bags, and a curtain side airbag system covered both front and rear occupants' heads. In 2022 and an additional standard lap belt tensioner for the front row of seats a center airbag was added between the front seats to prevent head contact.

The buildup to the Golf 8 launch was marked by stories about delays in getting its software in order, but it was the first Golf capable of receiving over-the-air updates, where the car could download software fixes via a Wi-Fi connection without needing to visit a dealer. Owners of more basic Golf 8s would also be able to add extra features at a later date through the on-air We Connect subscription service—depending on the market. Add-on elements, including ACC (Adaptive Cruise Control), Light Assist main-beam control, changes to the navigation system, App-Connect (integrating smartphone apps), Wireless App-Connect (wirelessly integrating iPhone apps), and a Wi-Fi hotspot and voice control, could be activated retrospectively.

2020—The Digital GTI Is Launched

Thanks to the COVID-19 pandemic, production of the Golf 8 was temporarily suspended in what was meant to be its first full year in production. The new-gen GTI had been set to be revealed at the Geneva Motor Show in spring, but the show was canceled and the car was launched online for all to access. Both the vehicles and the stand planned for Geneva were digitally processed for 360° viewing.

German-built only, the eighth GTI built on the aggressive front styling of the previous car, with the signature red highlights in the headlamps and along the top of the grille. "The full-width LED light

ABOVE: The performance Golf trio of GTE, GTI, and GTD had five LEDs arranged to create the fog lights in the front bumper. The new corporate logo was flanked by a light bar on the GTI. *(Volkswagen UK)*

graphic within the front end helps accentuate the new car's width," head of design Klaus Bischoff told *Autocar*'s Greg Kable (May 13, 2020). "It also gives the new Golf GTI a more confident appearance in comparison to the old model."

The front bumper (shared with the forthcoming Golf R) had black strakes at the sides, a honeycomb grille, and a front diffuser, and at the rear a diffuser with an exhaust opening on the left and right. Black side sills formed a line with the front splitter and rear diffuser. Five LED fog lights were integrated into the air intake grille in an X shape. The roof spoiler was extended rearward and merged with the black edging around the rear window.

The GTI interior markers returned: sports steering wheel featuring three silver double spokes and recessed Wolfsburg emblem, a golf-ball textured (but almost square) gear knob for the manual, sports seats in a new tartan pattern with black side bolsters, and, for the first time, integrated headrests.

With the new 245 PS EA888 Evo4, the claimed Mk8 GTI speed stats were 0–62 mph (100 kph) in 6.2 seconds and a governed top speed of 155 mph, which were almost identical to the Golf 7.5 GTI Performance five-door. A six-speed manual and seven-speed DSG gearbox with steering-wheel shift paddles (plus a tiny lever in the center console) were the choices, with the shift times of the DSG shortened and kick-down optimized.

The GTI sat 15 mm lower on the road than a regular Golf 8, with 17-inch alloy wheels as standard and optional 18- and 19-inch rims (Germany). The spring rates had been recalibrated—5 percent tauter up front and a notable 15 percent at the back, intended to give less front-wheel biased handling at the extreme. As expected, the rear suspension was multi-link with a new wishbone bearing and spring setup, reconfigured auxiliary springs, and new damping bearings and hydraulics. The aluminum front subframe from the previous Clubsport S was used to save a claimed 3 kg and boosted rigidity. Curb weight was 1,448 kg compared with 1,382 kg for a 2013 five-door GTI Performance manual.

The Progressive Steering system was carried over to the GTI Mk8, variable steering rack-and-pinion gearing and a more powerful electric motor to assist it. It took 2.1 turns of the steering wheel from stop to stop (usually 2.75).

Previously only fitted to the Performance, Clubsport, and TCR GTIs, the Golf 8 GTI had the VAQ limited-slip differential as standard, coupled to the electronic ESC, EDS, and XDS+ functions.

BELOW: As well as new rear light clusters and diffuser, the Mk8 featured GTI letters below the badge for the first time. Real twin exhaust tailpipes sat wider apart than on the Mk7. *(Volkswagen UK)*
OPPOSITE TOP: The covering for the EA888 Evo4 engine was plain and simple. Some owners missed having the hydraulic hood struts of the Mk7. *(Volkswagen AG)*
OPPOSITE BOTTOM: Only the door mirror and windows switches were carried over from the old Golf. There was a square button to start, not a key. Instruments were red, but there were 30 shades of ambient lighting. *(Volkswagen AG)*

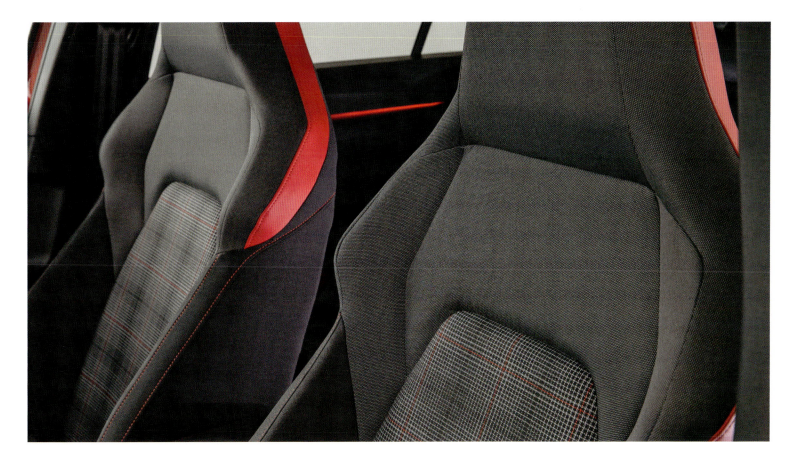

Specific to the new GTI, Volkswagen named the handling control unit the Vehicle Dynamics Manager, which juggled the throttle, brake, and steering responses, electro-mechanical running-gear functions, and (optional) electronically controlled shock absorbers of the Dynamic Chassis Control (DCC). It was claimed to adjust individual wheel damping 200 times a second, for particularly agile and accurate handling. According to Jon McIlroy in Britain's *Auto Express* (September 11, 2020), it worked: "You can tell the difference because the Mk8 GTI feels more alive than the outgoing model. It's quicker to respond to steering inputs, with a more direct front end that bites into the asphalt if you really commit to a corner."

The Manager lived in the central touchscreen where the choices between the Comfort, Eco, Sport, and Individual settings were found. At the extreme end of the slider for Individual, "Sport" gave the hardest suspension for track use and the possibility of the rear axle being allowed to lose traction to induce tail-out oversteer. This greater degree of adjustment meant that the firmer suspension settings could be dialed down for extra on-road comfort. The driver could set and store their personal driving profile.

To the displeasure of some of the more enthusiastic magazines, the button to turn off the traction control (ESC) of the previous GTI was gone. If you delved into the infotainment screen, you found an ESC Sport mode that increased the thresholds at which the slip systems cut in (reportedly preferred by racing drivers for the track), or ESC Off mode deactivated it altogether.

However, to the exasperation of both German and English magazine testers, the route to ESC Off was via five menu commands. If you got to this point a message popped up to say it was not recommended and asked you to confirm if you really did want to go ahead.

In the European hot hatchback power league, the 245 PS GTI Mk8 had less than most of its front-driven rivals. There was Hyundai's first hot hatch, the 275 PS Hyundai i30N Performance, the 2.3-liter 280 PS Ford Focus ST, and the 300 PS Renault Mégane R.S. 300. The Honda Civic Type R, with its whale-tail rear spoiler, still ruled the power game with 320 PS for GTI money but was a much more rowdy

OPPOSITE TOP: The haptic pads on either side of the steering wheel were a single molding with sensors below for each particular control marked on them. Not a fan favorite.
(Volkswagen AG)
OPPOSITE BOTTOM: There were four choices of chassis and steering setup within the GTI's Vehicle Dynamics Manager. Individual let you set any combination of Eco, Comfort, and Sport. *(Volkswagen UK)*
TOP: The new front sports seats had integrated headrests and a red highlight for GTI. The tops of seat backs had pockets for mobile phones. *(Volkswagen UK)*
ABOVE: The gear lever on DSG Golfs, Seats, Škodas, and Audis was reduced to a stub, as shifting was by wire rather than a mechanical linkage. This freed up space in the center console. *(Volkswagen UK)*

machine. In October, BMW announced a new direct GTI rival from its front-drive 1-Series, the 128ti, reviving a famous sporty badge from its past (Turismo Internazionale) and with 265 PS.

"Which is the best GTI?" asked Andreas Haubt of Germany's *Auto Motor und Sport* in April 2021, comparing the Volkswagen with the new (front-wheel-drive for the first time) BMW. There was some grumbling about the VW's glitchy software—the test car's onboard computer was slow to warm up, gave unwanted directions from the navigation, and developed a parking assistant fault.

Traction control off (the BMW had a button), thankfully for the GTI, a tight test track showed it cornered as if on rails, the rear end seemingly glued to the road. "This is where more than 45 years of experience culminate in a compact sports car."

Neither car was judged to sound very exciting, cabin comfort having taken preference, but the GTI still had an interior sound generator (the Soundaktor). The Volkswagen's EA888 Evo4 was rated as having more stamina in the upper rev ranges. Despite also having a limited-slip differential, the 128ti was more prone to understeer. Result: the GTI kept its crown, especially as the BMW was €5,000 more expensive.

2020 for 2021: The Fifth-Generation Golf R, with Some New Tricks

The final Golf 8 shown in 2020 was the flagship four-wheel-drive Golf R. It was once more an online launch, but interestingly, details were issued by Volkswagen of America on November 3, a day ahead of Europe, available to pre-order in 2021 as a 2022 model year car, and fully launched in July 2021 with the North American Mk8 GTI.

Thanks to a new Continental turbocharger instead of the GTI's Garrett, with 320 PS the new R was 10 PS up on the post-2017 fourth-generation R and rated at 315 hp in the US version, 27 bhp more than that market's outgoing model. The 0–62 mph (100 kph) figure was 4.7 seconds (over 5.1—and some testers managed 4.3 seconds) and top speed electronically limited to 155 mph (250 kph).

In Europe the seven-speed DSG auto gearbox was standard, with no manual option (Volkswagen said there was insufficient interest). It had an upgraded auxiliary oil cooler and was remapped. However, there clearly *was* sufficient interest in the US and Canadian markets, which would get an additional choice of a six-speed manual.

The new R sat 20 mm lower than a regular Golf (so 5 mm lower than the GTI) on 18-inch "Jerez" wheels. BorgWarner had re-engineered the 4Motion system with a new rear differential design, which provided faster apportioning of drive with a more rearward bias. This translated into a new feature called R-Performance Torque Vectoring (also seen on the Arteon and Tiguan R). Power was shared between the front and rear axles but also variably between the two rear wheels.

BELOW: In the signature R Lapiz Blue Metallic, the Golf R was once again introduced on a frozen lake. Volkswagen R ambassador Tanner Foust whisked one across the quickly melting snow of Michigan's Upper Peninsula. (*VWoA*)

OPPOSITE TOP: Blue was the instrument color for the R and a black roof lining was standard. On the left steering wheel haptic pad, a blue R button was a shortcut to the driving menus. (*Volkswagen UK*)

OPPOSITE BOTTOM: No eco setting here; the Performance Pack race profile opened more choices, including the new Drift mode and the Special, which was the Nürburgring profile. (*VWoa*)

The previous 4Motion system allowed no more than 50 percent of the power per rear wheel but the new Golf R's system allowed more torque to the outer rear wheel, pushing the car into the corner. Using a pair of electronically operated multi-disc clutches, the system could balance output across the rear axle from 0 to 100 percent within milliseconds. This was linked to the other running-gear components such as the electronic differential locks and adaptive chassis control by the Vehicle Dynamics Manager. DCC was standard.

There was a new version of the R Performance Pack (£2,000 in the UK), which increased the top speed to an unrestricted (autobahn-only) 168 mph (270 kph). Externally it included an (even) larger rear spoiler for extra downforce on the rear axle, 19-inch "Estoril" wheels, and two additional driving profiles, "Special" and "Drift." Unlike the GTI, all the driving profile selections could be rapidly accessed by lightly pressing an "R" button on the steering wheel.

"Special" was a dedicated Nürburgring track driving profile honed by VW race driver Benjamin Leuchter, set up to compensate for the undulations of the Nordschleife, with a specific vertical setup of the DCC adaptive chassis control and a modified lateral dynamics setup of the standard Vehicle Dynamics Manager. Volkswagen claimed that during in-house test drives the new R was up to 19 seconds quicker per lap around the Nürburgring Nordschleife than its predecessor (07:51 minutes).

However, Drift mode was the best party trick (and showed a rather naughty side of Volkswagen). All the power went rearward, so you could hang the tail out sideways on opposite (on a test track, of course, in the hands of an expert—a disclaimer popped up to that effect).

ABOVE: The R Performance Pack added a larger two-part spoiler with a supporting strut in the middle. *(Volkswagen AG)*
OPPOSITE: Pops and bangs were guaranteed with the Akrapovič titanium performance exhaust system, with a valve enabling the driver to adjust the volume. *(VWoA)*

In this mode the torque vectoring provoked oversteer instead of neutral vehicle handling—the maximum possible torque was available on the wheel located on the outside of the bend. In Drift mode the ESC was set to "Sport" as standard, meaning that the Golf R's control electronics kicked in at a very late stage. But full-on drifts were only possible if the ESC was switched to OFF (back through those pesky menus).

For the first time since the introduction of the DSG, the gearbox would stay in manual mode in both modes if the driver had selected this, without unintentionally slipping back into automatic mode, as previous cars could.

The European order books for the Golf R opened that November for 2021 delivery. The almost £40,000 people's car had arrived. Priced from £39,270 in the UK, it could be topped off with an Akrapovič titanium exhaust (7 kg lighter for £3,100), panoramic sunroof, Harmon/Kardon sound system, and a head-up display.

Golf GTI MK8 Clubsport

Announced alongside the new R, the GTI Clubsport was this time a regular production mode rather than special edition, with 300 PS in Europe replacing the former GTI TCR line as the flagship Golf GTI, and well above the regular GTI.

Available only with the seven-speed DSG gearbox (with shorter ratios), essentially it had a de-tuned Golf R engine without having to lose any power to a four-wheel-drive system. With a 0–62 mph time of 5.6 seconds, the new Clubsport was claimed for this new fastest-ever accelerating GTI, compared with the standard automatic GTI's 6.3 seconds.

Braking was boosted by the R's drilled discs and two-piston calipers. And like the R, it had a Nürburgring driving profile. Outside, there were restyled front and rear bumpers and a two-part rear spoiler from the R Performance Pack. Starting at £37,215, it slotted in just below the R.

By the end of the pandemic-marked 2020, the best-selling car in Europe was the Golf, with around 312,000 sales—and yet the Golf 8 had not met with the universal praise afforded to its predecessors. Journalists and owners were increasingly critical about the new digital approach, especially the lack of physical buttons for heating and ventilation.

Just like with the ID.3, early buyers of the Golf 8 had been bothered by the same software bugs, and in January 2021, 56,000 European customers were offered a "voluntary update" rather than a recall to fix issues with the infotainment system and reversing camera. Later in 202, readers of *Auto Motor und Sport* also reported (December 15, 2021) that car keys were not recognized, assistance systems reacted incorrectly or failed, emergency braking cut in needlessly, traffic sign recognition detected signs that were not even there, or the entertainment system sometimes packed up completely. The Golf reputation was taking a knock.

GTI Clubsport 45 Edition

In March 2021, the GTI Clubsport 45 edition followed the Clubsport 40 (chapter 7) to mark 45 years since the original Golf GTI was launched. The exterior included a black roof and roof spoiler, in homage to the black-framed rear window of the first GTI. No more power, but a Race Package was exclusive to this model and included the lightweight Akrapovič sports exhaust system. Removal of the speed limiter gave a 267 kph/166 mph top speed.

Summer 2021—The North American Performance Golfs

There had been a long buildup to the July launch of the Golf GTI and R after they were announced at the Chicago Auto Show, and the decision to focus just on the GTI and the R was welcomed.

In North American tune the GTI produced 241 hp and 273 lb ft of torque (identical to Europe) and the R produced 315 hp and 295 lb ft of torque with the DSG transmission (compared with the European R DSG's 310 lb ft), or 280 lb ft with the manual.

The US would not get the GTI Clubsport, but the GTI came in the usual range of trims of S, SE, and Autobahn, which gave buyers the choice of more equipment for one power output. The manual gearbox S began at $29,545 and the Autobahn topped out at $44,445 for the DSG and came loaded with all the options such as Vienna leather seats and DCC adaptive damping. The US equivalent of Volkswagen We Connect Wi-Fi and internet radio was Car-Net and SiriusXM. Car-Net was standard to all GTIs. The R came in one super equipped trim where the gearbox was the only choice and made a compelling prospect at $44,445 for the DSG.

Against the GTI, the North American hot hatch Class of 2021 was a small band made up of the Honda Civic Type R, the Hyundai Velostar N, and the Mini Cooper Works GP. The Hyundai and Mini came with eight-speed autos and the Civic was by far the most powerful at 306 hp.

OPPOSITE TOP: The GTI Clubsport had oval tailpipes, rather than the GTI's circular pipes, which sat further apart on either side of a new diffuser. *(Volkswagen UK)*
OPPOSITE BOTTOM: The GTI Clubsport had an exclusive front bumper incorporating a new front splitter for greater downforce on the front axle, VW claimed. *(Volkswagen AG)*
RIGHT: The markers between an Mk8 European and North American GTI were reflectors in the front wheel arches, and the red trim strip above headlights was omitted. *(VWoA)*

The Mk8 GTI was warmly welcomed by the US magazines. For the June 2021 issue of *Car and Driver*, Tony Quiroga took a DSG European spec car with DCC adaptive dampers barreling along Little Tajunga Canyon Road in the countryside outside of L.A. The headline read: "2022 Volkswagen Golf GTI Still Defines the Hot Hatch."

"The GTI surges out of bends with unbelievable ambition and confidence," he wrote. "Limited-slip diffs on front-drive cars can create unwanted tugs and noise at the steering wheel as load shifts from one side to the other, but the GTI's allows the car to maintain its path without drama and without disturbing steering precision or feel. You're left in awe of its magic."

The only negatives were aimed at the digital environment, bemoaning the lack of a volume control knob and the center screen's "dizzying menu structure but Apple and Android phone-mirroring capability would allow owners to "mostly avoid VW's obtuse infotainment system."

The Second Golf R Estate

In Europe, from September 2021 the new Golf R estate joined the Golf 8 range. It had the same 320 PS engine and four-wheel-drive as the hatch and also the R Performance package and torque vectoring. On the practical side there was an optional electrically retractable towbar, and it also gained in rear legroom over the R hatchback as the Golf estate had been allowed to grow, its 2,686 mm wheelbase a 66 mm stretch compared with the Golf 7. The fully loaded trunk volume had increased by 6 liters to 611.

Volkswagen Resets Itself

Summer 2022 saw new faces at the top of Volkswagen management. In July after four years, it was announced that Herbert Diess, the man chosen to lead Volkswagen out of the dieselgate crisis, was to leave his post as chairman of the board of management of Volkswagen AG on September 1, three years before the end of his contract. His major tasks included setting up CARIAD, Volkswagen's own software company, and investing heavily in electric vehicles, but according to Reuters (July 22), "In the end, Diess appears to have moved too fast for some on the company's supervisory board, and not fast enough for others." He was replaced by Porsche chairman Oliver Blume.

In July 2022 Thomas Schäfer, former CEO of Škoda, became a member of the group board of management, CEO of the Volkswagen passenger cars brand (replacing Ralph Brandstätter), and head of the brand group core. Acknowledging the setbacks of the software problems with the ID range, he told *Autocar* (August 24), "The first goal is to make the brand loved again." The first part of this task was the release of an updated ID.3 at the start of 2023 with a refreshed exterior and interior design, and the Golf would surely be next in line.

Golf R 20 Years and GTI 40th Anniversary Edition

Volkswagen having delivered a quarter of a million Golf Rs by 2021, the following year marked twenty years since the model was introduced, so in June 2022 the Golf R 20 Years limited edition was announced for European and North American markets—limited in the sense that it would only be produced for one year and about 1,800 cars allocated for North America, which retained the manual gearbox option.

Outside, there was "20" badging on the door pillars, contrasting mirror caps, optional blue accents on the black 19-inch "Estoril" wheels, and a larger rear spoiler. Inside, the dash panel and door trim decorative trim elements were in real carbon fiber and the same sports blue "R" logos as the regular car.

In Europe more power was served up for the price premium; remapped software gave an extra 13 PS to the four-cylinder EA888, bringing the total to 333 PS (328 bhp). On start-up the new Emotion Start function briefly took the engine up to 2,500 rpm for either a quick getaway, a sense of drama, or to annoy the neighbors. The tur-

OPPOSITE: Offered in all markets, the Golf R 20th Anniversary Edition was offered in Lapiz Blue Metallic, Deep Black Pearl, and Pure White, with a limited allocation of cars for each color. *(VWoA)*

TOP: The 2023 North American GTI 40th Anniversary had 19-inch wheels painted gloss black borrowed from the European Golf GTI Clubsport 45 model. *(VWoA)*

ABOVE: The second special R in two years, the 2023 Germany-only R333 was only in Lime Yellow. Trimmed in Nappa leather, each had a numbered plaque inside. *(VWoA)*

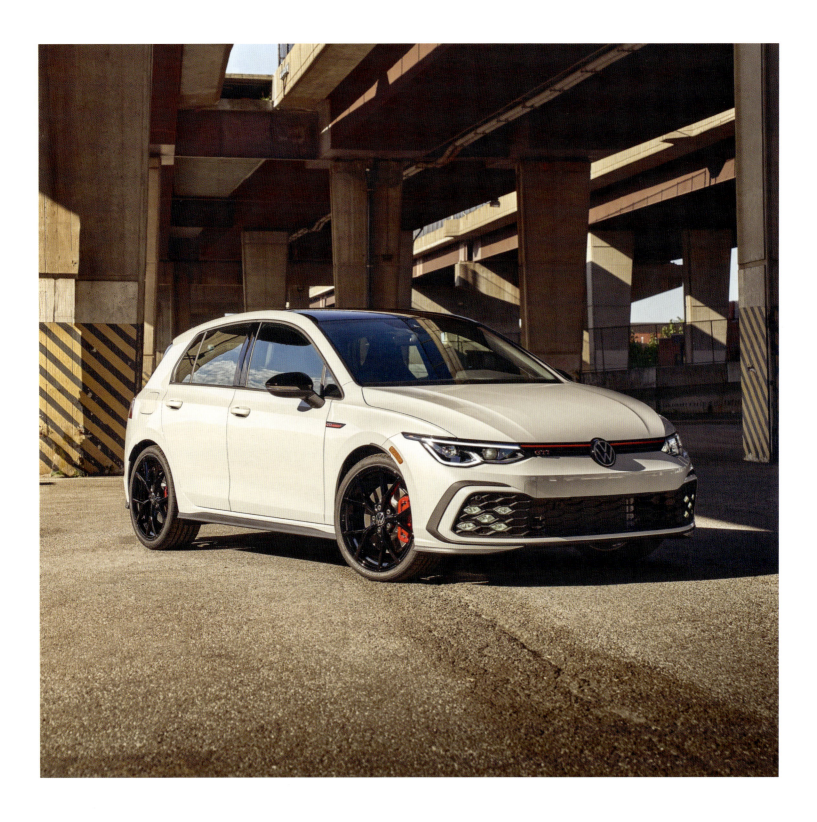

bocharger was allowed to keep spinning during periods of part-load driving, which, coupled with an open throttle valve in overrun phases, was claimed to provide even quicker reactions when the driver took their foot off the accelerator then pull it back quickly.

In October 2022 came a US-only GTI special for the 2023 model year, marking 40 years since the 1983 Rabbit GTI. Around 1,500 Golf GTI 40th Anniversary cars were offered for the US available in four colors, including Anniversary Edition–exclusive Tornado Red and Urano Gray, and with "40" badging inside and out. Based on the GTI S trim, the equipment bonus was performance summer tires, DCC adaptive damping, and speed-sensitive steering.

Looking back at 2022, at the first full year of GTI and R sales in North America, 6,924 GTIs had found owners, with 1,499 Golf Rs. As ever, the contrast was with the Jetta range—still fuller, including the GLI—at 38,260 cars, but now there was a five-strong choice of SUVs, including the electric ID.4 manufactured in Chattanooga from that year. The Mexican-built Taos found 59,103 buyers. In all, 83 percent of sales were SUVs. The GTI was a select niche.

ABOVE: Last call for the manual GTI, the 2024 model year GTI 380 stood out with a gloss black roof, mirror caps, and wheels. *(VWoA)*

THE ELECTRIC GTI FUTURE

After years of debate, at the start of 2022 the European Union (EU) committed to ban the sale of internal combustion engine (ICE) cars and vans from 2035 by requiring carmakers to only sell zero-emission vehicles or face huge fines.

Once Volkswagen launched its first purpose-built electric car, the ID.3 in 2020, given that it was very much Golf-sized and priced, how were the two to live alongside each other? Would Golf drivers switch loyalties, and would there even be a ninth-generation Golf?

In November 2023 Thomas Schäfer, CEO of the Volkswagen passenger cars brand, confirmed that there was a future for the Golf beyond gas power. In a wide-ranging interview with Carl Nowak of *Auto Motor und Sport*, he said, "The Golf and the whole segment are still very popular in Europe. And I believe that it will stay that way. That's why we're also bringing the Golf into the electric future."

By 2023, Volkswagen's massive investment in electric vehicles was evidenced by the ID.3 having been joined by the ID.4, ID.5, ID.7, and ID.Buzz. Audi, Seat (under the Cupra brand), and Škoda also had growing electric ranges.

A NEW ID OR A NEW GOLF?

Now, like many European manufacturers, Volkswagen was keen to show that it could offer an EV at an affordable price in the face of the growing wave of cheaper Chinese alternatives. In March 2023 it presented the ID. 2all, a five-door concept car said to be close to a production version coming in 2025 that would cost less than €25,000 with a range of up to 450 km (380 miles)

and would be "as spacious as a Golf, as inexpensive as a Polo."

At 4,050 mm long it was 234 mm shorter than a Golf 8, but it had many Golf design features. Volkswagen had already made a comparison to the Golf, so were we looking at the Golf 9 rather than a new member of the ID family? Schäfer quickly put a stop to this rumor, telling *Autocar*, "We want to reserve our iconic names for the true successor of it. If you make a Golf, it had better be a Golf. You know, proper." However, when he spoke to Germany's *Autobild* in August he avoided committing to a Golf 9. "The new Golf would be launched in 2027 and theoretically run until the EU's planned ban on combustion engines in 2035. Schäfer, however, sees the future in the ID. models, and this group strategy will not change even after Diess' departure."

THE FIRST ELECTRIC GTI WON'T BE A GOLF

If the ID. 2all caused a stir, the ID. GTI Concept at September's Frankfurt show was aimed straight at the hearts of Golf GTI fans. And it was for real said Volkswagen: "The ID. GTI Concept is more than just a show car—it is the first glimpse of the exciting GTI future because its series develop-

PREVIOUS PAGE: The first electric Volkswagen to wear the GTI badge, the ID. GTI Concept was both virtual and as two wooden mock-ups. Striking 20in wheels more concept than reality. *(Volkswagen UK)*

ABOVE: The GTI Concept's dash was only shown as drawings. A golf ball texture wrapped around the rotary control for the driving profiles—note how the "I" of GTI is a lightning bolt.
(Volkswagen AG)

LEFT: Looking very Golf-like from the rear, the two ID. GTI concepts were finished in Mars Red and Diamond Silver Metallic, both colors from the first generation GTI. *(Volkswagen UK)*

ment has already been decided." It would go into production in 2026.

"In my opinion, the powerful ID. 2all is the perfect basis for an electric GTI," said Volkswagen brand head of design Andreas Mindt. "I already had the GTI in mind when I first put pen to paper for the ID. 2all. It is now becoming reality and allowing us to project the GTI idea into the new age of electric mobility." In fact, the GTI badge was already primed for the electric age. In August *Autocar* reported that Volkswagen had trademarked a GTI logo where the "I" was replaced by a little bolt of lightning.

The two ID. GTI show cars only showed exteriors—they were built from clay on a wooden frame, so any clues on the interior were supplied by Volkswagen in the form of sketches. The ID. 2all had displays that could resemble an original Beetle's, and the GTI Concept's screens could be configured in Vintage mode where the instruments transformed into a set from the Mk1 Pirelli GTI. The virtual seat fabric pattern had a reinterpreted GTI pattern playfully called Jack-e (instead of Jacky, the name used for the fabric in the Golf GTI Mk6).

No power or performance figures were supplied for the single front-mounted electric motor but 300 PS was guessed at. We were told that it had an electronic limited-slip differential like the current performance Golfs.

Meanwhile, some ID models had gained a GTX version, and an ID.3 GTX arrived in 2024. GTI by another name? It seemed not. They were sporty-ish in looks but had suspension and steering more geared to comfort, despite the ID.3 GTX Performance having 326 PS.

And in May 2024 Schäfer told *Autocar* that the branding would be phased out after one generation, in favor of a new band of electric GTIs. The R would be electric-only from 2030. "GTX is the performance brand of the MEB [platform], but we'll work our way back to GTI and R in the next products going forward."

BELOW: Like the first time the badge was used in the 1970s, the new GTX Volkswagens (here an ID.3) were lightly sporty, not a new GTI. *(Volkswagen UK)*

Three Specials for 2023

Limited-run performance Golfs were sprinting out of Wolfsburg like never before. From June 2023 Golf R fans in Germany only could order a very select kind of R. As the name suggested, the Golf R 333 had the same power as the previous year's Golf R 20 Years but was limited to a production run of only 333 cars. Its Lime Yellow Metallic paint was new for the R range and echoed the one-off R400, with a black-painted roof and 333 logos on the sides. With prices starting at €76,410, it was the most expensive Golf yet (the R 20 Years had been €59,995).

Volkswagen was about to drop manual GTIs for Europe. North America looked to mark the final model year of the stick-shift GTI with the 2024 Golf GTI 380, a special equipment set standard on every 2024 manual-transmission GTI (available in S, SE, and Autobahn).

Sold from late 2023, the GTI 380 would quickly find buyers. In the first quarter of 2024, North American demand for the GTI jumped by 156 percent compared with 2023 to 2,412 units from January through June. Golf R sales increased by 125 percent compared with the same period with 1,233 sold, and 40 percent of them were manuals. From the 2025 model year, all Golfs sold in the US would come with the seven-speed DSG.

2024—A Fresh Golf for a Big Birthday

By 2024 a Golf 8 facelift was not a surprise and neatly coincided with the 50th anniversary of this automotive legend (March 29 being the first day a Golf came down the line), over 37 million having been sold worldwide. It was a facelift designed to take the Golf 8 to 2027, according to some magazines.

First shown in January 2024, the new Golf and Golf estate/Variant had a restyled lower front panel/spoiler, slightly narrower LED headlights, and for the first time the (new look) VW logo was illuminated. In the middle trim levels, the light bar continued from the headlight to the logo. The IQ. Light option continued with new patterns of turning indicator front and rear and on main beam could reach up to 500 meters away. A special edition Golf 50, based on the European starter Style trim, included extra equipment such as alloy wheels and Discover navigation.

The Big Screen

The biggest news was, of course, on the dashboard. You couldn't miss the jump in size of the central infotainment screen, which appeared freestanding, unconnected to the driver display, rather than blending into it as before. The central screen size grew across the range, with the Discover version jumping from 10 inches to 12.9. It was big—some people even thought it was too big.

RIGHT: The unmissably large central touchscreen resembled that of the ID models. Real carbon-fiber dash and door inserts were a new option. *(Volkswagen UK)*

This was the fourth-generation infotainment system software, MIB4, already rolled out on recent new Volkswagens such as the ID. Buzz and 2024 ID.4, with new graphics and menus, meant to be more intuitive to use and with faster processing speeds. And yes, the redesigned sliders for temperature and volume control at the base of the screen were now illuminated at night. All that customer and press feedback had worked.

Where previously fitted, the haptic steering wheel buttons were replaced by conventional ones from lesser Golfs. From the wheel, the new IDA2 voice assistant continued to be used to control functions, such as the air-conditioning, telephone, or navigation, but could also access online information from "all conceivable areas," said Volkswagen. Later in 2024 as standard in Europe (along with other Volkswagens) the IDA voice assistant would include the artificial intelligence–based chatbot ChatGPT, which would give a more natural interaction. As an example, when launched at the 2024 Las Vegas Consumer Electronics Show (CES) it could generate a random story about dinosaurs to keep the kids happy.

When it came to parking, the latest Park Assist Pro was available for the Golf for the first time, enabling drivers to guide the vehicle in and out of parking spaces with their smartphones While standing outside the car. The Area View system projected a 360-degree all-around view created by merging four cameras onto the infotainment system touchscreen.

Engine-wise regular Golfs continued with mild hybrid (eTSI), plug-in hybrid (eHybrid and GTE), turbocharged gas (TSI), and turbocharged diesel (TDI).

The GTE offered a useful upgrade. It was now based around the 1.5-liter TSI instead of the previous 1.4. Power went from 245 PS to 272 PS, and battery capacity from 13 kWh to 20 kWh, meaning it could be driven on electric power only up to a claimed 100 km/62 miles compared with the previous 80 km/50 miles. The GTE and the lower-powered eHybrid had a DC quick charging function. In the UK a Golf GTE was more about company car tax benefits based on zero emission range than being a GTI rival.

Clubsport 8.5

The updated GTI Clubsport was shown first in May 2024 as part of the Nürburgring 24 Hours, teasingly covered in a special paint film. It kept its 300 PS output but received the styling updates and new infotainment system with a new mult-function leather sports steering wheel with the welcome return of individual buttons (the R had to keep the haptic button as it contained the R profile switch).

ABOVE: Like all the Golf 8.5s, the Clubsport 8.5 had slimmer headlights and was set apart from the GTI by large wings in the front grille. *(Volkswagen UK)*

OPPOSITE: Early hours June 1, 2024, and the one-off Golf 24h makes a pit stop at the 24 Hours of Nürburgring. It's wearing the launch "camouflage" livery of the latest GTI Clubsport. *(Eibner-Pressefoto/Alamy Stock Photo)*

While there was no change to the headline power, the VAQ differential, adaptive dampers, and Vehicle Dynamics software were recalibrated to make it that little bit sharper. Within the Vehicle Dynamics Manager, the Clubsport 8.5 now had the Nürburgring profile accessed via "Special." The 19-inch Queenstown alloy wheels were new, meant to evoke the classic Detroit wheel from the Mk5 GTI. As an option, the new 19-inch Warmenau forged wheel reduced the unsprung masses with a weight of only 8 kg per wheel, about a 20 percent reduction. They were named after the headquarters of Volkswagen R in the town of Warmenau on the outskirts of Wolfsburg.

Test drives were offered to the international press, but in June 2024 Emmet White of *Road & Track* reported that, just like its predecessor, the GTI Clubsport would not be coming to America. Mark Gillies, Volkswagen of America's director of public relations, explained, "The reason the GTI Clubsport hasn't made it to North America is simply that we would have to homologate the powertrain for this market, and the cost to do that—based on limited potential volume—would ensure that the car would end up costing considerably more than a Golf R. Simple business case at the end of the day."

A parallel story reported that Volkswagen was allegedly planning a new Golf R Clubsport. "There's another interesting car we are working on at the moment," said Martin Hube, a global spokesperson for Volkswagen, in an interview with *Road & Track*. "They are thinking about and working on a Clubsport version of the Golf R." Nobody was commenting any further.

Golf GTI Clubsport 24h

The May 2024 Nürburgring 24 Hours brought forth a surprise return for the monster racing Golf. The one-off GTI Clubsport 24h was none other than the prototype Golf Mk8 TCR created by Volkswagen Motorsport before its demise and sent to the company museum in 2021 (see chapter 7).

So, only weeks before the race it was revived by VW factory driver Benny Leuchter then transferred to the Max Kruse Racing team, which was still successfully running GTI TCRs. The GTI Clubsport 24h ran in the AT3 class (SP3T/class for vehicles with alternative fuels) as its 348 PS 2.0-liter turbo was powered by a new bioethanol fuel from technology partner Shell called E20.

Driven by Leuchter, Johan Kristofferson, Nico Otto, and Heiko Hammel, its lap time was equivalent to a new lap record for TCR cars, and after securing pole position it went on to win its class.

Golf R 8.5

Of the facelifted performance Golfs, the flagship R received the most changes aside from the new cockpit. There was speculation that the Golf R 8.5 would be the last combustion-engine Golf R, as the brand was tipped to go all-electric in 2023 (see page 225).

Available as an estate and hatchback (for Europe), the previous 333 PS of the 2023 special was now standard on the 2024 R. Torque remained 310 lb ft but developed in a wider rev range of 2,100 to 5,500 rpm, and the torque split between the rear wheels was described as having been "softened" to apply the brakes more subtly (*Autocar*).

It made more exciting noises, too. The exhaust system was tuned so that a backfire could be heard from outside from engine speeds as low as 2,500 rpm. The sound of the R-Performance Akrapovič titanium exhaust system had also been made "even richer."

There were still Drift and Nürburgring modes, but the Digital Cockpit Pro in the versions with the Performance package had a new G-meter and a GPS lap timer. Executing a standing start in Drift mode launch control would leave a pair of dramatic tire tracks from the rear wheels.

Alongside the regular Rs came the most expensive and the fastest Golf ever—and possibly the most sinister looking—the Golf R Black Edition (there were other Volkswagen Black Editions, too) priced from £44,570. It was black from nose to tail, with darker VW badges and R logos, and black R brake calipers with a dark R logo (rather than the VW one). If this was too much, it came in white, with black accents.

The Performance Pack was standard, as were black 19-inch Estoril alloy wheels instead of the standard 18-inch Jerez alloys—or optionally, the Warmenau forged wheels seen on the Clubsport.

OPPOSITE: This 2024 facelifted R is wearing the new optional forged Warmenau wheels. They were lighter and increased cooling air to the brakes. (*Volkswagen UK*)

ABOVE: Because the VW logo was now illuminated, the front radar sensor moved from behind the badge to the lower part of the grille. The optional 19-inch Queenstown wheels were meant to evoke the 17-inch five-hole alloys of the Mk5 GTI. (*Volkswagen UK*)

GTI 8.5

Arriving last in European showrooms, the Golf GTI 8.5 shared the infotainment update of the other Golfs and the new frontal styling that more closely resembled the Clubsport. No major suspension changes were specified, but the 19-inch Queenstown alloy of the Clubsport was a new option.

The six-speed manual GTI had gone—although still present lower down the Golf range, which led to press grumblings. However, there was a slight power uplift by 20 PS to 265 PS, bringing it closer to the Clubsport. The engine had a new internal designation: EA888 LK3 evo4.

In its September 25, 2024, test, *Autocar* found the usual respect for the Golf GTI but not great enthusiasm (the unique rally-bred Toyota Yaris R was the new hot hatch darling, even if it cost £44,000). However, while the GTI's manual gearbox was missed it wasn't all bad, said the testers: "when it comes to engagement, but the combined effect of the 19 bhp (20 PS) uplift for the updated GTI and the DSG's rapid changes and launch control is that the 0–60 mph sprint took 0.9 seconds less than it did in the manual pre-facelift car we timed in 2021. Where that car struggled to find traction off the line, the new version simply takes off with no drama and keeps ripping through the gears until it runs out of road."

In North America, Jetta sales were in sound health (13,025 in the first quarter) and all models got a facelift for the 2025 model year, with a revamped interior and tablet-style infotainment display (although at a more modest 8 inches). The GLI kept its six-speed manual transmission. It's worth recalling that this generation first seen in 2019 was a distinct model on the MQB platform, so it trod a different path than the Golfs.

The facelifted automatic-only Golf GTI and R were launched for the North American 2025 model year in autumn 2024. While the R had a 13 horsepower increase to 328 hp, the GTI remained at 241 hp because emissions regulations would demand the exhaust system be re-engineered, according to VWoA.

At the close of 2025, Volkswagen announced a major rationalization in German production aimed at cutting costs. From 2027, production of the combustion-engined Golf would wholly move to Puebla, but from the end of the decade, the new electric Golf would be built in Wolfsburg. Meantime, as it looked toward its 50th birthday in 2026, the Golf GTI's status as an automotive legend stood firm, even as it too looked toward electric power. The great ride continued.

ABOVE: The 2025 model year Jetta GLI (right) had new front and rear styling. Within the lowest right honeycomb was a tiny graphic of a freeway and the words "LET'S GO!" (*VWoA*)

Golf GTI Mk8/8.5

Model	European Golf GTI Mk8/8.5	North American GTI Mk8	Golf GTI Mk8 Clubsport
Engine type/capacity	2.0-liter 16-valve 4-cylinder, turbocharged	2.0-liter 16-valve 4-cylinder, turbocharged	2.0-liter 16-valve 4-cylinder, turbocharged
Gearbox	6-speed manual or 7-speed DSG	6-speed manual or 7-speed DSG	7-speed DSG
Maximum power/at rpm	245PS from 5,000–6,500 rpm (from 2024 265PS)	241hp at 5,000 rpm	300PS at 5,000 rpm
Maximum torque/at rpm	320 Nm (273 lb ft) of torque between 1,600– 4,300 rpm (from 2024 273lb ft of torque between 1,600– 4,500 rpm)	320 Nm (273lb ft) of torque at 1,750 rpm	400 Nm (295lb ft) of torque between 2,000– 5,000 rpm
Acceleration 0–60 mph	Claimed (manual): 0–62 mph in 6.2 sec (from 2024 auto only 0–62 mph 5.9 sec)	0–60 mph 5.7 sec (DSG) Car and Driver	Claimed 0–62 mph time of 5.6 seconds
Maximum speed	155 mph (governed)	155 mph (governed)	155 mph (governed) 166 mph on Clubsport 45
Suspension front/rear	Strut and coil springs, wishbone, anti-roll bar/trailing arms, coil springs, multi-link axle, anti-roll bar, optional adaptive dampers (DCC)	Strut and coil springs, wishbone, anti-roll bar/trailing arms, coil springs, multi-link axle, anti-roll bar, optional adaptive dampers (DCC)	Strut and coil springs, wishbone, anti-roll bar/trailing arms, coil springs, multi-link axle, anti-roll bar, optional adaptive dampers (DCC)
Wheels/tires	18-in Richmond alloy wheels 225/40 tires optional 19 in Adelaide wheels (UK)	18-in alloy wheels 225/40 tires optional 19-in wheels	18- in alloy wheel 225/40 tires optional 19-in wheels
Brakes front/rear	Ventilated disc/ventilated disc with anti-lock and ESP/XDS+, VAQ limited -slip differential	Ventilated disc/ventilated disc with anti-lock and ESP/XDS+, VAQ limited -slip differential	Ventilated disc/ventilated disc with anti-lock and ESP/XDS+, VAQ limited -slip differential
Length	4,287 mm/4,289 mm (2024)	4,287 mm	4,287 mm
Wheelbase	2,627 mm	2,627 mm	2,627 mm
Width	1,789 mm	1,789 mm	1,789 mm
Height	1,470 mm/1,471mm (2024)	1,464 mm	1,456 mm
Weight (kg)	(curb) 1,448 DSG (2020)	(curb) 1,442 (manual) 1,447 DSG	(curb) 1,461
Years produced	2020 to date	2021 to date	2021 to date

BIBLIOGRAPHY

Books

VW Golf GTI Limited Edition Extra 1976–1991 (compiler Clarke, R.M., Brooklands Books).
Hayes, Russell: *The Volkswagen Golf Story: 40 Years of the Second People's Car* (Behemoth Publishing Limited, 2021).
Hayes, Russell: *The Volkswagen Golf Story, 2nd ed.* (Behemoth Publishing Limited, 2014).
Hayes, Russell, and Kuch, Joachim: *VW Golf Story, Alle Generation Seit 1974* (Motorbuch Verlag, 2021).
Hutton, Ray, ed.: *Volkswagen Golf GTI, the Enthusiast's Companion* (Motor Racing Publications, 1985).
Kuch, Joachim: *VW Golf 1 1974–1983, Schrader-Typen-Chronik* (Motorbuch Verlag, 2007).
Marek, Bjorn: *VW Golf, Meister Aller Klassen* (Komet Verlag, 2008).
Meredith, Laurence: *VW Golf Sutton's Photographic History of Transport* (Sutton Publishing Ltd., 1999.
Meyer, Jens: *Kult Klassiker VW Golf 1* (GeraMond Verlag, 2010).
Road & Track on Volkswagen 1968–1978 road tests (Brooklands Books, 1986).
Road & Track on Volkswagen 1978–1985 road tests (Brooklands Books, 1986).
Ruppert, James: *VW Golf with Scirocco, Corrado and Karmann Convertible Derivatives* (Crowood Autoclassics, Crowood Press, 1996).
Steiger, Christian, and Wirth, Thomas: *Audi 1965–1975 Die Entscheidenden Jahre* (Edition Oldtimer Markt, HEEL Verlag GmBH).
Wagstaff, Ian: *Golf GTI, First and Finest of the Hot Hatches* (Windrow & Greene Ltd., 1992).

Online

Autocar www.autocar.co.uk
Auto Motor und Sport www.auto-motor-und-sport.de
Car and Driver www.caranddriver.com
Edmunds car reviews and pricing www.edmunds.com
Evo magazine www.evo.co.uk
Road &Track www.roadandtrack.com

ACKNOWLEDGMENTS

Thanks to Zack Miller, Group Publisher at Motorbooks International, for entrusting me with this project and Acquiring Editor Jordan Wiklund. Many thanks to Mark Gillies, director, public relations and reputation Volkswagen of America, for the generous provision of images and fielding detailed questions for this book; also to Mike Orford, head of public relations and communications Volkswagen UK. Photos of the 1979 Mk1 GTI (DKU 709V) in chapter 1 by kind permission of Allen Kenny and Iconic Auctioneers: www.iconicauctioneers.com.

INDEX

A
A59, 78–79
Albrecht, Peter, 58
Apostolou, Konstantinos, 51
Audi, 8, 9, 11, 32, 44, 48, 71, 77, 78, 96, 99, 104, 114, 116, 122, 137, 141, 158, 163, 168, 225
    in motorsport, 50, 51, 52
Audi A1, 132
Audi A3, 88, 94, 96, 99, 100, 119, 130, 150, 156, 163, 181, 204
Audi A4, 66, 86
Audi 50, 8, 9
Audi 80, 9, 13
Audi 80 GT, 11, 20
Audi 80 GTE, 18
Audi 100, 8
Audi RS3, 148, 149, 197
Audi S3, 143
Audi TT, 88, 99, 106, 107, 108, 119
Audi TT RS, 142
Audi V6 engine, 71

B
Barker, John, 118
Beetle
    convertible, 12, 23, 116, 117
    discontinued, 194
    engine, 104, 147, 168
    ID. 2 all and, 227
    new, 88, 90, 92, 98, 99, 100, 102, 123
    recalled diesel, 181
    sporty, 9
    successors, 6, 8
Beetle RSI, 106
Beetle Turbo, 168
Bergmeister, Willi, 15
Bez, Ulrich, 148
Bischoff, Klaus, 133, 137, 172, 212
Blume, Oliver, 222
Bondil, Francis, 27
Bora, 96, 97, 98, 104, 108
brake horsepower (bhp), brake horsepower PS, 4
Brandstätter, Ralph, 222
Browning, Jonathan, 146, 147
Brunel, Alain, 27
Burt, Matt, 171

C
Callaway, Reeves, 45, 60
Caribe, 23
Ceppos, Rich, 54
Corrado, 5, 46, 58, 59, 62, 64–66, 70, 74
Corrado G60, 61, 65, 66
Corrado VR6, 66

D
Darniche, Bernard, 50
Design Vision GTI, 170–71
de Silva, Walter, 133, 137
Diekmann, Peter, 50, 51
diesel cars, 86, 101, 104, 112, 209
"dieselgate" scandal, 136, 173, 181, 184, 209, 222
Diess, Herbert, 222, 226

E
EA888 Evo4, 207, 212, 213
e-Golf, 175, 182, 194
Eklund, Per, 26, 27
electric cars, 181, 182, 194, 209–10, 225–27, 230, 234
engine power in this book, explained, 4
Eos, 115, 116–17, 133, 150
Eriksson, Kenneth, 51

F
Feltz, Matthias, 51
Fiala, Ernst, 11, 18
Ford Escort models, 17, 23, 37, 49, 59, 75, 78, 94
Ford Focus models, 94, 106, 110, 112, 114, 120, 128, 130, 141, 142, 161, 167, 178, 215
Frankfurt Motor Show, 18, 62, 74, 77, 92, 110, 119, 168, 202
fuel crisis of 1974, 9, 13
Fuller, Jim, 30

G
Gelb-Schwarzer Renner (GSR), 9
Gill, Jared, 178
Gillies, Mark, 231
Giugiaro styling, 6, 8, 12, 16, 34, 90
Goffey, Chris, 9
Goldstein, Karl-Heinz, 78
    Golf Blue-e-motion, 154
Golf Cabriolet
    discontinued, 181, 204
    Eos vs., 117, 150, 151
    1979 debut, 23
    1983–1985, 39
    1987 facelift, 54, 56
    1993 debut, 77
    1995 diesel, 86
    1998 debut, 98
    replacements, 59
    sales of original, 37
    2002 retirement, 116
    2011 return, 150–51
    2012 GTI launch, 151, 153
Golf 4Motion V5, 97
Golf GL estate, 77
Golf GT, twin-charged, 120
Golf GTD, 25, 142, 165
Golf GTE, 182–83, 209, 210, 230
Golf GTE Sport 2015, 173
Golf GTI Clubsport, 180–81, 186, 187, 219–21, 235
Golf GTI Clubsport Edition 40, 181, 191, 201, 221
Golf GTI Clubsport 8.5, 230–31
Golf GTI Clubsport 45 Edition, 221
Golf GTI Clubsport S, 184–87, 191, 201
Golf GTI Clubsport 24h, 233
Golf GTI Edition 30, 126
Golf GTI Edition 35, 150
Golf GTI 8.5, 234, 235
Golf GTI 40th Anniversary cars, 224
Golf GTI G60, 58, 62–63, 65, 67
Golf GTI G60 Limited, 58, 62
Golf GTI Mk1
    design and engineering features, 9, 16–17, 18, 19
    development, 6, 8, 9–11
    launch, 9, 18, 19
    in motorsport, 26–29
    naming, 8, 11
    1977, 23
    1980–1981, 24
    1982, 25
    1.8-liter engine, 25
    right-hand drive, 19, 20, 23, 24
    16-valve, 21
    special editions, 31
    specifications, 33
    tuning, 20–21
    turbocharged, 21, 25
    at Wörthersee festival, 32
Golf GTI Mk2
    design and engineering features, 34, 36–39, 40
    in motorsport, 50–53
    1987, 54–56
    1988–1991, 56–59
    16-valve, 48–49, 54–56, 58, 59, 67
    specifications, 67
    supercharged, 60–63

Golf GTI Mk3
  anniversary models, 68–69, 87
  design and engineering features, 72–75
  diesel, 86
  European, 74, 77, 80, 82, 86
  GTI Color Concept, 86
  launch, 68, 88
  North American, 74, 80, 88
  16-valve, 76, 77
  specifications, 89
Golf GTI Mk4
  anniversary models, 108
  design and engineering features, 90–96
  diesel, 101, 104
  European, 96–97
  1998–1999, 98–99
  North American, 101–2
  specifications, 109
Golf GTI Mk5
  automatic, 119
  debut, 110, 118
  design and engineering features, 112–15, 118–19, 122
  diesel, 112
  end of, 127
  special editions, 126–27
  specifications, 129
Golf GTI Mk6
  Adidas Edition 2010, 144–45
  Blue-e-motion, 154
  design and engineering features, 132, 137–41
  Driver's Edition, 154, 168
  Golf GTI Edition 35, 150
  GTI Cabriolet, 150, 152–53, 155
  launch, 127, 130, 137
  specifications, 155
  2010, 144
  Wolfsburg Edition, 154, 168
Golf GTI Mk7
  design and engineering features, 156, 158, 161–67
  launch, 154
  Mexican-built, 167–68, 175
  specifications, 200–201
  three-tier, in North America, 178
  2017 updates, 187–89
Golf GTI Mk8
  all-digital, 210
  design and engineering features, 202–5, 210–16
  diesel, 209
  European, 202, 204, 207, 215, 216, 219, 221, 222, 225, 228, 233, 234, 235
  GTI Clubsport, 219–21
  launch, 202, 210, 216
  mild hybrid, 206, 207
  North American, 221, 222, 223, 224, 228, 234, 235
  plug-in hybrid, 209
  preview, 194
  sales, 224
  specifications, 235
  2024 facelift, 228–30
Golf GTI TCR Concept road car, 191–92
Golf GTI TCR racers, 196–99
Golf GTI 380, 228
Golf GTI VR6, 68, 70–72, 80–85, 88, 89
Golf Harlequin, 86
Golf Plus, 115, 123
Golf R, 5, 135, 142–44, 150, 168–69, 180, 194, 207, 216, 217, 218–19, 224, 234
Golf R 8.5, 233
Golf R 20 Years limited edition, 222, 224, 228
Golf R32, 106–7, 119, 120, 143
Golf R 333, 228
Golf R400, 176–77, 181
Golf R Black Edition, 233
Golf R Cabriolet, 153, 168
Golf R estate, 222
Golf R Variant, 179
Golf24, 148–49, 150
Grundel, Kalle, 50
GTI
  evolution of, 5
  meaning of, 11
GTI Color Concept, 86
GTi Engineering, 20, 23, 24, 26, 60, 61
GTI GLX, 101–2, 109
GTI Pirelli special edition, 126, 127
GTI Roadster Concept 2014, 172
GTI Sport, 189
GTI W12-650, 124–25, 126, 170
GT TDi, 86
Günak, Murat, 116

H

Hablitzel, Hermann, 9, 10
Hackenberg, Ulrich, 128, 134
Hahn, Carl, 30, 71
Hammel, Heiko, 233
Hammerbeck, Malte, 172
Hansch, Andreas, 26
Haubt, Andreas, 216
Hauk, Franz, 9
Hinterleitner, Ferdinand, 51
Hofbauer, Peter, 71
Hohenadel, Werner, 51
Horntrich, Herbert, 9, 11
Hube, Martin, 231
hybrids, 182–83, 209, 230
  mild, 206, 207, 230

I

ID. 2all, 225–26, 227
ID.3, 194, 195, 202, 209, 222, 225
ID. GTI Concept, 226–27
Iroc, 133

J

Jetta, 23–24, 30, 37, 49, 52, 56, 71, 75, 80, 82, 86, 102, 234
Jetta GLI, 5, 37, 41, 47, 56, 57, 58, 59, 104, 105, 107, 108, 120, 121, 122, 145–47, 168, 179, 182, 192, 193, 194, 195, 207, 234
Jetta GLI Edition 30, 169
Jetta GLS, 102
Jetta GLT Fahrenheit, 127
Jetta GLX VR6, 80, 102
Jetta GLX wagon, 104
Jetta GT, 39, 49
Jetta GTI 16V, 54, 56, 57
Jetta hybrid, 182
Jetta SportWagen, 123

K

Kable, Greg, 212
Kacher, Georg, 167
Karmann, 12, 23, 37, 44, 46, 59, 77, 108, 117, 123, 150
Karmann-Ghia coupé, 12
Kleint, Jochi, 26, 50–51, 52
Konrad, Anton, 9, 10, 11
Kottulinsky, Freddy, 10
Kreyer, Norbert, 78
Kriadis, Mihalis, 51
Kristoffersson, Johan, 233
Kuch, Joachim, 12, 13, 14, 66

L

Leiding, Rudolf, 6
Leuchter, Benjamin, 184, 185, 233
Lichte, Marc, 125, 137, 170
Liljequist, Gunhild, 16
Lloyd, Richard, 20, 26, 60
Löwenberg, Alfons, 9, 11

M

McIllroy, Jon, 215
Mignot, Guillermo, 172
mild hybrids, 206, 207, 230
Miller, Duane, 30
Mindt, Andreas, 170, 227
Modular Transverse Matrix (MQB), 156, 158, 159, 161, 163, 171, 175, 178, 191, 196, 204, 234
motorsport
  Audi in, 50, 51, 52
  Golf GTI Mk1 in, 26–29
  Golf GTI Mk2 in, 50–53
  Golf GTI TCR racers in, 196–99
  Golf24 in, 148–49
  Sciroccos in, 14–15, 26, 134–35, 148
  24 Hours of Nürburgring, 128, 134, 135, 148–49, 150, 230, 233
Mouton, Michèle, 52

N

net horsepower, defined, 4
Neuwirth, Erwin, 32
Nissen, Kris, 128
Nowak, Carl, 225
Nowak, Hans, 15
NSU K70, 8, 9

O

oil crisis of 1974, 9, 13
Opel/Vauxhall models, 59, 62, 72, 74, 75, 150, 163, 167
Ostmann, Bernd, 128
Otto, Nico, 233

P

Passat, 8, 9, 11, 12, 13, 14, 30, 34, 59, 62, 64, 65, 68, 70, 71, 74, 90, 92, 96, 97, 98, 116, 117, 120, 145, 163, 164, 171, 191
Passat CC, 132, 156, 181, 194
Passat 2.0 TDI, 209
Perkins, Chris, 194
Phillips, John, 82
Piëch, Ferdinand, 11, 71, 79, 94
Pikes Peak Twin Golf, 52–53
Polo G40, 61, 96, 204, 226
Porsche models, 9, 10, 20, 46, 65, 134, 135, 148, 153, 158
PS *(Pferdestärke)*, 4

Q

Quiroga, Tony, 122, 222

R

Rabbit
    add-ons, 21
    features, 18
    1978 arrival, 23
    power steering and, 37
    tuning, 20
    2006 revival, 123, 144
Rabbit Edition, 192
Rabbit GTI, 30–31, 40, 123, 224
    specifications, 33
Rabbit S, 30
Rabe, Matthias, 210
Ricketts, Brian, 20
Robinson, Peter, 62–63
Röhr, Walter, 78
Römers, Philipp, 170
Rosorius, Klaus, 78
Rucigaj, Domen, 172

S

Sainz, Carlos, 134
Schäfer, Herbert, 16, 34, 44, 72
Schäfer, Thomas, 222, 225, 226, 227
Schebdstat, Karsten, 184
Schmidt, Konrad, 78
Schmuck, Paul, 27
Schuster, Herbert, 11, 77
Scirocco, 5, 8, 9, 10, 31, 34, 40, 132, 141
    convertible, 23
    discontinued, 181, 204
    engine, 18, 24, 48, 49, 52, 60
    in motorsport, 14–15, 26, 134–35, 148
    1974–1981, 12–14
    1981–1992, 44–46, 54, 64, 65, 66
    revival, 133–34
    tuning, 20
Scirocco GTI, 14, 19
Scirocco GT-24, 148
Scirocco R, 135–36, 142
Scirocco TS, 13, 16
Scott, Bill, 15
SCR technology, 209
Seat Leon models, 88, 99, 108, 112, 128, 141, 163, 167, 179, 180, 184, 204
Siegrist, Jörg, 15
Škoda Octavia models, 88, 99, 100, 112, 119, 156, 163, 167, 204
Smeets, Sven, 197
Stock, Alfons, 27
Stocker, Anton, 15
Stuck, Hans-Joachim, 134
Sylvan, Hans, 27

T

24 Hours of Nürburgring, 128, 134, 135, 148–49, 150, 230, 233

V

Vento, 74, 75, 77, 80, 86, 98
Volkswagen GTI, 40
Volkswagen GTI 2010, 144
Volkswagen K70, 8–9
Volkswagen Karmann-Ghia, 12
Volkswagen management changes, 222
Volkswagen Motorsport, 14, 15, 50, 51, 52, 62, 106, 128, 196, 199, 233
Volkswagen-Porsche 914, 9
VR6 engine development, 71

W

Warkuß, Hartmut, 90
Weber, Erwin, 51, 52
Weidl, Eduard, 78
White, Emmet, 231
Winkelhock, Manfred, 14–15
Winterkorn, Martin, 124
Wittmann, Franz, 51
World Rally Championship (WRC), 26, 50–51, 52, 61, 78
Wörthersee festival, 32, 184, 186

Y

Yamauchi, Kazunori, 172
Yongfeng, Guo, 209

Quarto.com

© 2025 Quarto Publishing Group USA Inc.
Text © 2025 Russell Hayes

First Published in 2025 by Motorbooks, an imprint of The Quarto Group, 100 Cummings Center, Suite 265-D, Beverly, MA 01915, USA. T (978) 282-9590 F (978) 283-2742

EEA Representation, WTS Tax d.o.o.,
Žanova ulica 3, 4000 Kranj, Slovenia.
www.wts-tax.si

All rights reserved. No part of this book may be reproduced in any form without written permission of the copyright owners. All images in this book have been reproduced with the knowledge and prior consent of the artists concerned, and no responsibility is accepted by producer, publisher, or printer for any infringement of copyright or otherwise, arising from the contents of this publication. Every effort has been made to ensure that credits accurately comply with the information supplied. We apologize for any inaccuracies that may have occurred and will resolve inaccurate or missing information in a subsequent reprinting of the book.

Motorbooks titles are also available at discount for retail, wholesale, promotional, and bulk purchase. For details, contact the Special Sales Manager by email at specialsales@quarto.com or by mail at The Quarto Group, Attn: Special Sales Manager, 100 Cummings Center, Suite 265-D, Beverly, MA 01915, USA.

29 28 27 26 25   1 2 3 4 5

ISBN: 978-0-7603-9374-1

Digital edition published in 2025
eISBN: 978-0-7603-9375-8
Library of Congress Cataloging-in-Publication Data available

Design and page layout: Justin Page

Printed in China